It's Not Personal

ALSO AVAILABLE FROM BLOOMSBURY

It's Not Personal

Post 6os Body Art and Performance

SUSAN BEST

BLOOMSBURY ACADEMIC
LONDON · NEW YORK · OXFORD · NEW DELHI · SYDNEY

BLOOMSBURY ACADEMIC
Bloomsbury Publishing Plc
50 Bedford Square, London, WC1B 3DP, UK
1385 Broadway, New York, NY 10018, USA
29 Earlsfort Terrace, Dublin 2, Ireland

BLOOMSBURY, BLOOMSBURY ACADEMIC and the Diana logo are trademarks
of Bloomsbury Publishing Plc

First published in Great Britain 2021

A catalogue record for this book is available from the British Library.

A catalog record for this book is available from the Library of Congress.

ISBN: HB: 978-1-3501-4413-2
PB: 978-1-3501-4414-9
ePDF: 978-1-3501-4415-6
eBook: 978-1-3501-4416-3

Typeset by Deanta Global Publishing Services, Chennai, India

To find out more about our authors and books visit www.bloomsbury.com and
sign up for our newsletters.

Contents

Figures

Acknowledgements

This book draws upon a course called 'Art, Gender, Sexuality and the Body' that I have taught for nearly twenty years. I'd like to start by acknowledging all of the art and art history students who have taken this course over the years and who have sharpened my thinking about body art and performance. In a classroom situation, this kind of art never fails to set off passionate debates. To me, this is evidence of its significance and relevance for both art and life.

Each of my books is deeply indebted to my reading groups both past and present. At the beginning of my writing career, the Silvan Tomkins Reading Group was crucial (Elizabeth Wilson, Gill Straker, Anna Gibbs, Melissa Hardie, Maria Angel and the late Doris McIlwain). Currently, I really enjoy monthly catch-ups with (kylie valentine, Elizabeth Wilson and Gill Straker). Another ongoing debt is to Liz Grosz. I feel incredibly lucky to have her friendship and support. Her formidable intellect, curiosity, generosity and kindness are the model of how to be an engaged and thoughtful intellectual.

Dear friends and colleagues have very generously read sections along the way and given me fantastic feedback: Tim Bass, Jess Berry, Chari Larsson, Justin O'Brien, Ann Stephen and Gill Straker. I want to especially thank Gill Straker, whose close reading of the whole manuscript has been invaluable. I think she might just be my perfect reader: no nuance is lost, argumentative weaknesses are spotted and brilliant strategies of redress are suggested. Thanks to Helen Hughes, editor of the Australian art journal *Discipline*, for permission to reprint an earlier version of Chapter 3, 'Intimacy with Strangers: Nat Randall and Anna Breckon's *The Second Woman*', *Discipline* (2019): 17–20.

Thanks also to the colleagues and friends who invited me to talk about this research and for the invaluable feedback that resulted. In Dunedin, I enjoyed the amazing hospitality of Rebecca Stringer and her family. In Toronto, I had a wonderful time thanks to Gabby Moser and Keith Bresnahan. In Melbourne, thanks to the invitation of Linda

Williams and Daniel Palmer, I really appreciated the opportunity to speak to RMIT postgraduate students.

Thanks to my friends and colleagues at Griffith University for keeping me sane. What would I do without you? I'd especially like to acknowledge the support, intellectual stimulation, fun, friendship and frivolity of Bianca Beetson, Laini Burton, Elisabeth Findlay, Julie Fragar, Rosemary Hawker, Natalya Hughes, Chari Larsson, Vanessa Tomlinson and Justene Wiliams. Other friends are also immensely important to me. Thanks for your comradeship: Nick Aloisio-Shearer, Judy Annear, Claire Armstrong, Amelia Barikin, Ellie Buttrose, Jacquie Chlanda, Beck Davis, Geraldine Donoghue, Mikala Dwyer, Joan Grounds, Sarah Hetherington, Tim Laurence, Donna Marcus, Callum McGrath, Andrew McNamara, Eva Rodriguez Riestra, Toni Ross, Lydia Rusch, Vanessa Tomlinson, Tim Walsh and Dirk Yates.

Thanks always to my brilliant editor at Bloomsbury, Liza Thompson. I feel very lucky to have her ongoing support and interest in my work. Editorial assistant Lucy Russell has done a wonderful job of keeping everything on track. Thanks to both for supporting this book every step of the way.

Introduction

In a review of the recent biopic on German artist Gerhard Richter, *Never Look Away* (2018), film critic Adrian Martin discusses the perverse desire to unveil the purportedly hidden biographical underpinnings of art about concepts.[1] Richter's emotionally cool dispassionate painting would seem an unlikely fit for this biographical model but as Martin observes this is the stock in trade of most films about artists. As he notes, there has yet to be a filmic representation of the complexity of Andy Warhol's art and ideas – he is invariably just shown as a sad shut-in man – and the latest film on Richter simply follows suit. It would seem that the idea of art as primarily a form of personal expression is so deeply entrenched in Western thinking that it is applied indiscriminately. Visual art that aims to be 'impersonal', on the other hand, has virtually no registration in the pop cultural imaginary. Why is this key modernist idea, adhered to by so many artists, writers, philosophers and critics throughout the twentieth century, so singularly absent in such accounts of artists and art making?

Curiously, the German title of the Richter film *Werk ohne Autor* (*Work without Author*) does signal allegiance to this idea. The title points to two classic essays that query our fixation on the subjectivity of the author: 'The Author as Producer' (1934) by Walter Benjamin and 'The Death of the Author' (1967) by Roland Barthes. These essays were essential reading for art and art history students when I was an undergraduate in the mid-1980s. And, I now realize, they first signalled to me the importance of impersonality in art. While neither essay uses the specific terms 'impersonal' or 'impersonality', nonetheless they both promote a move away from personal expression.

The first essay, as many will be aware, advocates for politically engaged art in the service of revolution rather than the 'me, me, me' of bourgeois art derided in the Richter film by one of his East German art teachers. The artist is entreated to transform the techniques of art making in order to make them suitable for revolutionary purposes; Benjamin's friend and interlocutor Bertolt Brecht called this manoeuvre a 'functional transformation' of art to serve the class struggle.[2] And like Brecht, Benjamin believed techniques must be radical both in artistic and political terms. In other words, avant-garde innovation is in the service of political progress, not the exploration of self.

This collective function of art was an important ideal for the historical avant-garde, that is advanced art in the West produced from the late nineteenth century through to the 1930s. That ideal is particularly vividly demonstrated by art movements of the early part of the twentieth century inflected by utopianism, such as Russian Constructivism and the art and design of the Bauhaus. The Russian constructivists, like Benjamin, were key advocates of the interests of the collective over the individual in art making. For example, Russian constructivist artist Vladimir Tatlin wrote in 1919: 'Invention is always the working out of impulses and desires of the collective and not the individual.'[3] His assertion of the irrelevance of personal expression is echoed by his contemporary, Russian literary critic Osip Brik. Brik rejects the idea that poetry is about the poet's individuality; he wrote of poetry's relationship to the poet that it is 'totally worthless as an expression of his I'.[4] Other revolutionary art movements of the twentieth century echo similar sentiments. For example, in 1922 Mexican muralist David Siqueiros asserted 'art must no longer be the expression of individual satisfaction which it is today, but should aim to become a fighting, educative art for all'.[5] The impulse to serve a social purpose rather than a personal one recurs throughout the twentieth century returning most forcefully with socially engaged art from the 1990s onwards. The orientation towards something larger than the self, whether political cause or social movement, is one way to understand the impersonal urge in art. More on this shortly.

The other classic essay, Barthes's 'The Death of the Author', perhaps more controversially points to the fiction of originality, and the impossibility of the purely personal voice by pointing out how indebted all art is to pre-existing visual and verbal languages. Barthes begins this essay by succinctly summarizing the popular image of the artist or author that we find in the Richter film:

> The image of literature to be found in ordinary culture is tyrannically centred on the author, his person, his life, his tastes, his passions . . . the *explanation* of a work is always sought in the man or woman who produced it, as if it were always in the end, through the more or less transparent allegory of the fiction, the voice of a single person, the *author* confiding in us.[6]

Now, over fifty years later, his account of the positioning of the author or artist in ordinary or popular culture remains strikingly true. In *Never Look Away* the explanation for Richter's particular style of painting is to be found in his person, his life and his passions. More specifically, his use of photography as a model for painting is linked directly to his biography. In the film, his breakthrough moment occurs when he paints a newspaper headline that uncannily (and unbeknownst to him) relates to his father-in-law's role in the Nazi regime. Films about artists love these light bulb moments: Richter's 'signature' style comes from his very personal relationship to recent German history. For viewers, these biographical explanations are immensely appealing; they promise to deliver the secret of artistic innovation and to remove the troubling uncertainty about how to interpret art by delivering a singular meaning. Furthermore, such biographical explanations of art reinforce the idea of the artist as a special person with unique skills and capacities to transform their life into meaningful form, or in the case of Richter to magically intuit culturally and personally resonant sources for art.

To unsettle this fixation on the author, Barthes's essay begins by questioning the view that the author or artist is the sole source of meaning, the one who delivers 'a single "theological" meaning (the message of the Author-God)' as he puts it.[7] In the place of this idea of the text as a simple conduit for personal communication, he suggests it is, instead, a space where 'writings, none of them original, blend and clash'.[8] He thereby shifts our attention from the myth of art as person-to-person communication to a highly impersonal way of thinking about art. Writings or visual languages, severed from their producers, are what we actually confront when we engage with art. And these writings, he continues, are not the specific property of an individual; the text, he says, is just a 'tissue of quotations drawn from the innumerable centres of culture'.[9] This account of art underscores the second-hand nature of expression; what is taken to be self-expression, according to Barthes, is actually a patchwork of quotations from others. Infamously it is the reader that benefits from this challenge to conventional accounts of the sources of artistic meaning: 'the reader is the space on which all the quotations that make up a writing are inscribed without any of them being lost; a text's unity lies not in its origin but in its destination.'[10] It is at the point of reception, then, that art's meaning is found according to Barthes.

These two accounts of authorship seem to almost cancel one another out. On the one hand, the impersonal dimension of art is inevitable (all art is quotation, the author is dead à la Barthes) and yet on the other, moving away from personal expression requires a transformation of technique by the author (now very much alive) in order to serve a higher purpose (Benjamin). How do we reconcile these divergent approaches? Curiously, when I read these articles as an undergraduate student, I synthesized them into a joint rejection of personal expression and as underscoring the importance of the social and/or political dimension of art. I did not perceive the differences that intrigue me now.

For my purposes, the key difference is that Benjamin pushes us to think about the agency of artists, their capacity to transform techniques and artistic languages even when it comes to the paradoxical aim of cancelling themselves out. Barthes, on the other hand, highlights the shared social dimension of the language of art, the background which makes all expression possible, personal or otherwise, and to which new expressions inevitably contribute in order to maintain and revitalize the 'tissue of quotations'. In each example, despite the ostensible rejection of the personal dimension of art, it cannot be entirely excluded or eradicated. Theorist and poet Denise Riley expresses this interdependence of the impersonal and the personal very succinctly. In relation to language, she writes: 'Language is impersonal: its working through and across us is indifferent to us, yet in the same blow it constitutes the fiber of the personal.'[11] Our inner lives, including our most intimate thoughts, beliefs, emotions and desires, are woven from that impersonal resource.

Shifting back to art practice, there is then an interplay between what we take to be personal and particular to an artist (signature style, artistic innovations, their person, tastes, intentions, thoughts, feelings and passions) and the non-personal means and methods they might either use or invent. Indeed, as Sharon Cameron has astutely observed in her book length study of impersonality in American literature, personality and impersonality are not in a binary relation and thus they are not mutually exclusive.[12]

My title, 'It's not personal', is intended to signal this interplay between the personal and the impersonal. The phrase, when used to excuse some action, perceived criticism or slight, seems almost always to confirm what it is denying. Hence as soon as someone says 'it's not personal', most of us immediately assume the opposite. Yet, taken as a sincere communication, it could also mean the offending statement is not motivated by the speaker's subjective feelings towards the addressee, such as anger, envy, hate or dislike. Instead, like the impersonal operation of justice or the impersonal order of the universe, to use Canadian philosopher Charles Taylor's terms, there is no personal bias, particular intention or prejudice involved.[13] Whether delivered with sincerity or as a form of subterfuge, the phrase registers the speaker's awareness of reception as something to pre-empt or clarify. In other words, the speaker acknowledges that their comment might offend, while insisting things are not as they seem. Despite appearances to the contrary, their speaking position is intended to be dispassionate, neutral and fair. This complicated fusion of the horizons of enunciation and reception is, I believe, also a key feature of the art I discuss in this book. The artists use a variety of means and methods to think about the reception of their work and to thereby make it broadly conceptual and a little impersonal.

Curiously, the term 'impersonal' is not much used in art historical discourse despite its prevalence in both modern and contemporary art. Indeed, it is barely recognized as a key approach to modern art making, or a recurring and important aim for artists. In art history, then, conditions are not so different from the pop cultural domain with which I began. Yet, as I indicated earlier, impersonality shapes and frames many art practices and movements, particularly in post-1960s art which is the period covered in this book. The best way to understand this blind spot would be to note that the rejection of personal expression is consciously known and registered, but that the orientation towards an impersonal mode, tenor or tone is not. The impersonal urge in art history is, then, in a strange liminal zone that psychoanalyst Christopher Bollas calls the 'unthought known'.[14] It is part of our aesthetic experience, but not consistently identified and thematized as such.

Certainly, terms like 'deadpan', 'affectless', 'detached' and 'anti-aesthetic' are frequently used in the visual arts literature of the late modern and contemporary period, but the consistent aim of self-effacement or self-minimization is not discussed in any depth. The exception to this general rule is art historian Yve-Alain Bois who is preparing a book on what he calls the impersonal urge in twentieth-century art. In a lecture presentation for the Institute of Advanced Studies in 2007, titled 'The Difficult Task of Erasing Oneself: Non-Composition in Twentieth-Century Art', he outlines the scope of the book. He traces the 'impersonal impulse' in modern art from Seurat to American minimalism, finding in the reduction of the artist's aesthetic choices, or compositional actions, the desire to efface or erase the self.[15] In his published work, Bois has touched on the quest for impersonality in relation to the work of Polish constructivist artists Wladyslaw Strzemiński and Katarzyna Kobro, as well as American artist Ellsworth Kelly and American composer John Cage.[16] In relation to Cage, Bois observes that his 'ascetic detachment' owed much to the thought of Zen Buddhism and particularly his exposure to the thought of D. T. Suzuki at Columbia University in the 1950s.[17] Bois's work is discussed in greater detail in Chapter 1.

Impersonality is, of course, a much more familiar term in modernist literature, associated most often with poet T. S. Eliot whose essay 'Tradition and the Individual Talent' (1919) famously advocates for impersonal feeling in poetry. In a much-cited passage, he argues that poetry 'is not a turning loose of emotion but an escape from emotion; it is not the expression of personality but an escape from personality'.[18] Clearly in this essay emotion and personality are very closely linked; rejecting one, it is implied, means a rejection of the other.[19] Later in the same essay he recalibrates his stance on emotion and personality by arguing that the emotion of art 'is impersonal. And the poet cannot reach this impersonality without surrendering himself wholly to the work to be done'.[20] It is by anchoring emotion outside the person in what he calls an 'objective correlative' that Eliot seeks to enable impersonal emotion. As he puts it in his essay on Hamlet of the same year:

> The only way of expressing emotion in the form of art is by finding an 'objective correlative'; in other words, a set of objects, a situation, a chain of events which shall be the formula of that *particular* emotion; such that when the external facts, which must terminate in sensory experience, are given, the emotion is immediately evoked.[21]

This indirect way of representing emotion shifts away from the more typical expressive model where an inner world of feeling is brought out or released by the author or artist. Instead, feeling is spread across a whole scene or set of actions and is evoked in the audience rather than coming directly from the character or author.

Despite the importance of impersonality for Eliot, the idea has been in critical abeyance until relatively recently. Literary theorist Tim Dean puts the case more strongly, arguing that impersonality had fallen into 'disrepute' since the pioneering study of Eliot by Maud Ellmann and had become a marginal concern in literary theory.[22] He notes that the bracketing out of the author's thoughts and feelings closely resembled the concentration on the text associated with conservative formalist criticism.[23] Dean's work has sought to reconsider that assessment. He calls Eliot's strategy an 'experiment with self-dispossession rather than self-advancement'.[24] While Dean takes a positive view of this strategy of self-abnegation and surrender, he also notes that Eliot's stance is very frequently read through a biographical prism as motivated by his desire to conceal facts of his life.[25] In other words, Eliot's advocacy of the author's extinguishment is turned back into a personal concern. It would seem that personality and impersonality are not so easily separated.

While Eliot ties impersonality to emotion, British novelist and philosopher Iris Murdoch presents it as a clarity of vision. She asserts that the greatest art is 'impersonal'. It is so, she continues, 'because it shows us the world, our world and not another one, with a clarity which startles and delights us simply because we are not used to looking at the real world at all'.[26] Here the impersonal is aligned with surprise and delight, and most particularly with the illumination of the world and reality. In contrast, the self in her work is often aligned with selfishness: the 'self-centred rush of ordinary life', the 'greedy organism of the self', the 'fat relentless ego'.[27] She writes approvingly of art that is able to 'silence and expel self, to contemplate and delineate nature with a clear eye'.[28] In other words, clarity of vision and openness to the world come from silencing the self; the ego clouds our vision. Like Benjamin's promotion of committed art and literature, this account or theory of impersonal art stresses an orientation outwards beyond the self. In literary theory typically Murdoch's metaphor of the mirror is contrasted with the lamp that illuminates the self; in contrast, Marxist theories of art usually favour the hammer. The famous quote from Leon Trotsky (sometimes attributed to Brecht) states: 'Art is not a mirror held up to reality, but a hammer with which to shape it.' The purpose of art is to illuminate or change the world.

So far, I have not mentioned the specific type of art examined in this book, namely body art and performance from the 1960s until the present. In these forms of visual art practice, the medium of art is the very volatile material of the human body so that impersonal techniques become even more important: they subdue, harness and convert that material for aesthetic purposes. Using something as deeply personal, singular and particular as the body or bodies as an art material, of course, makes the task of self-effacement or self-diminishment significantly more challenging. That challenge is indirectly registered in the early literature on body art, which demonstrates how anti-expressive strategies developed in late-modern art movements, like minimalism and conceptual art, are transferred to body art. That alignment of performance and conceptual art is also registered in early accounts of conceptual art by writers such as Lucy Lippard and John Chandler, where body art and performance were considered alongside other forms of dematerialization. In their essay of 1968, 'The Dematerialisation of Art', Lippard and Chandler identified two forms of dematerialization: art as idea and art as action. The latter form, 'art as action', includes body art and performance; art has been transformed into 'energy and time motion', as they put it.[29] This description fits many performances of the 1960s and 1970s and, in particular, those that attempted to shift the emphasis away from the body to the tasks performed.

Despite these shared origins, much writing on performance, like writing on photography, has split off from visual art discourse, creating its own language of concerns. This situation is changing in the wake of the recent 'choreographic turn' and the 'performative turn'. The 'performative turn' is linked by Sigrid Gareis, Georg Schöllhammer and Peter Weibel to the current museum interest in the presentation of historical performances from the 'heroic' period of the 1960s to the early 1980s, a period they characterize as informed by an 'interdisciplinary dialog' between performance, dance and the visual arts.[30] Peter Weibel frames the relationship between visual arts and performance even more tightly, arguing performance results from the tendency in the visual arts in the twentieth century to seek an 'exit from painting'. That impetus away from painting, he continues, explains the advent of body art and performance: 'Thus, visual art brought forward a new type of action: happenings, Fluxus, actions, performances.'[31]

Key scholars contributing to the choreographic turn, like Andre Lepecki, also draw parallels between visual and performing arts, such as the consonance between the ready-made in the visual arts and the use of everyday or vernacular movement in dance and performance.[32] The involvement of museums has also spurred the interest of art historians who have begun to engage more consistently with movement and dance. For example, art historian Claire Bishop has transferred the idea of deskilling from visual art to dance and movement.[33]

One aim of my book is, then, to contribute to this interdisciplinary dialogue by reconnecting body art and performance to the concerns of late-modern art history and in particular the legacy of conceptual art. The acknowledged importance of conceptual art for the art of the present is perhaps most strongly expressed by philosopher Peter Osborne's recent book that characterizes the art of the present as post-conceptual contemporary art.[34] I would suggest an overlooked and crucial part of that legacy is impersonality which has become so naturalized that we barely notice it.

* * *

The book is divided into four chapters. The first chapter sets the scene by interrogating some of the meanings of impersonality in art. The remaining three develop a typology of body art and performance based on the number of bodies involved – one body, two bodies, a group of bodies – and the kinds of subjective and intersubjective relations they construct or address.[35] The singular body points to the issue of gender, the couple raises the question of intimacy and the collective body investigates the social dimension of life. A key contemporary work, conceived as a kind of case study or strong example of the genre, concludes each chapter.

Examining the psychological appeal of impersonality is the aim of the first chapter. The chapter establishes the recurrent nature of the impersonal urge in modern and late-modern art, considering both formulated strategies to attain it (non-composition, deductive structure) and more nihilistic approaches like minimalist Carl Andre's desire for an art 'utterly free of human associations'. Andre's admission of both his desire to eliminate the human element of art and its impossibility captures the way impersonality functions as an unattainable ideal. His desire for an inexpressive concrete art of literal substance is shared by many other artists of the 1960s and 1970s. Artists during this period eschewed the manual techniques, skills, protocols and procedures associated with the modern system of the arts and with the production of a signature personal style. Often understood as a form of deskilling, this moment is then interpreted in negative terms as founded on subtraction, negation or reduction. That negativity is interpreted using French psychoanalyst André Green's idea of death narcissism. Death narcissism speaks to a desire to minimize stimulation, describing experiences ranging from the ordinary letting go of sleep to an ascetic desire for non-existence. This idea allows us to consider the satisfactions and pleasures of this reductive self-effacing art and to explain why this recurrent approach to art is so psychically appealing to artists and audiences alike.

Chapter 2 examines performance works that focus on one body. In the visual arts, these performances often involved the artist's body. This chapter, 'The self, without autobiography: From Nauman to Ulman', examines how the self is presented and yet autobiography is negated – another twist of the personality/impersonality couplet. The aim of self-negation or self-erasure is always easier for male artists than for women artists – men have mastery and recognition to give up. In contrast, the use of the artist's own body produces a predictable problem for women artists. Women artists of the 1960s and 1970s using their own bodies had to contend with objectification by the male gaze. They needed to arrest, deflect or attenuate the gaze or risk being labelled narcissistic. Consequently, artists like Ana Mendieta, Joan Jonas and Eleanor Antin framed the nude female body (or partly nude body) in non-erotic ways. I argue that contemporary artist Amalia Ulman is a fitting successor to these earlier feminist efforts, even though in her work the female body is explicitly sexualized. Her five-month-long Instagram performance, *Excellences & Perfections* (2014), involved three invented persona and has been dubbed the first Instagram masterpiece. How do we understand this shift in feminist practice from attenuating the objectifying gaze to explicitly addressing it? The unveiling of *Excellences & Perfections* as an art project, rather than an example of the relentless display of the self associated with contemporary selfie culture, adds a new complication to how we might understand the self without autobiography.

Chapter 3, 'Cool intimacy: Pairs, couples and duos', examines various two-person works. The chapter begins with Marina Abramović's *The Artist Is Present* (2010) and ends with a contemporary participatory performance that centres on a romantic couple: a 24-hour performance work by Anna Breckon and Nat Randall called *The Second Woman* (2016). This work uses the serial method established by conceptual art as an impersonal mode to present 100 intimate encounters between Nat Randall (or her delegate) and the various men who answered a call out to participate. The work repeats a scene between a woman and her lover where disconnection and repair figure. The men are at once highly individual and yet also interchangeable, disposable and substitutable (like a contemporary Tinder dating app, the men slide past quickly into a blur). I analyse Breckon and Randall's approach to seriality using the idea of 'the law of the mother' developed by British psychoanalyst Juliet Mitchell.

In between these bookends, I consider various ways in which performing couples are forged and how the temperature of intimacy is lowered to make the connection less personal. The works range from participatory works, to two-person performances, to works with actual romantic couples. In all cases, the intense relationship between the two bodies is both figured and subdued.

The final chapter, 'Collective effervescence: Group formation from fusion to virtual togetherness', considers performances that involve more than two bodies. There are many works now shown in art galleries and museums that borrow group formats from dance and music. I am less interested in these group formations, mainly because they work with established protocols and traditions and tend not to 'make the group strange'. In contrast, the group works I have selected experiment with the group form, at times illuminating social cohesion, at others, rendering it absurd.

The social quality or dimension of these group formations is quite difficult to make visible. Some of the techniques used to depict or enact solidarity are very literal (actually joining bodies together), while others use more attenuated spatial means: gathering or drawing bodies into a clump, pile or huddle. The most impersonal of these works tend to deal with bodies as though they are mere indifferent matter – the social side of the group is barely evident. The challenge of group works is, then, to articulate connection between members of the group without enabling particular personalities to emerge or dominate. The idea of a collective will or shared aim needs to be the image of impersonality produced by the work – the 'we' discussed by philosopher Axel Honneth in his article 'The I in We: Recognition as a Driving Force of Group Formation'.

The final part of the chapter focuses on Angelica Mesiti's *Citizens Band* (2012), a four-channel video work that assembles a band of four distinct and isolated individuals that come together only in the space of exhibition. The band members share an immigrant experience, and their displacement is underscored by performances that hark back to their countries of origin rather than their current place of residency and citizenship. The group thus is only very tenuously sharing a collective experience, although the title *Citizens Band* makes it clear that the isolated participants are in some way united across time and space into a band of citizens. The attenuated connection is an example of the kind of coming together that doesn't form a 'we' – to use Byung-Chul Han's analysis of contemporary group formation. Han's ideas about contemporary group formation will be used to analyse Mesiti's work. His work perpetuates the idea of the group as a negative formation – a rabble, crowd or mob. He rejects the more optimistic terms for groups and their agency such as the multitude and the collective.

By focusing on this typology of one, two and many bodies, I hope that a new more psychologically and socially attuned account of body art and performance in late-modern and contemporary art will be revealed. Taking bodies and their mode of assembly as a means of classification certainly has the advantage of bringing up these psychological and social issues with clarity and force. The number of bodies points very viscerally to the relationships involved: couple, group and lone individual. In other words, this method foregrounds the subjective and intersubjective qualities of art that often go unnoticed when art is framed as about ideas or materials. At a time when isolation and togetherness have come in for renewed investigation, these aesthetic models of being together and apart take on a new urgency. These models, inflected by the impersonal urge, show us how to move away from a preoccupation with the self and yet still think about ourselves and our relationships.

1

'Utterly free of human associations'

Impersonality in modern and late-modern art

In an interview in 1979, American minimalist artist Carl Andre described his work as dedicated to the task of making art 'utterly free of human associations'.[1] He acknowledged the peculiar character of this desire, concluding: 'It is exactly the absurd impossibility of that task which made my art possible. If I had known that it is impossible to make art devoid of human associations because the essence of art is human association, I never would have been able to do what I have done. Human beings, alas, are the one indispensable necessity for art.'[2]

'Devoid of human associations' is a curious phrase. I assume he is referring to the desire to shear away symbolism and expressiveness in order to emphasize bare materials, often referred to as minimalist literalism. In his writing on the painter Frank Stella, Andre spells this out more clearly. Stella famously said of his own work: 'what you see is what you see.'[3] And according to Andre, all you see in Stella's stripe paintings are stripes: 'There is nothing else in his painting', he insists.[4] Stella, Andre continues, is not interested in expression, sensitivity or symbolism – just stripes. There should, then, be no associations, human or otherwise. The viewer simply sees the stripes, or in Andre's

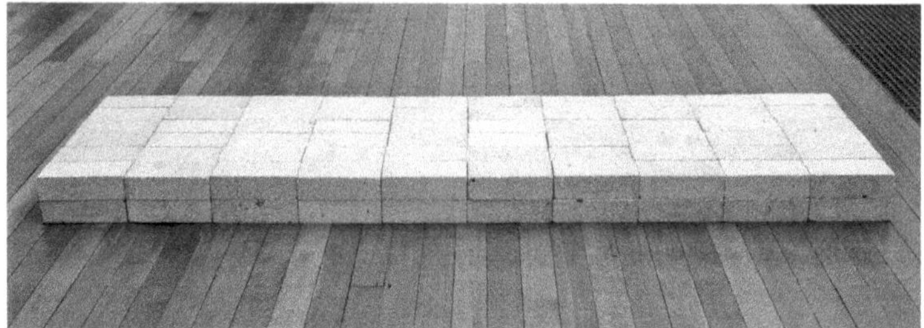

FIGURE 1.1 *Carl Andre,* Equivalent VIII *(1966)* © *Carl Andre/ARS. Copyright Agency, 2020.*

case, the bricks. A work like Andre's *Equivalent VIII* (1966) which is comprised of ordinary mass-produced materials – 120 firebricks arranged into a rectangle on the floor – would seem to have achieved the barest minimum of human associations (Figure 1.1).

In the 1960s and 1970s, Andre's desire for an art devoid of traditional human associations is echoed by many artists associated with minimalism, conceptual art, body art and land art. His acknowledgement of the impossibility of eradicating the human element, however, is a rare concession.[5] Why is this impossible impulse so prevalent in this period and yet so strangely generative?

Typically, the former question is answered by following the approach laid down by the social history of art, which assumes that shifts in art practice, particularly formal ones, can be deciphered as reflections or constructions of historical circumstances. For example, art historian Yve-Alain Bois has argued that in the 1950s American artist Ellsworth Kelly's dream of impersonality, his rejection of 'the romantic and modernist conception of art as self expression', can be partly understood as a response to the atrocities of the Second World War.[6] He writes:

In the immediate aftermath of the Holocaust and Hiroshima, it comes as little surprise that young painters would ask: what does it mean to be an artistic subject, an author, at the very moment when the humanity of any individual has been cast in doubt by the massive demonstration of the inhumanity of our whole species?[7]

An ethical withdrawal from authorship, agency and intention, it is implied, is a suitable response to wartime barbarity. In a similar vein, Liz Kotz reads the deliberately inexpressive linguistic turn of American art of the 1960s as aiming to not only '"wreck" language and wreck art' but perhaps thereby to respond to the growth of mass cultural words and images supporting the expanding consumerism of that moment.[8] Like Bois, she sees the emptying out of meaning performed by artists using language as a strong ethical and political stance to take in the face of the dramatic upheavals of the 1960s in the United States.[9] Dance historian Sally Banes identified this same refusal of meaning in the dance and performance work at Judson Memorial Church in New York in the early 1960s, what she calls 'a refusal to capitulate to the requirements of "communication" and "meaning"'.[10] Withdrawals of the ego, traditional aesthetic labour and communicative intent are then presented as responses to both the upheavals and the traumas of the twentieth century. Changes large and small, events catastrophic and merely capitalist and consumerist, are all sufficient to provoke the retraction of the self. Yet the persistence of this aesthetic tone and intention throughout the twentieth century and into the twenty-first century makes these specific historical accounts less than convincing. Surely if the impersonal current recurs and persists, it is not simply a reaction to the immediate historical context.

This chapter considers the recurrent quest for impersonality, focusing in particular on late-modern art, the period that has seemingly set the tone for current practice. I briefly consider some earlier precedents from the modern period, specifically those identified by key analysts of this phenomenon: Yve-Alain Bois and Maria Gough. However, my concern is not so much with the historical coordinates of this impulse, the 'why' I gestured to above, but rather with the curious appeal and strange generativity in evidence. Think of the range of strategies that has been invented to counteract the expression of subjectivity and feeling. Serial or modular methods, chance operations, task-like actions, non-composition, revealing the medium, ready-made objects and already made compositions, collective production, delegated production and performance, appropriation – these are just some of the ways in which artists have sought to reject personal expression across the twentieth century.

These art strategies developed to enact or approximate impersonality have now become part and parcel of contemporary art, perhaps not even perceived as operating in an anti-psychological mode. Perversely perhaps, in the final section of this chapter I consider the psychological appeal of the longing for impersonality, using in particular the work of French psychoanalyst André Green who has developed an account of the tendency towards self-extinguishment that he calls 'death narcissism'. Drawing together everyday forms of surrender, such as falling asleep, along with deep-seated needs for an absence of stimulation, he develops a compelling account of the opposite pole of narcissism – the unmaking of the self.

1 Ways to eliminate personal expression in late-modern art

While Carl Andre framed the motivation for his practice in terms of the exclusion of human associations, other American artists in the 1960s and 1970s articulate their efforts to eliminate the personal or subjective aspects of art in different ways. To name just some of the approaches, they include the evacuation or suppression of the ego; the minimization of agency; the orientation of artworks towards the public, the world and information; and an interest in systems, materials and propositions as generators of work. These aims and desires can be found in the writings of minimal and conceptual artists such as Sol LeWitt, Robert Morris, Mel Bochner and Yvonne Rainer. This selection of artists could easily be extended, partly because this generation of university-educated American artists frequently contributed to criticism and speculation about the nature and purpose of art. Indeed, Harold Rosenberg contends that impersonal art is a corollary of art education conducted in universities, as he puts it: 'Can there be any doubt that training in the University has contributed to the cool, impersonal wave in the art of the sixties?'[11] In this section and the next, I want to sketch in some of the strategies developed by these artists to diminish the personal dimension of art and consider some of the recent interpretations of this anti-aesthetic impulse.

In the case of dancer and choreographer Yvonne Rainer, her approach aimed principally to suppress the ego. Rainer is often included in accounts of minimalism and conceptualism as her work adheres to their broadly anti-expressive, anti-aesthetic aims. In her classic essay of 1968 with the rather cumbersome title 'A Quasi Survey of Some "Minimalist" Tendencies in the Quantitatively Minimal Dance Activity Midst the Plethora, or an Analysis of Trio A', she compared minimalism in the plastic arts with her own efforts in minimal or postmodern dance, drawing out some of the ways in which movement in dance could be rendered as impersonal. She coins a particularly apt phrase that is often quoted: the performer should be a 'neutral "doer"'.[12] Her 'No Manifesto', published in 1965, spells out very clearly the kinds of things she thought needed to be rejected to achieve the desired neutrality:

No to spectacle.
No to virtuosity.
No to transformations and magic and make-believe.
No to the glamour and transcendency of the star image.
No to the heroic.
No to the anti-heroic.
No to trash imagery.
No to involvement of performer or spectator.
No to style.
No to camp.
No to seduction of spectator by the wiles of the performer.
No to eccentricity.
No to moving or being moved.[13]

This series of negations are typically understood as a type of deskilling that aligns with the other reductions and subtractions that characterize this period in the visual arts.[14] Bertolt Brecht's *Verfremdungseffekt*, the alienation effect, or A-effect, which opposes the seduction of the viewer, is also in evidence. Minimizing identification and what Brecht called 'crude empathy' that entangles the spectator with the spectacle allows for a detached audience to match the neutral presentation.[15]

Against the spectacle and virtuoso movements associated with classical and modern dance, Rainer poses the performer as simply someone who does things, who acts. This matter-of-fact, ordinary, everyday way of moving is intended to prioritize action. It is in the context of this affirmation of action that impersonality and neutrality are introduced: 'action can best be focused on through the submerging of the personality; so ideally one is not even oneself, one is a neutral "doer"'.[16]

The alienation from oneself described here – 'not even oneself' – responds directly to a question posed by a writer about the kind of dance Rainer and her collaborators produced at Judson Dance Theatre in the early 1960s. Rainer reports that the critic reacted negatively to the new dance, querying in particular the mundane quality of movement by asking: 'Why are they so intent on just being themselves?' Her riposte indicates the stance to be adopted: submerging one's personality so that the performer becomes synonymous with the action. The result of this reduction is then what she calls 'a more matter-of-fact, more concrete, more banal quality of physical being in performance'.[17] She poses this egoless type of dance as in opposition to classical ballet movements such as the '*grand jeté* (along with its ilk)'.[18] These heroic and highly skilled accomplishments of classical dance she dismisses summarily, they have run their course; such 'displays', as she calls them, entailed 'overblown plot' and were involved with 'connoisseurship, its introversion, narcissism and self-congratulatoriness'.[19]

Rainer's embrace of impersonality is then very much in accord with a principled refusal of illusion on the one hand – there's a literalness to her choreography that matches the minimalist focus on unencumbered materials sought by Andre – and a movement away from the concentration on the highly skilled performer as the source or focus of any production. Her version of impersonality does not entail the removal of all reference to the human, as Andre might have wished, a task that would be much harder to conceive when the medium of the art form is the body itself. Rather, she tamps down the expression of the self through a deliberate democratization of dance movement. The movements she used in her classic dance of 1966 *Trio A* – walking, toe-tapping, kneeling, performing a backward roll, skipping, lying down – are recognizable to all and thereby accessible to all, perhaps even able to be enacted by all, they are task-like, ordinary and 'found', as she puts it, certainly not expressive or personal.[20]

While in comparison to the overblown and specialized poses of classical ballet, her work has a modesty, simplicity and lack of ostentation; nonetheless *Trio A* is described as a 'mini-masterpiece'.[21] In this brief dance-work of approximately ten minutes, while many of the individual movements might be recognizable and everyday, the complex transitions between them, and their assembly into a seamless flow demonstrates a new kind of motile virtuosity. And indeed when Rainer revised her 'No manifesto' in 2008, like Andre, she conceded that many things she rejected were unavoidable and that virtuosity was 'acceptable in limited quantity'.[22] However, in *Trio A*, she achieved a recalibration of the role of the performer: their ordinary clothes and ordinary movements did indeed shift the emphasis to the assembly of movements and the complex choreography. Carrie Lambert-Beatty uses particularly acute linguistic analogies to capture the inventiveness of that choreography: the 'suppression of phrasing', slurred 'syntax', the dance equivalent of a 'run-on sentence'.[23]

American conceptual artist Mel Bochner's article of 1967, 'Serial Art, Systems, Solipsism', advances other ways to make art less personal. He shares with minimal-conceptual artist Sol LeWitt a kind of ceding of agency through the ascendancy of the idea. Bochner wrote: 'the idea is carried out to its logical conclusion, which, without adjustment based on taste or chance, is the work'.[24] His use of passive voice here mimics the desired automaton-like quality of an artwork driven by an idea. LeWitt's earlier article on seriality characterizes the artist's role more explicitly but in very similar terms. In his article from 1966, he wrote:

The aim of the artist would not be to instruct the viewer but to give him information. . . . One would follow one's predetermined premise to its conclusion, avoiding subjectivity. Chance, taste or unconsciously remembered forms would play no part in the outcome. The serial artist does not attempt to produce a beautiful or mysterious object but functions merely as a clerk cataloguing the results of the premise.[25]

While the artist's labour is typically characterized as relatively free and self-directed, particularly when compared to a wage labourer, here LeWitt models artistic labour on the unthinking obedient drudgery of the lowly clerk cataloguing results. Artistic labour acts in conformity to a pre-established schema, carrying out the appointed task with a minimum of personal intervention – 'avoiding subjectivity', as he puts it. Bochner similarly advocates ways of making art 'based on the application of rigorous governing logics rather than on personal decision making'.[26] The reduction of personal decision-making allows ideas to gain ascendancy in a manner akin to Rainer's advocacy of movement.

Bochner also advocates a kind of inhuman literalness or concreteness: matter, as it were, devoid of human associations. For example, in his account of LeWitt's serial work, Bochner speaks of '"things-in-the-world" separate from both maker and observer'.[27] This way of conceiving of things in radical isolation runs totally counter to our contemporary sense of knowledge as always situated and relative, the work of perspective, and skewed or shaped by embodiment and experience. Bochner's various epigrams in this article underscore the philosophical lineage of this now-very-foreign idea. He cites analytical philosopher J. R. Weinberg who claims it is a misnomer to even speak of 'my experience'. He explains: 'Experience is simply whatever experiential facts there happen to be. It is quite impersonal and is not in any sense mine.'[28] The idea that even my experience is not specifically or particularly mine, that experience is actually impersonal, also sits awkwardly in an era that worries about the effects of hyper-individualism. The confidence of mid-twentieth-century philosophers that subjectivity can be kept at bay and that things are stable and discoverable reflects a world view extremely distant from contemporary sensibilities that routinely acknowledge the effects of subject position and how that is refracted and informed by factors such as race, ethnicity, class, gender and sexual orientation.

Bracketing perspectives and their contribution supposedly allows an objective, accumulative account of knowledge, where we might finally get to the bottom of things. Such a world view is reflected in another of Bochner's citations from British logical positivist philosopher A. J. Ayer. Ayer writes: 'There is nothing more to things than what can be discovered by listing the totality of the descriptions they satisfy.'[29] The optimism of positivism is very much in evidence here: things can be neatly demarcated, they have a knowable essence, what we know of them, or rather descriptions they satisfy (to cut out the primacy of the human), is all that there is.

At the beginning of his essay, Bochner also refers to the opposing tradition of continental philosophy to underscore the separation of subject and object. The epigram from the German phenomenologist Edmund Husserl is his famous clarion call to turn 'to the things themselves', a call which posed the possibility of finally knowing or getting to things outside of human understanding and mediations – in other words, the infamous phenomenological reduction, or bracketing of experience is championed.[30] Experience becomes very strange here: it is impersonal in the analytic tradition and can somehow be voided of subjectivity in this much-vaunted return to things from the continental tradition. For Bochner, LeWitt's work can be understood as about 'things themselves', because the artist follows 'a rigid system of logic that excludes individual personality factors as much as possible'.[31] A system carefully followed, it is suggested, delivers an impersonal objective outcome.

Finally, a further more formal means to overturn the 'intimate mode' of apprehending art and its private and personal connotations is offered by minimalist artist Robert Morris.[32] In his article of 1966, 'Notes on Sculpture, Part 2', he refers to large-scale objects that create distance between the sculptural object and viewing subject as enabling a 'nonpersonal or public mode'.[33] For him the key to maintaining the 'public external quality of the object' is to reduce detail, rich surface and internal relationships. Large simple forms, he suggests, keep the viewer in the space in which the object exists. His sculptural works of the mid-1960s fit the bill: they used large simple geometric shapes – L-shapes, beams, rectangles, cubes, triangles – often rendered in dull pilgrim grey that echoed the architectural language of the gallery. In this fashion, the sculpture includes the non-fabricated elements of the situation. As Morris famously put it: 'the better new work takes relationships out of the work and makes them a function of space, light, and the viewer's field of vision.'[34] In other words, the artist is no longer responsible for the totality of the work: a large part is contributed by the non-personal public site or situation.

Typically, these ways of thinking about art have been brought together under the rubric of the anti-aesthetic, the idea being that traditional aesthetic problems and concepts – such as the autonomy of art, beauty, taste and the expressive genius – have been jettisoned. More recently Eve Meltzer has argued that such approaches can be framed as varieties of anti-humanism. In her book *Systems We Have Loved: Conceptual Art, Affect, and the Antihumanist Turn* (2013) she suggests that artists in the late 1960s and 1970s shared with structuralism and poststructuralism an investment in anti-humanism.[35] Partly taking her cue from artists such as Robert Smithson and Robert Morris who used this term explicitly, Meltzer responds to the consistent efforts in word and deed to negate and recalibrate the traditional meanings of the human.[36] Curiously, she ignores the contribution of British analytic philosophy, evident in Bochner's article and the writings of conceptual artists associated with Art & Language.[37] Nor does she mention Judd's investment in empiricism and behaviourism teased out by David Raskin.[38]

Leaving aside Meltzer's unexplained rationale for stressing the importance of structuralism, nonetheless the frame of anti-humanism makes possible another way of thinking about the impersonal tendencies I am tracing. This is most evident in her discussion of the American critic Rosalind Krauss. Meltzer lists the myths about art dismissed in Krauss's book about the avant-garde, most of which reformulate the artist as a detached, impersonal performer. The myths to be extinguished include

> the myth of genius, the myth of authorial inspiration and determination, the myths of artistic evolution and aesthetic intention; the prioritizing of biographical context and psychological models of creativity; the belief in the existence of private worlds of allusion; and the humanist notion of the human subject as a set of relations, actions, causes, and effects generated from a coherent, unified, internal or true self.[39]

The result, Meltzer says, is 'the end of the humanist understanding of the subject as in command of not only himself and a consciousness fully transparent to itself, but also the historical process'.[40] This account of the opposition to humanism is now very familiar; it has dominated the humanities for decades. It is curious, however, that when Meltzer defines humanism, she cites a version not entirely consonant with its negation. She quotes from the art historian Erwin Panofsky, who describes humanism as

> not so much a movement as an attitude which can be defined as the conviction of the dignity of man, based on both the insistence on human values (rationality and freedom) and the acceptance of human limitations (fallibility and fragility); from this two postulates result – responsibility and tolerance.[41]

As this definition makes clear, the stakes are high when humanism is rejected – in everyday life to oppose responsibility and tolerance would be foolhardy to say the least. Meltzer ignores the issue of human limitations raised by Panofsky, concluding from this passage only that the antihumanist subject enjoys 'neither self consciousness nor freedom – only the illusion of such things'.[42] Just as impersonality is desired and impossible, so too anti-humanism is a necessary deflation of human self-importance, as well as an absurd and exaggerated understanding of our capacity for self-negation. What is useful to take from the analysis, however, is the intensity and banality of the continued desire for self-negation. Furthermore, considering the quest for impersonal art as part of anti-humanism more securely links late modernity to the present where this impetus continues to grow in the form of new materialisms, anti-intentionalism and varieties of post-humanism.

2 The return of the repressed: Subjectivity, feeling

Over the last two decades various art historians have been gnawing around the edges of this anti-aesthetic interpretation of minimalism and conceptualism, myself included. The first interventions, however, came from artists and critics at the time – most notably, the American artist Eva Hesse, who is typically interpreted as indebted to minimalist precepts, while also fundamentally refiguring them.

Hesse certainly saw associations in Andre's work. Of all the minimalists she felt the closest affinity to Andre; his work, she said, did 'something to my insides'.[43] Asked what his work represented for her, she said of his metal floor pieces that they reminded her of the 'concentration camp'.[44] More specifically: 'It was those showers where they put on the gas.'[45] Pushed further by her interlocutor, to think about what Andre would make of her comments, she replied, 'because we like each other maybe he'd understand, but it would be repellent to him that I would say such things about his art.'[46] Hesse's comments on Andre's work are used by American art historian Anna Chave in her more broad-ranging project to rethink the anti-subjective characterization of minimalism.[47] She points out that while minimalism might be 'more emphatically depersonalized than any prior visual art idiom' biographical details are still manifest in the artists' work, most particularly, of course, in the work of women artists like Hesse and Rainer.[48]

In turn, Hesse's work is used by Briony Fer to question the seeming rationality of minimalism.[49] Fer argues that the 'particular compulsions' of Hesse's art 'dislodge the rationalist frame' through which minimalism is typically viewed.[50] Repetition-compulsion is, of course, one way of responding, or giving form, to a traumatic event or a troubling unconscious idea. But what is the idea that makes dispassionate machine-like seriality the symptom? I will return to this in the final section of this chapter and to the image Hesse conjures of utter annihilation.

Other re-readings of minimalist and conceptualist rationality and its avowed anti-humanism have sought to reintroduce the bracketed question of feeling. For example, David Raskin has argued that Judd's work is deeply concerned with feeling; he rejects its affectless characterization.[51] While Raskin asserts this several times in his landmark monograph on Judd, he does not actually mount an argument to support this reading.[52] Certainly Judd himself indicated that while 'painterly feeling' was not his concern, he did not reject feeling altogether.[53] More to the point, however, he rejected the idea that his work is impersonal. In a lecture delivered at Yale University in 1983, he said his work was wrongly called 'objective' and 'impersonal'.[54] Peculiarly for an artist often identified with hard-edged geometry and slick manufactured materials, he said his 'largest interest is in my relation to the natural world'. He continued: 'This interest includes my existence, a keen interest, the existence of everything, and the space and time that are created by the existing things. Art emulates this creation or definition by also creating, on a small scale, space and time.'[55]

Judd's way of seeing his own work as about his existence and his relationship with the natural world contrasts markedly with the views of many of his critics, who continue to underscore the cool affectless quality of his work that, like other minimalists, is purged 'of authorial feeling and demonstrable intent', as James Meyer put it.[56] Jonathan Flatley reads the avowed affectless quality through Judd's declared regard for the interesting, arguing that rather than a withdrawal, his work should be interpreted as a particular form of affect appropriate to his time, namely a new type of boredom associated with 'mental relaxation'.[57]

The positive reading of minimalist boredom is actually a feature of contemporary reception, as Frances Colpitt notes.[58] As I have argued elsewhere, the withdrawal of legible feeling that minimalism effects provoked a range of emotions: from experiencing minimalist objects as aggressive, as involving both negative and positive boredom, and supposedly generating new emotions all together.[59] The range of responses, however, does not displace the impersonal tone of the slick industrial manufacture. I think James Meyer and Jonathan Flatley are correct in their characterization of minimalism as affectless. Or to pose a compromise that complements Flatley's interpretation, impersonal feeling could be how this work is characterized; impersonal feeling is precisely what the modernist poet T. S. Eliot advocated as the way to move beyond the personal. Eliot argues that the poet has to practise self-sacrifice and perform a continual extinction of the personality – this submerging of the self is akin to Rainer's account of impersonality. The process he calls 'depersonalization' is what makes possible the expression of impersonal feeling. As he puts it, emotion in poetry is 'not in the history of the poet', their biography, rather 'the emotion of art is impersonal'.[60]

In relation to conceptual art, Eve Meltzer has also brought up the question of feeling as the repressed bodily domain structuralism rejected, which returns, albeit in shadowy form, in the work of conceptualist artist Mary Kelly.[61] Again, it is the work of a woman artist that sits uneasily in the established late-modern art narratives. Here, conceptual art scientism – the characteristic provision of neutral information in a deadpan manner – is unsettled by her highly personal subject matter: the development of her infant son, charted in *Post-Partum Document* 1973–9.

The repression of affect also concerned another woman artist – Yvonne Rainer. James Meyer discusses Rainer's return to the question of feeling in his intriguing reconsideration of minimalist authorship. He also observes the generativity of this impossible desire to purge art of authorship and feeling on the part of this generation of sculptors, dancers, painters and musicians based in New York. He draws attention to the point in Rainer's autobiography of 2006 *Feelings Are Facts*, where she revisits that strange desire. Rainer's later conviction was that the feelings excluded from minimalist art returned with a vengeance in artists' unconscious lives. As she put it:

> Ignored or denied in the work of my sixties peers, the nuts and bolts of emotional life comprised the unseen (or should I say 'unseemly'?) underbelly of high U.S. Minimalism. While we aspired to the lofty and cerebral plane of a quotidian materiality, our unconscious lives unravelled with an intensity and melodrama that inversely matched their absence in the boxes, portals, jogging and standing still of our austere sculpture and choreographic creations.[62]

The contrast here is telling: the mess of emotional life is kept apart from austere cerebral art. What Meyer takes from this contrast is the idea of an underbelly or unconscious of minimalism where the subjective dimension returns like the repressed.

All of these re-readings of the 1960s and 1970s return us to the affective complexity underpinning this cool impersonal art, but they do not explain why the impossible task of eliminating human associations had such purchase. While impersonality is a recurrent theme in literary modernism, and in particular in British modernism, in the visual arts, Yve-Alain Bois is the main, if not the sole, investigator of this recurring tendency. Certainly, other art historians have noted this tendency; for example, Benjamin Buchloh has noted the prevalence of what he calls 'desubjectivisation' in art; however, as his term suggests, his characterization operates principally as a negation, rather than as an investigation of a positive value.[63] To date, it is only

Bois who has formulated impersonality as a meaningful strategy, impelled by a search for the absolute, among other things.

According to Bois, a desire like Andre's to eliminate human associations from the work of art is one variant of a broader tendency that he calls an 'impersonal urge' in modern art.[64] Bois coins this expression while discussing various strategies for the self-effacement of the artist employed in twentieth-century art. His lecture on this topic is called 'The Difficult Task of Erasing Oneself: Non-composition in Twentieth-Century Art'. As the title suggests, Bois focuses on a recurring strategy he calls 'non-composition', that is, the refusal of the purposeful language of artistic composition; the intention and labour of composition are to be avoided. He examines a range of strategies that artists have adopted to create works that eschew composition arguing the desire to eliminate personality has generated 'a good portion of modernist production'.[65] Avoiding composition is intended to eliminate, or at least minimize, the artist's personal touch or taste from the work of art. Curiously, Bois does not provide social or historical explanations for this tendency in this broader survey.

This desire for self-effacement can also be understood, following both Ruth Leys and Michael Fried, as an anti-intentionalist strategy – anti-intentionalism is another way of describing the diminution of the importance of authorship underpinning minimalism and conceptualism.[66] The effacement of the artist is to be achieved by minimizing authorial intentions and artistic choice.[67] Non-composition is simply one variant of this broader tendency to cancel or diminish agency and intention. To return to my main concern, the difficult question to answer is why anti-intentionalism has such ongoing appeal.

3 Yve-Alain Bois and Maria Gough: Deductive structure

Bois first raised this issue of non-composition in his discussion of the work of the Polish artists Wladyslaw Strzemiński and Katarzyna Kobro, and it is perhaps by returning to that early article that some sense can be made of the impersonal urge, particularly as, in this article, Bois positions the paintings and sculptures of Strzemiński and Kobro as important precursors to minimalism, even though their ideas were not widely known before the end of the Second World War. In this vein, he uses their work to contradict the account of European painting given by American minimalists Frank Stella and Donald Judd in a well-known interview conducted by Bruce Glaser. In that interview, Stella famously dismissed European painting as relational, asserting: 'The basis of their whole idea is balance. You do something in one corner and you balance it with something in the other corner.'[68] Judd in the same interview said he wanted to 'get rid of any compositional effects'. Those effects, he continues, 'tend to carry with them all the structures, values, feelings of the whole European tradition'.[69]

Bois's interrogation of the Polish constructivists, as they are sometimes called, highlights the problem of motivation that is at the core of anti-intentionalist strategies. In other words, he asks what can generate the work of art when traditional conceptions of expression and composition are rejected. If the labour of art is not motivated by self-expression, what else can organize its structure? Or to put this another way, how can the arbitrary mark making of expressionism be replaced with something that is not arbitrary? The solution proposed by Kobro and Strzemiński is a theory of artistic unity they called Unism. Unity is understood as a way of avoiding the figure/ground opposition or any other compositional device that privileges one part of the canvas over another, or that creates tensions and dynamism. As Strzemiński puts it, the 'law of organic painting requires: *the greatest possible union of forms with the plane of the picture*'.[70] The quest for pictorial unity reduces the opportunities for expressivity and reduces the artist's need to make compositional decisions.

A picture, Strzemiński says, 'should not be an interaction of forms, but a simultaneous phenomenon'.[71] In this proposal there is a remarkable anticipation of minimalist ideas of unity as Bois notes.[72] We find very similar sentiments in Judd's desire to oppose a hierarchy of parts, or Andre's desire for particles to be united into molecules. Strzemiński identifies the importance of what he calls the innate properties of the picture: square boundaries and the flatness of the picture plane. Pictorial forms need to emerge in relation to them, he argues. 'They must be dependent and closely connected.'[73] The idea of flatness is, of course, a key issue in the account of modernist painting associated with American critic Clement Greenberg. In the work of Stella, this same idea of using the dimensions, proportions and shape of the picture plane itself to generate form is reiterated. In Stella's painting the width of the stripes in his stripe paintings was determined by the width of the canvas' stretcher bar, which was also the width of Stella's brush. I will return to this idea of pictorial structure determined by aspects of its production, as it is a central issue in Maria Gough's discussion of Russian Constructivism.

The theory of Unism was also applied to sculpture. Here, the question of the integration of the artwork with space, which occurs in the work of both Judd and Morris, is anticipated. Judd remarked, 'I'm using actual space because when I was doing paintings I couldn't see any way out of having a certain amount of illusionism.'[74] Literal space is preferred to the illusion of space that two-dimensional pictorial language cannot entirely eliminate; even when the figure/ground relationship is radically refigured, colour recession and projection can suggest the spatial relations of in front of and behind. As noted earlier, Robert Morris describes the move from compositions that are part and parcel of painting or sculpture to installations in real space and time, as serving this desire for literalness. He argued that 'The object is but one of the terms in the newer aesthetic'.[75] Lifting the relations out of the pictorial plane reduces the importance of the work; it is dispersed into the quotidian world of space, light and viewers.

The issue of space is addressed more directly by Strzemiński and Kobro, in the co-written article of 1931 'Composition of Space: Calculations of Space-Time Rhythm'. They compare Unism in painting with Unism in sculpture: 'Unism in painting tends towards flat visual unity, closed in upon itself and indifferent to its environment. A unistic sculpture aims at accomplishing the unity of the sculpture with the surrounding space, a spatial unity.'[76] So the limits that are an intrinsic feature of painting are not a feature of sculpture. Sculpture's unity is with its spatial situation. The question is then how to make space part of the sculpture. In this article, the main strategy they discuss is rhythm. An open rhythm of shapes is advocated to integrate sculpture and space. By rhythm they mean 'a regular sequence of shapes in space'.[77]

Bois's ideas about the problem of motivation are amplified by his student Maria Gough in her study of the debates around composition and construction in the early 1920s formulated by the Russian artists associated with the Working Group of Objective Analysis. Construction is clearly a mode of artistic labour that is more closely aligned with architecture and engineering; it suggests a more purposeful mode of assembly than the subjective and arbitrary mode of composition.

In the Working Group's debates, the participants were attempting to delineate how the new concept of construction departs from traditional composition. Wassily Kandinsky features here, as he does for the minimalists, as hopelessly mired in subjective and arbitrary practices. Building on Bois's work, Gough uses Michael Fried's term 'deductive structure' to describe Alexander Rodchenko's solution to the problem of construction.[78] In other words, there are now at least two European precedents for the minimalist rejection of composition.

Significantly, Fried used this term, 'deductive structure', to discuss the work of Frank Stella and in particular it describes a formal problem, as he put it, the 'self-aware and strictly logical relation between the painted image and the framing edge'.[79] In the work of Rodchenko and Karl Iogonson, Gough observes that structures are generated by 'either deductive of nonrelational progressions of modular units'.[80] Stella's solution to this formal problem is to have the paintings seemingly generated by or deduced from the shape of the canvas. In Stella's shaped canvases of the early 1960s the painted stripes are deduced from the shape of the canvas: they repeat or reiterate the central void and the stepped canvas edge or outline.

A similar strategy was adopted by Rodchenko in works such as *Hanging Spatial Construction no. 10* (1920–1), which consist of concentric shapes cut from a single plane of plywood. When the shapes are rotated, they create a three-dimensional geometric form that is completely permeated by space. Gough notes that Rodchenko avoids what Nikolai Ladovskii regarded as 'the excess and relationality of composition': the structure of the work reveals its process of production. She reports that each work in the second series of spatial constructions was produced in the same way: Rodchenko drew a geometric figure on a sheet of plywood using a compass or ruler and then repeated 'the given figure to form a regularly diminishing pattern'.[81] Gough argues that while the geometric figures and the width of the ribs are products of the artist's subjective choice, this is 'somewhat mitigated by Rodchenko's recourse to a universal planar geometry'.[82] She sees deductive structure as inverting the conventional significance of material, as Russian critic Nikolai Tarabukin puts it: 'the material [now] *dictates* form to the artist.'[83] In these earlier iterations of the impersonal urge, the desire to shift authority and agency from the artist to something external and public such as material can already be seen. Inanimate objects and substances are relied upon to generate form.

4 Death narcissism, the zero degree of relations

To return to the minimalists, while they share the rejection of composition with the Russian and Polish constructivists, there is no longer the same sense of an alternative theory that Unism or the concept of construction provided. Certainly, there are principles of artistic production articulated in the 1960s and 1970s, for example, LeWitt's idea, cited earlier, of following a preconceived proposition to its conclusion; the idea once selected drives the work, as it were automatically. Similarly, Donald Judd's reduction of composition to the conveyor belt logic of 'one thing after another'[84] also suggests the minimization of intention, and the elimination of excess or 'compositional fussiness', as Stella called it.[85]

Yet these production principles are not elaborated sufficiently to elevate them into an alternative theory of art production, such as you find in Unism or Constructivism. It is as though there is a more nihilistic dimension to minimalist work that brings up the idea of impersonality indirectly but perhaps no less forcefully. I say indirectly as this is not a term that is frequently used by the artists themselves, although it is peppered throughout critics' responses. Following Bois's use of the phrase 'impersonal urge' as a summative concept, however, brings together the variously articulated projects of a long line of twentieth-century artists.

In this section of the chapter, I want to consider not so much how this urge might have motivated various minimalist artists, although this is an important consideration, but rather to account for the appeal of art that aims to be utterly free of human associations. In particular, I will explore why it might be psychically appealing to the audiences of minimalist and conceptual art, as much as to its producers. An early answer to this problem comes from a surprising source, the German art historian – Wilhelm Worringer.

In his book of 1908, *Abstraction and Empathy*, Worringer describes how what he called the urge towards abstraction in art can be characterized as a repudiation of empathy, vitality and life. According to Worringer, when a beautiful object elicits empathy, we project vital feeling into it, with abstraction, however, we yearn for the object purified of life. Contrary to what one might expect, he argues that both impulses address our 'need for self-alienation': in empathy we lose ourselves in the object; in abstraction we seek deliverance from the arbitrariness of existence.[86] It is an interesting coincidence that arbitrariness is the feature of composition consistently targeted by artists aligned with the impersonal urge. For those artists, and for Worringer, arbitrariness is something we want to be delivered from. Worringer poses those two tendencies as the twin poles of artistic expression, that is, empathy and vitality versus abstraction and the inanimate – the life drive and death drive of art.

This same opposition of the life and death impulses was also used by Lucy Lippard in her catalogue essay for 'Eccentric Abstraction', the 1966 exhibition of post-minimalist works at Fischbach Gallery in New York. She argued that minimalists had introduced a new type of funereal monument. She explains: 'funereal not in the derogatory sense, but because their self-sufficient unitary or repeated forms are intentionally inactive.'[87] In contrast, she argues: 'Eccentric abstraction offers an improbable combination of this death premise with a wholly sensuous, life-giving element.'[88] Significantly, Lippard's brief reference to the 'death premise' here aligns the dead or inert quality of minimalism with self-enclosure, unassailable sufficiency and inactivity.

It is precisely these qualities that feature in French psychoanalyst André Green's recent account of death narcissism. His idea of death narcissism provides the most promising account of this death premise and the pull or attraction of things that tends towards zero, or to recast this tendency in the language of the visual arts, the desire for a 'zero degree of form'. The 'zero of form' is, of course, Malevich's characterization of his infamous painting, *The Black Square* of 1915, which features prominently in Bois's account of non-composition.[89] This austere image of a black square consuming most of the picture plane shares some of the rejective, reductive qualities of minimalism: the square is like a void in the centre of the canvas draining away meaning.[90] In the case of minimalist artists like Andre, Stella and Judd, the impetus towards zero might be more accurately described as a tendency towards a zero degree of relations. This description does not cover the work of Robert Morris and Dan Flavin as adequately, although it might pertain to some of their works. With this in mind, I will confine my argument to Andre, Judd and LeWitt.

André Green proposes the idea of death narcissism as a way to think through the problem of narcissism opened up by Freud's second topography (Id, Ego, Superego) and his final theory of the drives introduced in the essay of 1920, 'Beyond the Pleasure Principle'. The new model of the drives refigures the major forces of instinctual life. Freud replaces his earlier account of the two opposing drives, sexual instincts versus instincts of self-preservation, with the opposition between Eros (the sexual drive) and the death drive. As Green points out, when that new theory of the drives was adopted, the theory of narcissism was curiously left in abeyance.[91]

Narcissism, of course, is popularly known as love of the self. In his essay on narcissism, Freud contrasts this investment in the self with the investment in others. Jean Laplanche and Jean-Bertrand Pontalis use the image of a seesaw to capture the relationship between the two: libido invested in others depletes the investment in the self, and vice versa.[92] Freud himself on several occasions used the metaphor of an amoeba with pseudopodia to describe the extension and retraction of libido.[93] As the latter metaphor indicates, narcissism is more usually associated with the outline of the self that is formed and stretched through the sexual instincts.

Green retrieves narcissism from its unwarranted neglect, reformulating it in accordance with not just the sexual instincts but also the death drive. For him, narcissism is characterized by two faces, which he calls death narcissism and life narcissism. In other words, his aim is to refigure narcissism as having the same dual orientation as the final theory of the drives. The implications of this are considerable: it means admitting that at the core of our being there is an aspiration towards non-existence. In order to unpack this idea, let me briefly outline the implications of Freud's death drive and then consider how Green uses this idea to refigure the ego-making activity of narcissism by including a tendency of the psyche also called narcissism but bent on unmaking. This idea might enable us to better understand the desire for self-annihilation that is at the core of the Freudian account of the self and seemingly much twentieth-century art.

In Freud's second theory of the drives, the death instinct or death drive is introduced to account for the repetition of unpleasant things. He introduces what he calls an 'opposition between the ego or death instincts and the sexual or life instincts'.[94] Prior to the introduction of the death drive, Freud assumed that the psychic apparatus was geared towards self-protection and minimizing or discharging unpleasure, hence the repetition of unpleasant feelings or experiences was anomalous and in need of explanation. As he put it: 'the course taken by mental events is automatically regulated by the pleasure principle . . . [which is associated] with an avoidance of unpleasure or a production of pleasure.'[95] Through clinical work, however, he discovered behaviour that did not fit this model: war veterans repeatedly dreaming of traumas of war, as well as patients acting out or repeating unpleasant experiences instead of remembering them. As he put it, the patient was 'obliged to *repeat* the repressed material as a contemporary experience instead of . . . *remembering* it as something belonging to the past'.[96] Freud uses these instances of human beings caught in what he terms a seemingly 'daemonic' compulsion to experience pain, to argue that there is an instinct or drive to return to an earlier state, a return to inorganic existence.[97] In sum, there is a drive that moves us away from pleasure and towards self-annihilation.

André Green takes up this idea of returning to a state of inorganic existence and incorporates it into the formation of the ego. He calls it negative narcissism or death narcissism: an ascetic desire for non-existence and zero stimulation that would characterize such a state. Death narcissism, 'under the influence of the Nirvana principle',[98] is a tendency towards withdrawing investments (or disinvesting); it is, he says, 'the quest for indifference'.[99] This narcissistic withdrawal, he notes, is 'one of the most natural tendencies of the ego, which, each night, withdraws its investments from the world to find refreshment in sleep; and not just to dream'.[100] The appeal of this state is that it promises a complete lack of relations, the tendency towards zero, 'null' as Mel Ramsden might put it, or blankness.[101] As Green elaborates, 'slipping back regressively towards the point zero' is a tendency towards 'non-existence, anaesthesia, emptiness, *blanc*, . . . from the English "blank"'.[102]

Attributing the appeal of blankness to death narcissism, rather than the death drive, removes the need to invoke compulsion as the motor for machinic seriality. Death narcissism is an ever-present state or structure of the psyche. We could dispense, then, with Briony Fer's idea that compulsion underlies minimalist repetition. Certainly, compulsion is not consistent with the affective tone of minimalist works. Repetition in minimalism is deadpan; there is no sense of a compulsive return to something distressing, nor is there a sense of a conflictual dynamic; otherwise the desired unity of the pieces would not have been achieved. Andre's components are not in tension, despite his insistence on never joining them and his idea that this produces uncertainty.[103] Even his scatter pieces, where parts are not assembled, have the sense of the molecular unity he strived for, delivered by the all-over non-hierarchical patterning produced by identical parts either randomly distributed, or subject to the force of the tide, in the case of works like *Walnut Water Scatter* (2001) where floating squares of walnut are scattered by the river (Figure 1.2).[104]

Judd's many and varied permutations of the box do not suggest compulsion. Nor do Sol LeWitt's grids, despite Rosalind Krauss's interpretation of them as both obsessive and compulsive.[105] Instead, as she also indicates by pairing her analysis of his grids with the work of Samuel Beckett, there is a quietly absurd quality to LeWitt's work, which as he insists follows a logic that is not rational.[106] As LeWitt said of the grid: 'The grid system is a convenience. It stabilises the measurements and neutralizes space by treating it equally.'[107] And if we focus on the components, rather than the space of the grid, we could follow Jonathan Flatley's reading of the cubes in *Variations of Incomplete Open Cubes* (1974), which he argues achieves likeness because they are all missing the same thing.[108] In the refusal of expressivity and the hand-made there is here a kind of democratization

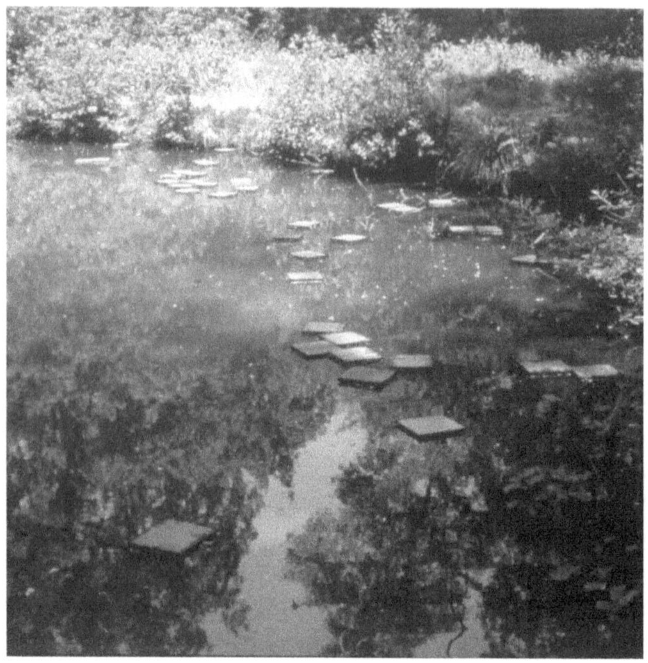

FIGURE **1.2** *Carl Andre,* Walnut Water Scatter, *sheets of walnut, Installation, Middelheimmuseum, Antwerp, 2001 © Carl Andre/ARS. Copyright Agency, 2020.*

of the elements assembled; they are all equally lacking. In other words, there is none of the sense of energy or tension between components that one might see in the repetitions of Eva Hesse, for instance. Her later works, which deploy what Yve-Alain Bois has called her 'additive' mode of production, generate a subtle tension between the parts that is not evident in the work of Andre, LeWitt or Judd.[109] In *Repetition Nineteen III* (1968), for example, the nineteen components are peculiarly isolated but in a group (Figure 1.3). William Wilson describes this strange spatial balancing act in Hesse's late sculptural work as causing 'parts to stand together, but not to do much more than stand together'.[110] He suggests she wanted to 'preserve in visibility the threshold where the parts begin to enter a system but have not done so completely'.[111] Wilson's analysis perfectly captures the tension between parts and whole: a system does not subsume

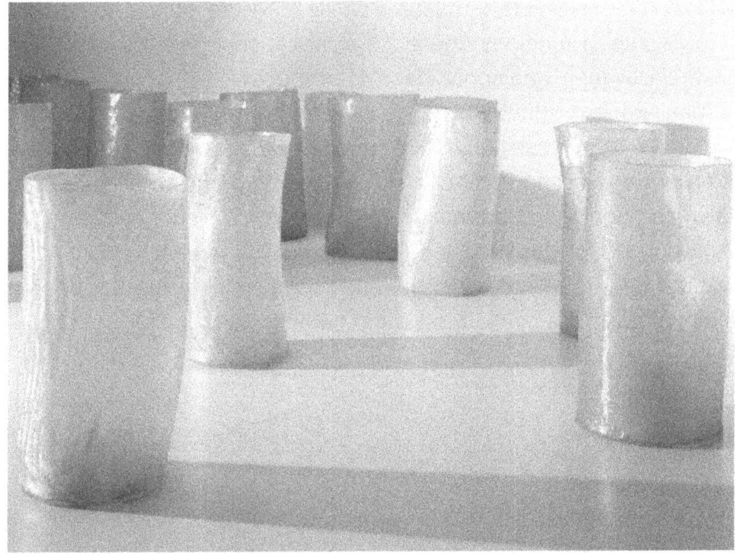

FIGURE 1.3 *Eva Hesse,* Repetition Nineteen III, *July 1968. Fibreglass, polyester resin. Installation variable, 19 units. Museum of Modern Art, New York, gift of Anita and Charles Blatt, 1969 © The Estate of Eva Hesse. Courtesy Hauser & Wirth. Photo: Abby Robinson.*

the individual elements. This cannot be said for Andre, LeWitt or Judd; they manage to fuse components so that they enter their system; the parts don't hover on the threshold. And it is the careful rejection of part-by-part compositional logic, and the minimization of the relation between parts, that creates the kind of blankness André Green describes as the major feature of death narcissism. The aspiration towards blankness is explicitly articulated by Andre. He described his most difficult task as an artist as 'ridding my mind of that burden of meanings which I've absorbed through culture'.[112] He continues: 'You have to really rid yourself of those securities and certainties and assumptions and get down to something which is closer and resembles some kind of blankness.'[113]

To conclude, it is of course impossible to separate life narcissism from its dark double death narcissism; both are part of what André Green calls narcissism's 'Janus' face.[114] Hence the desire to make art that is utterly free of human associations is always going to be caught up with its opposite: arbitrariness, intentionality, subjectivity.

And in minimalism this means that despite the efforts to reach a zero degree of relations, there are still relations, perhaps much less hierarchical than traditional ideas of composition might deliver, but human relations nonetheless. We can only conclude that just as there is a desire to express subjectivity through artistic labour, so too there is an equally strong desire to express nothing and to evacuate the self. The ongoing importance of minimalism – by most accounts it is as important for the second half of the twentieth century as cubism was for the first – speaks to the profound appeal of the impersonal, the minimum, the blank, the almost nothing.

2

The self, without autobiography

From Nauman to Ulman

In a brief description of a video by Bruce Nauman, legendary American curator Marcia Tucker perfectly pinpoints the impersonal nature of much art practice. She writes:

> A one-hour videotape of Nauman walking back and forth in this wall-board channel . . . indicates his attitude toward his own experience of the world. His pieces are about himself without being autobiographical.[1]

Clearly it is not possible to eliminate human associations in art, as the previous chapter indicated, and using the human body as a medium of expression makes this task infinitely more difficult. Tucker's formulation, 'about himself without being autobiographical', captures the peculiar nature of using the body in a deadpan inexpressive manner. The work is not about the particularity of Nauman – his unique existence, thoughts, feelings, desires – but the pared-back nature of the work using little more than his body in motion means that the work is to some degree about himself.

The description is drawn from the exhibition catalogue for *Anti-illusion: Procedures/Materials*, an important show at the Whitney Museum in New York in 1969, known for bringing together minimalist art and music, post-minimalism, conceptual art, structuralist film and body art/performance. In the monotonous action of walking up and back in a narrow corridor for an hour, Nauman demonstrates what Tucker calls the 'phenomenological' approach to art making that united the very diverse artists assembled in the exhibition. Such art is characterized by the elision of symbolism or narrative, offering instead a focus on simple materials and actions, or 'procedures' to use her term. Her succinct summary indicates the importance of the rejection of illusion for this concept of art:

> There is, in the exhibition, no illusionism that is relevant to the past tradition of art. We are presented with a non-symbolic, non-ordered approach, one which does not depend upon a conceptual framework to be understood. The work is realistic in the fullest sense, because it does not rely on descriptive, poetic or psychological referents. The approach is phenomenological in nature, dealing with appearances and gestural modes by means of which physical things are presented to our consciousness.[2]

The kind of literalness usually ascribed to minimalism is here spread across to a broader range of practices.

While the work in question wasn't identified in the catalogue, and nor was it actually in the show, I am assuming from the images reproduced in the catalogue that it is *Walking with Contrapposto* 1968, which perfectly fits Tucker's description and is an hour in duration.[3] The narrow 'wall-board channel' or corridor used in the filming of that work was in the exhibition.[4] In *Walking with Contrapposto*, Nauman mimics the well-known asymmetrical pose of classical statuary where the weight of the body is shifted to one foot, thereby throwing out the hips in a mildly comical manner when the body is in motion. This classical reference clearly contradicts the tabula rasa version of avant-garde art Tucker is advocating, but the opacity of the action, its inscrutability and seemingly pointless repetition remain in play.

This work is certainly about the body, its ideal form and the absurdity of that archaic pose or posture, which is perhaps only exaggerated by its newfound usefulness as a method for navigating a very narrow corridor. It is a senseless task for which there are nonetheless methods that are fit for purpose, setting up a humorous tension between purposefulness and purposelessness. Tucker's language draws attentions to such tensions and the contradictory nature of the work: hence her phrase 'about himself without being autobiographical' and later 'highly personal without being psychological'.[5] While she does not tease out precise meanings for these phrases, like a good critic she delivers the terms that are at the heart of the work's significance.

To continue her line of thinking, the work is certainly about Nauman as it conforms to the genre of the artist's self-portrait – it is a display or representation of the artist's body and shows the artist engaged in the practice of making art – hence it is about himself and personal in that limited sense. Yet it reveals almost nothing of that self, certainly nothing psychological, nothing autobiographical. Shearing away autobiography, but holding on to the idea of a self, is one of the tactics that enables the singular body to be made available for art and one that has far-reaching consequences for late-modern and contemporary art.

This chapter unpacks this idea of the self without autobiography and some of the different ways this is figured. The focus of the chapter is works using one body, mostly the artist's own body, although on occasions the performance is delegated. The use of a singular body often raises the issue of gender, or at least that has been the case for many women and non-binary artists. White male artists, like Nauman, can make works about tasks, gestures and materials and procedures, but can women? Generally, I think the answer to that question has been no. Women must work to suppress the objectifying male gaze – and a certain undesirable type of depersonalization – while developing other strategies to neutralize the body, to cut it free from an autobiographical reading.

The contemporary work I focus on in the second part of the chapter, Amalia Ulman's *Excellences & Perfections* (2014), plunges into the diaristic and the autobiographical, only to withdraw from both when the illusion of the confessional narrative is unveiled. It is a fitting successor to the first generation of feminist work on the gendered body. And, indeed, this work draws the kind of ire about narcissism and the nature of femininity previously directed at certain women artists of the 1960s and 1970s.

1 How to lose yourself

The spectre of autobiography and the return of expressiveness seem to haunt the early reception of body art. Hence critics and artists are overly emphatic about the exclusion of such personal references and qualities. For example, the early chronicler of this emergent art form Italian critic Lea Vergine is adamant that this way of making art 'always involves . . . the loss of personal identity'.[6] Similarly, pioneer of performance art, Ulay claimed the overarching aim of his work with long-time collaborator Marina Abramović was to be like an object, a status to be attained by 'the noninvolvement of self, of consciousness, of decision, of realization'.[7]

A zealous tone of denial can also be found in an important early article on American body art by critic and curator Willoughby Sharp. He makes a series of pronouncements about how to regard the use of the body, starting with the idea that it is just another 'sculptural material'.[8] Art historically, he frames body art as a reaction to conceptual art, which he argues tried to 'remove experience from sculpture'. He cautions, however, that this interest in experience does not mean that 'body works are a return to some kind of expressionism'.[9] He then very explicitly outlaws any personal connotation or meaning: 'The work is not a solitary celebration of self', 'It's more about using a body than autobiographical', 'The artists feel no need to vent their personal emotions in their work. The artist's own body is not as important as the body in general', 'The personality of the artist refines itself out of the work, impersonalizes itself'.[10] Citing James Joyce, he concludes that the desired impersonality can be obtained when the artist 'remains within or behind or beyond or above his handiwork, invisible, refined out of existence, indifferent, paring his fingernails'.[11]

Sharp's article provides a useful taxonomy of single-person body art, focusing on works involving the artist's body. In each instance, the body becomes something else, so that there is a tension between the brute materiality of the body and the metaphorical way the body is said to operate: the body as tool, the body as place, the body as backdrop, the body as prop. In short, in his account the 'body' in body art is modelled after inanimate things – the objective rather than the subjective end of the spectrum. It is perhaps not surprising that all of his examples are by male artists. The desire to relinquish agency and presence that animates these practices is, for Sharp, a solely masculine renunciation.

The contrast between male and female artists is, of course, very well worn terrain in discussions of body art and performance. As Jane Blocker remarks: 'It is rather commonplace to think of women's performance art as having a more diaristic, personal quality and of men's performance art as transcending the narcissism of personal reflection.'[12] Men can transcend the personal, women apparently cannot. To be able to transcend the personal one needs to be self-possessed in the first place and broadly that has not been the case for women artists. As Amelia Jones writes, women body artists, like Hannah Wilke, were 'removed from the lure of potential transcendence' relegated to exploring instead how her 'body/self is always already not her own'.[13] The colonization of the female body is a recurring theme of feminist art and feminist art criticism.

Interestingly, feminist opposition to the gendering of the impersonal urge was most evident in literary studies in the 1980s, rather than the visual arts in the 1970s. Feminist literary critic Nancy K. Miller famously bewailed the impact of antihumanist approaches to authorship that sought to deny or suppress the self, signature and identity. As she put it, women writers had rarely 'felt burdened by too much Self, Ego, Cogito, etc'.[14] She makes an incisive point about the deliberate ceding of authorship and the denial of the personal signature: 'Only those who have it can play with not having it.'[15]

While opposition to poststructuralist versions of anti-humanism were widespread in literary studies, the central issue – who could abrogate authorship – did not have the same purchase for feminist art historical scholarship. Perhaps that is why masculine renunciation continues unabated. It continues, for example, in the solo performance of French choreographer Xavier Le Roy, *Self Unfinished* (1998). This work follows the tracks laid down by early body art advocates of impersonality. As the title signals, this work questions the idea of a complete coherent self. Le Roy describes his choreography as making the body 'become something else' – a strategy, as we have just seen, that is very well aligned with earlier body art practices.[16] Similarly, his statements about the work perfectly echo typical impersonal

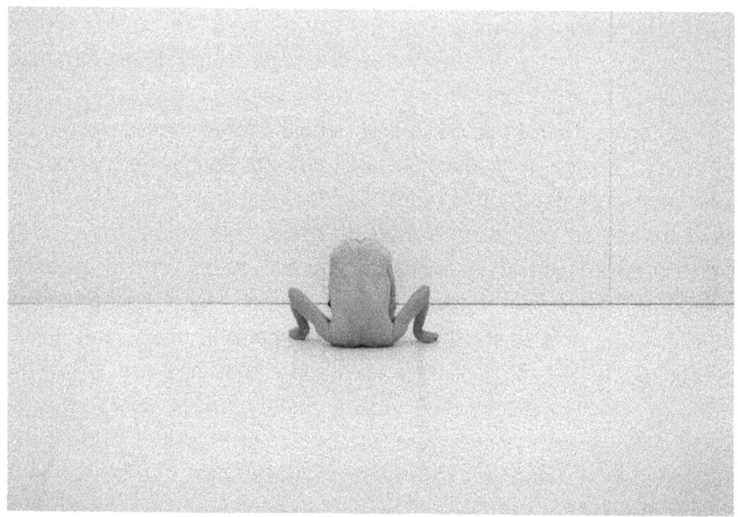

FIGURE 2.1 *Kaldor Public Art Project 31: Xavier Le Roy,* Self-Unfinished, *Carriageworks, Sydney, 17–19 November 2015 © Xavier Le Roy. Photo: Pedro Greig.*

strategies: 'I flee from identities', 'I try to become an object', he aims to 'to disappear in the space'.[17]

And indeed the fifty-minute performance is a mesmerizing transformation of his body through movement and costume. He appears as both animate and inanimate things, to me at one point he looked like a roast chicken, at another a human pretzel (Figure 2.1). The strange and wonderful forms he adopts are aptly described by François Piron as 'hallucinogenic'.[18] The costume he uses serves this purpose well. At the beginning of the performance he is simply dressed in dark trousers and shirt, but the shirt somehow shapeshifts to become a black skirt which when worn upside down transforms him into a kind of double-ended body without a head. Yvonne Rainer vividly describes her experience of the surreal corporeal transformations from that point in the performance:

By the time you're into the contortions with the dress, we're given this extraordinary hybrid creature which confronts us with a multiplicity of interpretations. For me it alternated variously as insect, martian, chicken, watering can, caterpillar into pupa, et al. What saved it from being a Pilobolus-like entertainment (a crowd-pleasing American group that combines bodies to create biomorphic oddities) were the stillnesses and extended durations. We must sit with our attention riveted, waiting for the next stirring. Like watching a spider or snail. Your timing in this piece is exquisite: no pandering to short attention spans here.[19]

White male bodies, we can conclude, are able to connote bare life, materiality and literalness, as well as becoming quite other things. They can even reject stable selfhood, embrace a type of objectification and seek to challenge the attainment of subjectivity. It is possible for Le Roy to speak of 'the body' and its transformation as his focus because he does not have to contend with gender – his body is generic, or 'the body in general' to cite Willoughby Sharp's terms. In contrast, female bodies cannot stand for a generic body and they rarely connote transformed material or pure action in this fashion. The familiar gendered dichotomy immanent/transcendent ensures women are at once mired in the bodily and the world of mere appearances, and yet unable to represent the body's various states and meanings.

When it comes to the nude body, the contrast is even more marked. Think of the naked torso of Bruce Nauman spurting a perfect jet of water from his mouth in the photograph *Self Portrait as a Fountain* (1966–7), or Vito Acconci's performance for camera *Trademarks* (1970) a humorous riff on unique marks where he is shown biting parts of his naked body and then using the bitten cavities as stamps. These two works, wry in the first instance with its knowing art historical reference to Marcel Duchamp's urinal of the same name and masochistic in the second example, do not direct you to think about masculinity or the male body. The actions of the artists are what draws our attention as well as the particular manner of treating the body as material – a readymade material in one, a crafted substitute art material in the other.

In an interview with Carolee Schneemann, American performance artist Barbara Smith summarizes with great precision the approach of male body artists like Acconci and Nauman:

When men like Acconci, Nauman, and Burden began to work with the body it was with a focus on its behaviour and permutations.

They used their bodies as tools for self-discovery with a kind of self-disengagement. It seemed to me that they were exploring things in a quasi-scientific way but not really exploring maleness.[20]

Smith's phrase 'self-discovery with a kind of self-disengagement' is another carefully calibrated expression, like the 'self without autobiography', that captures the operation of the impersonal mode of male body art. Her expression honours the peculiar ambivalence: an investigation of subjectivity that also seems to cancel that out.

In contrast to the latitude accorded to male artists to explore the body, female artists in the early days of body art were often criticized if their work used the naked body and particularly if they appeared to take obvious pleasure in their bodies. Lucy Lippard in a widely cited essay on women's body art made the point very clearly and forcefully. She writes:

> Men can use beautiful, sexy women as neutral objects or surfaces, but when women use their own faces and bodies, they are immediately accused of narcissism . . . . Because women are considered sex objects, it is taken for granted that any woman who presents her nude body in public is doing so because she thinks she is beautiful. She is a narcissist, and Acconci, with his less romantic image and pimply back, is an artist.[21]

Certainly, this contrast describes the reception of work by conventionally attractive women artists, such as Hannah Wilke and Carolee Schneemann, as Lippard reports. These two women had extraordinary bodies and the expression and exploration of female sexuality was certainly part of their art. There are, however, practices by women that display the kind of complicated impersonality captured by the phrases 'the self without autobiography' or 'self-discovery with a kind of self-disengagement'. I want to consider some of these practices before turning to the intriguing way in which Amalia Ulman continues this history.

Three works will suffice to outline the way women artists operated within the seemingly contradictory formulation of the self without autobiography: Joan Jonas's *Mirror Check* of 1970, Eleanor Antin's *Carving: A Traditional Sculpture* (1972) and Ana Mendieta's *Corazón de Roca con Sangre* (*Rock Heart with Blood*) (1975). Each of these works involved the artist's nude body and thereby risks the accusation of narcissism and the sexualization of the body.

Mirror Check (Figure 2.2) is now performed as a delegated performance, but was first performed by Jonas herself. She reports that it was originally shown to a small artworld audience, largely of people she knew. The performance involves the slow self-inspection of the body using a small round mirror. She describes it as 'a very meditative piece' and certainly the delegated version of it I saw in Sydney in 2013 for '13 Rooms' had that quality.[22] The slow and dispassionate investigation of virtually the entire surface of the woman's body was gently involving. With the movement of the mirror, the viewer's attention was shifted to consider each part of

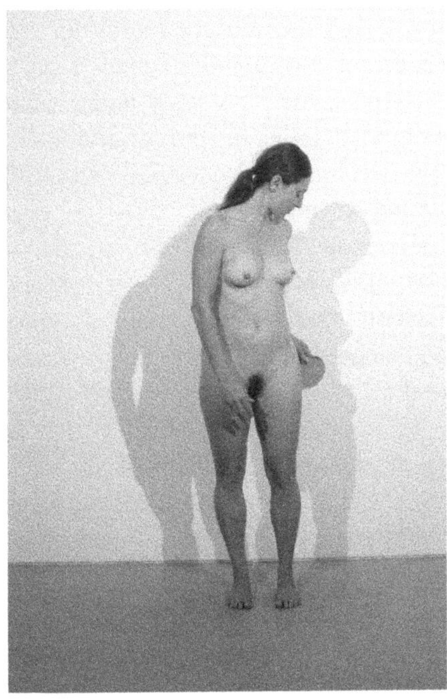

FIGURE 2.2 *Kaldor Public Art Project 27:13 Rooms, curated by Klaus Biesenbach and Hans Ulrich Obrist. Joan Jonas,* Mirror Check, *1970, performed for 13 Rooms, Pier 2/3 Walsh Bay, Sydney, 11–21 April 2013 © Joan Jonas. Photo: Anna Mckay.*

the body, rather like a yoga relaxation exercise. Jonas describes the delegated performance as 'intimate' given the small room in which it is performed; the work, she says, is one of her simplest and thus 'modest' in that sense.[23] In the version I saw, the audience was close to the action and yet strangely excluded by the performer's self-absorption; that negation of the audience made viewing less awkward or embarrassing.

Jonas explains that the work was influenced by the Women's Movement and thus it was about reversing the gaze: the performer claims her body as her own.[24] There's an interesting feminist insertion here into art historian Michael Fried's idea of the negation of the 'primordial convention' that art (or at least painting) is 'made to be beheld'.[25] Fried famously argued that paintings depicting people absorbed in tasks, where the subject is clearly preoccupied, tend to negate the beholder and deny their gaze. In *Mirror Check*, it is as though the closed circuit of the performer's self-examination precludes or makes redundant the audience's gaze. That coupled with the deliberateness, the slow pace and continuous nature of the self-examination dictates a kind of meditative detachment on the part of the viewer. The work becomes an object lesson in how to look at a woman's nude body in a cool disinterested way. We see a woman occupied with a task that demonstrates ocular self-possession, in other words, a self turned inwards, but without autobiography. When asked about the vulnerability nakedness usually connotes, Jonas drew attention to the absence of that kind of self-representation:

> It seemed to other people I had made myself vulnerable, but it really wasn't the case. It wasn't autobiographical. Also, I was protected by the distance from the audience, and in my work, no one breaks the wall – or they haven't so far. I don't know any performance artists who have been heckled.[26]

The alignment of autobiography and vulnerability is an astute assessment of what might lead to feelings of exposure and openness to shame. While *Mirror Check* does not use masking, persona or egoless surrender to shield the self, self-absorption delivers a similar protection. The performer might explore every inch of her naked body in a public situation but not in a way that invites commentary, sexual fantasy or sexual objectification.

Intriguingly, Eleanor Antin refers to some of her works, such as *Carving: A Traditional Sculpture*, as taking an autobiographical turn. She writes of this turn as a shift in her practice in the early 1970s:

> Around this time I began to use myself as material and I must confess to an almost voluptuous pleasure in moving from biography into autobiography. *Carving: A Traditional Sculpture* was a naturalist transformation, a piece consisting of 148 sequential photographs of my naked body 'carving' down 10 pounds over a period of 37 days of heavy dieting.[27]

It is curious that Antin invokes autobiography for a serial project that presents her body in the deadpan and dispassionate manner of the mug shot, or given the full-length view, like an anthropological specimen with front, back and profile shots. The diet and weight loss depicted in the series are certainly 'real' aspects of her life but would hardly qualify as autobiographical detail of her particular character or circumstances. The humour of the piece also creates a considerable distance from documentary protocols. The title wryly aligns her use of her body with traditional sculptural methods: the removal of substance to produce a form. Here, of course, it is her own body that is the sculptural material subject to reduction. The absurd but fitting comparison of the often feminized activity of dieting and the high art technique of carving is one of the sources of amusement. The work is also argued to satirize the humourless monotony and pseudo-science of conceptual art of the day.[28] Antin herself said:

> The early conceptualists were primitives. Contrary to their belief, documentation is not a neutral list of facts. It is a conceptual creation of events after they are over. All description is a form of creation. There is nothing more biased than scientific documentation. It presents a non-psychological image of the 'natural order' with no more claim to objective truth than William Blake's symbolic universe.[29]

Her sophisticated critique of the claims to objectivity and scientific truth of documentary and deadpan conceptual art aligns well with

Abigail Solomon-Godeau's recent re-evaluation of feminist art of the 1970s. Solomon-Godeau argues against the dominant view that first-generation feminist art was naïve essentialism that aimed for '"authentic" self-representation'.[30] She says of this work by Antin that it is 'fundamentally deflationary of an ideal, not revelatory of an authentic self'.[31] She sees such work as showing a prescient attitude to selfhood, asserting that artists like Eleanor Antin, Lynda Benglis, Hannah Wilke and Ana Mendieta, among others, anticipated the theoretically complex postmodern approaches to identity of the 1980s and 1990s where the self is constituted by, and entangled with, representation, and authenticity is debunked as an impossible construction.[32] Referring to the work of Francesca Woodman, Birgit Jurgenssen, Marina Abramović, Yoko Ono and Ana Mendieta, she writes: 'in all of these instances, the artist presents herself as an impersonal screen, a field of projection.'[33]

While impersonality is not Solomon-Godeau's chief concern in this article, she identifies a key way in which women's body art utilizes impersonal blankness. Presenting the body as an impersonal screen perfectly describes works such as Cindy Sherman's Film Stills series as well as performances by Antin involving her invented personas, like ballerina Eleanora Antinova and the King of Solana Beach. While the dieting images of *Carving* suggest the inscription and internalization of societal expectations, they are also simultaneously funny and very raw. They bring a different inflection to the self without autobiography. The naked dieting self is displayed unflinchingly and yet we are not privy to Antin's thoughts or feelings – her facial expression conforms to institutional portraiture's demand for neutrality. Her standardized poses, identical across the series, similarly indicate nothing of her personal feelings or attitude. The humour creeps in at the level of the title, which contains the vulnerability that is also on show. Her recent reprise of the work *Carving: 45 Years Later* (2017) as an eighty-two-year-old woman underscores the vulnerability of nudity and the dieting female body (Figure 2.3).[34]

In the homage to this work by trans artist Cassils, *Cuts: A Tradition Sculpture* (2010), there is neither humour nor vulnerability. Instead this durational performance encourages visual scrutiny of the gradual appearance of a bodybuilder's cut body – the gaining of 23 pounds of weight over twenty-three weeks. Moving towards the body builder's

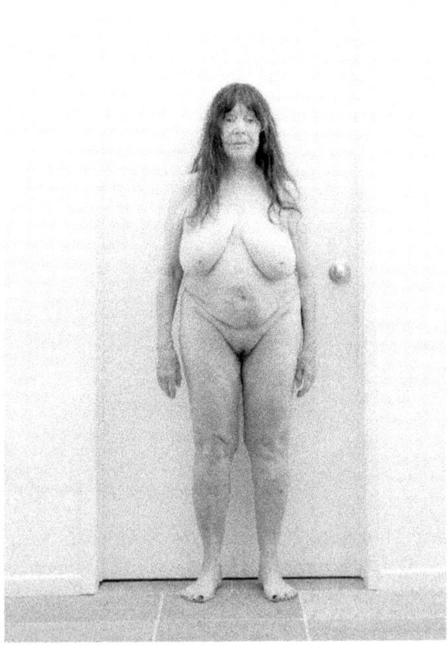

FIGURE 2.3 *Eleanor Antin,* CARVING: 45 Years Later, *2017, 6 3/4 × 4 3/4 inches, 5 images per day, 100 days starting 8 March 2017 © Eleanor Antin. Courtesy of the artist and Ronald Feldman Gallery, New York.*

idea of perfection shifts the oppressive feeling of needing to conform to societal norms that framed Antin's work. It is a subcultural set of choices that are centre stage in this glitzy, self-conscious, highly stylized performance.

The raw quality of Antin's *Carving* is also an attribute of Ana Mendieta's use of the body. While it is certainly true that Mendieta's Silueta Series, based on just the outline of her body, presents an impersonal blankness, the shapes pressed and moulded in the landscape also suggest transience and exposure to the elements. That openness and vulnerability to the erosion of time and the elements is particularly evident in *Corazón de Roca con Sangre* (*Rock Heart with Blood*). The short three-minute film shows her nude body from above, isolated and alone on an inhospitable mud flat beside a body of water (the Iowa River) just visible as a murky triangle in the right hand corner (Figure 2.4).

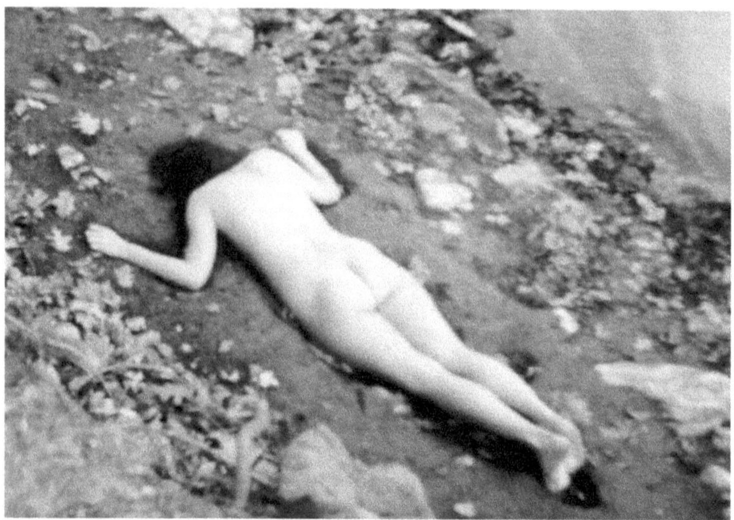

FIGURE 2.4 *Ana Mendieta,* Corazón de Roca con Sangre *[Rock Heart with Blood] 1975. © The Estate of Ana Mendieta Collection, LLC Courtesy Galerie Lelong & Co. © Ana Mendieta/ARS. Copyright Agency, 2020.*

The camera is tightly focused on the patch of ground where an ash silhouette has previously been gouged and burnt into the earth. In that cavity, Mendieta paints a bright red heart – the rock heart covered with blood indicated in the title. Her spare movements preparing the site are at once ritual-like and strangely poignant. Her body seems vulnerable and small, a slight pale body with neat and precise actions that terminate with her motionless body placed face down, united with the heart and her own perfectly fitting outline. The positioning of the rock heart on the right hand side of the silhouette gives an outward facing orientation to the depicted body, making Mendieta's downward gesture into an intimate meeting of the two bodies – a kind of embrace. Despite this intimate gesture, the body is not sexualized; the precarious context and angle of observation make that an unlikely reading.

Mendieta's desire to commune with the earth is strongly conveyed by the simple action, a gesture that emphasizes connection rather than individuation. Although, the performative action to camera also presents her as a solitary figure in the landscape. There is an autobiographical dimension to the desire for communion articulated by her as a response to her exile from her homeland, Cuba.[35] That feeling of yearning for return, not necessarily precisely legible in the work itself, nonetheless colours the work, giving it an atmosphere that pulls her body away from being an impersonal screen. Her nudity in the muddy landscape makes the action seem primal and raw: a self that is seeking to merge with the context, to lose the self perhaps in an egoless fashion.

All three works use the deadpan impersonal language of early body art with careful additional inflections to render the female body less visible. Jonas subtly negates the beholder by withholding the results of the actions of self-scrutiny (only the performer sees her self-image). Antin uses the distancing mechanism of humour, and the title shifts what could be a humiliating exposure of the less-than-perfect female body, to a clever comparison. Mendieta limits visual access to the body; its depiction largely from behind and at an oblique angle shifts the emphasis to the strange ritual she performs in the seemingly remote location. These clever calibrations of bodily presentation aim to downplay the typical objectification of women's bodies routinely found in Western art history. Hence the reception of these practices was not dogged by the accusation of narcissism, nor threatened by the return of expressionism or autobiography.

To work against stereotypes in this fashion is one way in which feminist artists have operated; the adoption and amplification of stereotypes is another strategy developed in this period. In her close analysis of the work of Hannah Wilke, Amelia Jones argues such practices forgo distance, embracing seduction yet 'exceeding the framing apparatus of art critical judgment'.[36] Jones is critical of the equation of distancing techniques with criticality: a result of the valorization of Brechtian approaches to cultural production by feminist scholars in the 1970s and 1980s.[37] She aims to develop a different account of criticality. Her argument rests on the idea that Wilke's work seduces by pulling the viewer close and that the ensuing collapse of the distinction between viewing subject and viewed object serves a feminist purpose. She argues: 'Without distance, one has no "perspective", no vantage point from which to construct or reaffirm the borders of the frame – one is emphatically *not* disinterested but fully and pleasurably implicated in the process of determining meaning'.[38] The issue of proximity to the image is key to Mary Ann Doane's classic analysis of the female gaze (analysed in the final section of this chapter) and is crucial for understanding practices that encourage identification and lack of distance.

Curiously, Jones notes many times that Wilke uses the distancing technique of exaggeration yet does not comment on how this interferes with the asserted collapse of distance and distinctions. For example, Jones writes: 'Wilke's works exaggerate', 'Wilke's "feminine" narcissism exaggeratedly solicits the viewer's "masculine" desires', 'Wilke's self-presentation through exaggeratedly erotic, "feminine" poses', 'her work through the rhetoric of the pose, reiteratively exaggerating it beyond its veiled patriarchal function of female objectification'.[39] Like parody, exaggeration underscores artificiality, making whatever is amplified seem unnatural, humorous, perhaps even ridiculous. The presence of humour, however, does not cancel out the operation of seduction that Jones identifies. I believe she is right to draw a sharp distinction between works such as Wilke's that reiterate 'normative femininity', albeit in an exaggerated fashion, and artists working in the Brechtian vein.[40] The latter often concentrated on the repudiation of 'the male gaze', consider for example the work of Martha Rosler, VALIE EXPORT, Mary Kelly, to name just some of Wilke's contemporaries.[41] Wilke's exaggerated postures are perhaps better described as seductive and parodic; she is both feminist and flirt to use Lucy Lippard's apt characterization.[42]

I am underscoring the role of exaggeration here not only to open up the complexity of Wilke's practice but also because in the work of Amalia Ulman exaggeration went largely undetected. In an era when popular female figures like Kim Kardashian and Laura Lux have astonishingly artificial bodies, augmented by innumerable additives and procedures, the parodic exaggeration of femininity is much harder to determine.

Significantly, Amalia Ulman's web-based performance *Excellences & Perfections* (2014) also brings together the two approaches Jones polarizes. It has a type of modernist unveiling that retrospectively operates as a kind of Brechtian distancing technique and yet it is keenly attuned to the seductions of amplified clichéd femininity. How do we make sense of this contemporary body art that dwells upon the traditional feminine pleasures of food, fashion, flowers and fetishized femininity? Ulman's durational performance of five months on the picture-sharing social network Instagram is an interesting heir to the legacy of feminist one-body strategies. *Excellences & Perfections*, in fact, perfectly embodies the performance of the self without autobiography.

2 *Excellences & Perfections*: The diaristic, deception and social media

Unusually for an artwork, *Excellences & Perfections* began in a clandestine fashion on 19 April 2014. The performance was discreetly but enigmatically introduced into Ulman's existing Instagram feed by a white screen announcing 'Part 1', with the title of the work 'Excellences & Perfections' less conspicuously displayed as a caption below that image. Perhaps barely noticed by anybody (it had only twenty-eight likes), that post established the framework for the ensuing project. When Ulman posted her regular updates, mostly a couple per day, it was not widely known that she was playing a character (or characters), rather than documenting her life. She had created a 'fictional alter ego', as the *New York Times* put it, which ostensibly fooled her thousands of followers.[43] At the conclusion of the project Ulman had over 88,000 followers on Instagram.[44]

The final post in the series is a blank white shot, posted on 19 September 2014.[45] This metaphorical closing of the curtain is preceded by a number of posts on 14 September, including two of her new boyfriend, a close-up of roses and a video of the artist waving and blowing kisses, subtended by a caption that thanks her 'followers for being so nice and supportive'. A month later, she posts a link to her talk at the ICA in London where she discusses the project as an artwork. In between these book ends there were over 180 posts, through which a loose life narrative is threaded that includes major events such as her break-up with one boyfriend, followed by selfies taken before, during and after subsequent dates, and eventually the introduction of the new boyfriend who appears at the project's conclusion. The narrative thus moves in a familiar romantic arc from heartbreak to happily ever.

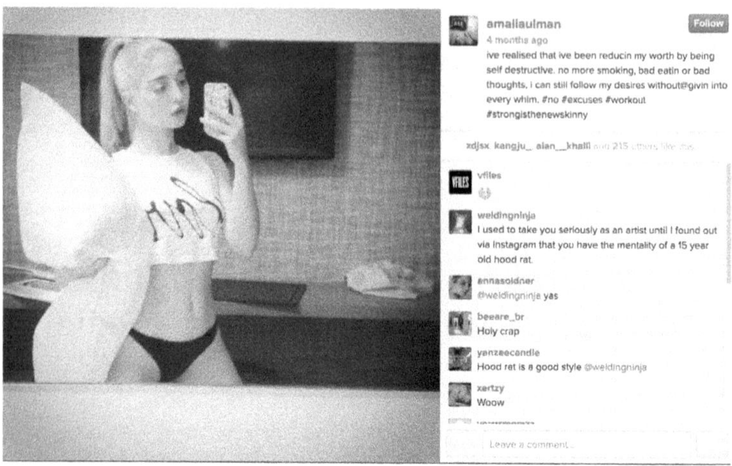

FIGURE 2.5 *Amalia Ulman,* Excellences & Perfections *(Instagram Update, 28 June 2014), courtesy: The Artist.*

Interestingly, even artists who knew Ulman as an artist (she has an honours degree from Central St Martins) did not twig that *Excellences & Perfections* was not recording her life.[46] A comment from 28 June 2014 underscores the effectiveness of the deception: 'I used to take you seriously as an artist until I found out via Instagram that you have the mentality of a 15 year old hood rat'(Figure 2.5).[47] The caption for this selfie, like many other posts, has a squirm-making message about self-worth and self-destruction, while also registering a preoccupation with weight and appearance. The mirror selfie shows her semi-clad body with midriff exposed, gazing into her phone like a mesmerized Narcissus. The poster clearly doesn't recognize Ulman as 'performing' the vacuity she demonstrates. As art critic Gilda Williams put it, Ulman's mimicry of 'self-absorbed-sexy, aspirational, objectified, weirdly blank' femininity was 'pitch-perfect'.[48]

Ulman's work before this project was clearly informed by feminism and was critical of the endless body maintenance required of women. In an interview published on 30 April 2014 when the project was in train, she said, 'I'm fascinated by people's obsession with their bodies and the quest for self-improvement.'[49] She clearly indicates she is researching body modification and the so-called wellness industry:

> So, right now, I'm doing lots of research on plastic surgery and the body as a screen where culture sees itself reflected. One of my favorite websites is realself.com, where people keep track of all the pre- and post- surgery processes, with all their insecurities and expectations. . . . The world of the aesthetic clinics is only a part of the project; I will also be focusing on the inner side of beauty, like nutrition, meditation, exercise and breathing techniques – and clichés on what is expected of women in terms of character and presence.[50]

Her clarity about the concerns of her practice make it very curious that the Instagram performance was not uniformly recognized for what it was by art insiders, at least. Perhaps there was no precedent for using Instagram in this fashion. Certainly, Ulman has since argued that a project like hers is no longer possible, that it was 'very specific to its time', that is, the early days of Instagram (it was invented in 2010) when the platform was relatively new.[51]

Instagram is generally assumed to be a diaristic medium: part of the paradigm shift from memorialization as the dominant trope for photography, to the new trope of 'showing' that the internet and smart phones have effected. The photograph on social media, or the 'social photo' as Nathan Jurgenson calls it, generally signals immediacy and veracity – here's who I'm with and what I'm looking at, eating, wearing.[52] It does not have the more complex temporality of the photograph so succinctly summarized by Roland Barthes as the 'illogical conjunction of the *here* and the *formerly*'.[53] That temporal paradox is loosened if not completely lost by the sliding scroll of social media images where photographs are rarely viewed again – *here* has swallowed *formerly*. These networks are worlds of eternal presents, an endless stream of images into which it is extremely hard to step twice.

Interestingly, when Ulman was interviewed in 2015 following the revelation of her fictional production, it was in the context of a well-established literary genre – the diary. The article framed diaries as 'the slipperiest of all literary forms'.[54] To use the epistolary form of the diary to discuss her work instantly gets to the heart of the project – the unreliable narrator and suspect self-presentation. Ulman has certainly said that she wanted to underscore the idea of the unreliable self-reporting of social media.[55] Her impetus for the performance is also described in terms of wresting control of her own image, to try to limit its interpretation, not unlike first-generation feminist pronouncements. She said:

> Among the still lifes and portraits, I take selfies – mostly to remind my later self of where I've been. But after being contacted by men who seemed to feel that they knew me from my photographs alone, I began to worry about my online presence, the lack of control I had over it.
>
> And so the performance that I now call 'Excellences & Perfections' began. I decided to fake an Instagram account to tell the story of a 25-year-old girl who was, in many ways, an absolute stereotype.[56]

The parallels to classic feminist projects examining feminine stereotypes such as Cindy Sherman's *Untitled Film Stills* (1977–80) or Martha Wilson's *A Portfolio of Models* (1974) would not be lost on feminist art historians. Clearly, role-playing is at work in all of these practices, the self is concealed by an array of personas, but in Ulman's performance the selves on display were not clearly identified as roles. This deception or concealment is the most salient difference that separates Ulman's work from these other feminist artists working more directly with the unveiling or the demystification of feminine stereotypes.

Aligning *Excellence & Perfections* with more enigmatic public art actions might better serve Ulman's tactics; for example, the confronting public performances of Adrian Piper have a similar unannounced quality. Piper took to the streets in drag in works like *The Mythic Being* (1973–5), adopting deliberately offensive masculine patterns of behaviour and harassment that are registered by the horrified faces of bystanders caught in documentation shots. In other works, like her Catalysis series (1970), she performed various unannounced public actions designed to confront and perplex. In *Catalysis 1* she travelled on the D Train in New York during rush hour in unpleasant smelling clothes soaked in vinegar, egg and cod liver oil.

The work of Sophie Calle aligns most closely with Ulman's diaristic approach. For example, Calle's major installation for the Venice Biennale *Take Care of Yourself* (2007) brought together the responses of 107 women enlisted to make sense of an email ostensibly sent to her by her lover telling her their relationship was over. It is unclear whether Calle's work is really based on her life or not, although that is certainly how she represents it in interviews.[57] With *Excellence & Perfections*, there isn't this kind of ambiguity; during the performance Ulman seems to fully inhabit the stereotypes and then the fictional nature of the performance is unveiled after the performance concluded. In other words, demystification had a temporal lag that substantially changes how it operates; I will return to this in the final section.

3 Archiving Instagram art

Ulman's project is now archived as part of 'First Look', a joint venture between digital arts organization Rhizome and the New Museum in New York. The collaboration is intended as a kind of curation or 'showcasing' of art on the net, as they put it.[58] Selected digital works appear on both organizations' websites. The creation of this shared platform enables art using social media, such as Ulman's, to be preserved, while also signalling the museum's somewhat belated acknowledgement of the importance of post-internet art.

Excellences & Perfections was until very recently also still on Instagram, albeit widely known to be an art project. Viewed on either of these platforms, it was possible to see the work in close approximation to its original *visual* presentation – that is, the posts appear along with the comments from Ulman's many followers as well as her replies to some comments. The archived version captures the comments only up until the end of the performance. On Instagram, the project was still open to comments and Ulman appeared to be still maintaining her own account.

There are of course a number of important differences between the original Instagram feed and its archived presentation. First, the project's presentation is now massively temporally telescoped: the serialized presentation is lost. The gradually unfolding narrative is replaced by the replete presentation of the on-demand repository. It is possible to, as it were, binge watch Ulman's performance in one sitting or to digest it more slowly. In other words, the temporal unfolding is now controlled by the viewer rather than the producer. Second, the distracted mode of its original unfolding is lost: it is no longer possible to view *Excellences & Perfections* as just one part of a complex feed of images.

Finally and most importantly, the project's presentation on Rhizome is unambiguously understood as a performance. Ulman's elaborate hoax – her ability to pass as a hood rat – can't be recaptured. In that sense, the project has the unrepeatability and ephemerality much vaunted by performance theorist Peggy Phelan.[59] As she famously put it:

> Performance's only life is in the present. Performance cannot be saved, recorded, documented, or otherwise participate in the circulation of representations *of* representations: once it does so it becomes something other than performance.[60]

Phelan's pronouncement about the importance of real time apprehension of performance applies to only the first moment of *Excellences & Perfections*. The work has two modes of existence: the original unrepeatable performance by Ulman, which was barely perceived as a performance, and the project after the reveal when it is perceived as a durational performance but it is already over. The audience, then, is paradoxically either too early or too late to witness the performance.

Another avenue for viewing the work is the 2018 art publication that documents the complete performance. Strangely here the images are divorced from the comments, and the comments are presented in an appendix. Presented in this way, the banality of the individual photographs and memes comes to the fore. Ulman's images are mostly not visually inventive or complex.[61] Rather like postmodern uses of photography, as described by Douglas Crimp, originality and uniqueness were not the intent. Emulating and inhabiting circulating clichés and stereotypes was the aim of the work.

4 Three acts, three Amalias

As one would expect of a well-made play, *Excellences & Perfections* has typical dramatic features: there is dramatic tension, a climax and of course narrative resolution. And borrowing from the visual arts, there is the courting of controversy and shock. For example, Ulman appears to have a breast enlargement in July 2014. The augmentation – that apparently didn't actually occur – is represented by a post-operative shot of the upper part of her torso with bandages. From then onwards, in her selfies and other images, Ulman appears to have larger breasts. From a feminist point of view this action could be interpreted as pandering to the male gaze, although very frequently the justification provided by women for undergoing cosmetic surgery is that they did it for themselves. Indeed, this is how Ulman justifies her augmentation in a post on 19 July:

> reasons I wanna look good
> for myself
> for myself
> to plant the seeds of envy in other bitch's hearts
> for myself[62]

Less antagonistic to a feminist sensibility, there is the suggestion of drug taking. On 17 July an image is posted of what looks like lines of cocaine arranged in the trademark interlocking Cs of Chanel. The climax, however, is some kind of minor breakdown. I say 'minor' as the duration is incredibly brief, she cries twice on 8 August then seems back to usual form by 14 August when she apologizes for her behaviour. She writes:

> Dear everyone,
>
> I'm really sorry for my behavior recently. I was acting weird and committed many mistakes because I wasn't at a good place in my life tbh.
> I'm recovering now and feel better, all thanks to the help of my closest friends and family. I'm very grateful to my family from [*sic*] rescuing me from such dark void. I was lost.
> Also, feeling blessed for all my internet friends who sent wonderful recovery messages on fb.
> I'm really sorry if I have offended you.
> Everything came out from a soul full of pain, anger and darkness.
>
> Thank you so much for being patient with me,
> Blessings,
> Amalia[63]

A comment from a follower reads: 'Drugs?' No reply. The audience could only speculate, but the carefully planted clue certainly pointed in that direction.

The radio silence that may have once resonated for assiduous followers between the posts is hard to recapture in the documentation. Certainly, a five-day absence from social media by a regular poster would be cause for concern. An artist I spoke to who was following her posts, but unaware it was just a performance, was indeed deeply unnerved by the five-day silence.

The two short videos of Ulman crying posted on 8 August bring to the surface typical internet behaviours: a nasty hater, a typical internet spat between this hater and a fan, and also more knowing art historical references. One person comments with the hashtag #basjanader, another with the title of the Dutch conceptual artist's 1971 film of him crying *I'm too sad to tell you*. One follower says: 'Euh why are you filming this? Is Instagram your real life?'[64] These comments show the reception of this work is more uncertain than the media hype would suggest. As noted earlier, while the work is regularly presented as fooling thousands, the comments demonstrate a range of responses. Intriguingly, the media release for 'First Look' on 7 August 2014 identifies Ulman as one of the chosen artists well over a month before *Excellences & Perfections* had concluded.[65] Similarly, the journalist Anna Soldner who interviewed her eleven days after the project began frequently comments on Ulman's feed.

Alongside these apparently autobiographical details there are photographs of food and drink, other women's bodies, flowers, potential purchases, outfits as well as innumerable inter-titles or memes so often shared on social media platforms that dispense banal life advice, such as: 'do not compare yourself to others', 'make time for yourself', 'don't worry about those who talk behind your back they are behind you for a reason'.

Visually, there are three colour schemes that divide the work into acts. The first part is very pink and cute. The second part favours browns: chocolate, coffee and clothes that match. The final part becomes more colourful, while in content it is much more oriented towards food and lifestyle. These colour schemes and accompanying visual styles map onto the three roles Ulman reports she adopted: 'cute girl', 'sugar baby' and 'life goddess'. Each act has a different profile image and description, and as Kimberley Henze points out, Ulman's use of language also changes dramatically to match the assumed persona.[66] These characters were chosen, Ulman says, because 'they seemed to be the most popular trends online (for women)'.[67] Her reiteration of 'normative femininity' to cite Amelia Jones, is drawn from online trends of young women's self-representation.

The cute girl images refer to the Japanese idea of cute, 'kawaii' (Figure 2.6). One follower queries the taste for such childish cuteness in a woman of her age. Some guy comments: 'Aren't you like 35 lol'.[68] Ulman's caption for this post is written like a breathless teen, sharing the purchase of a pink rabbit and asking her followers to respond with 'yay or nai' to her pink wig. Despite the child-like taste and demeanour the body shot is highly sexualized: her nipples (if indeed this is her body) appear above the line of the pink plaid bra-top, placing the image in the realm of self-styled porn as much as cute girl.

The pink images create an easy play between food and the female body – all are consumable. The female body appears alongside moulded jellies and flowers and anaemic strawberries (Figure 2.7). These bleached things are often softly out of focus. While the images blend together effortlessly, the narrative often jars. For example, below

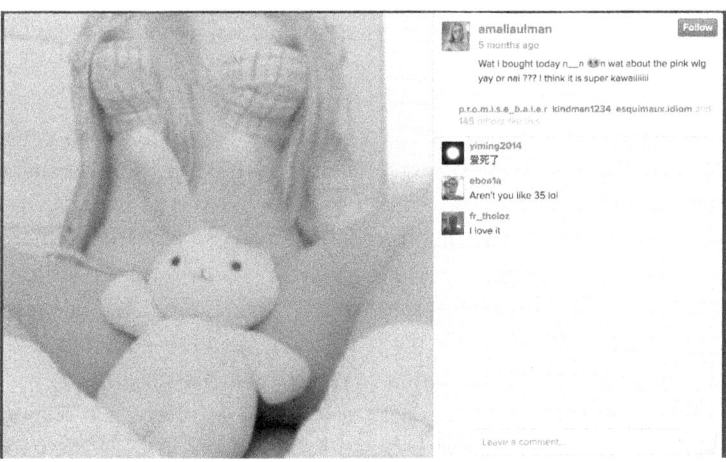

FIGURE 2.6 *Amalia Ulman*, Excellences & Perfections *(Instagram Update, 30 May 2014), courtesy: The Artist.*

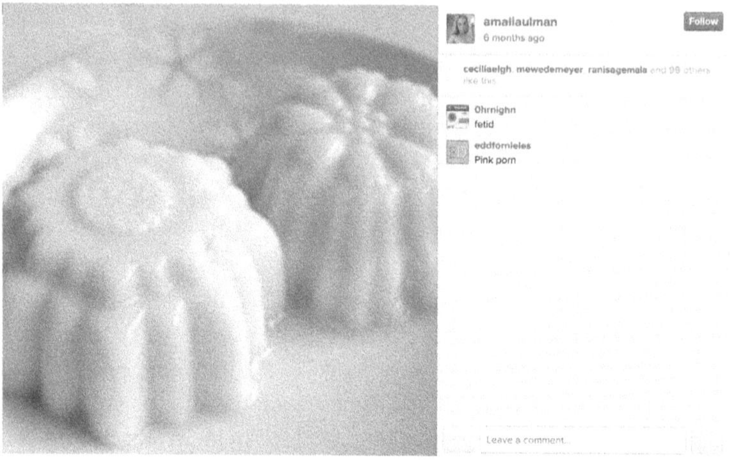

FIGURE 2.7 *Amalia Ulman,* Excellences & Perfections *(Instagram Update, 29 April 2014) (Pink porn), courtesy: The Artist.*

a softly pink butt shot posted on Thursday 22 May 2014, she writes that she is going to start juice fasting for a photo shoot on Sunday, yet a day later an albino strawberry tart appears for breakfast (Figure 2.8). The lack of continuity is an interesting hint at the fabricated nature of the narrative, although insufficient on its own to trigger awareness of the nature of the project given the distracted way in which it would originally have been consumed, interspersed with whatever else the audience was following.

In this sugary pink phase which runs from 19 April 2014 to 22 June 2014, parts of the female body come more sharply into focus when they are objects of desire or envy: I want those knees, those breasts. Parts of the body, it is suggested, can be purchased as easily as hair colour. In the second part of the work (23 June 2014 to 8 August 2014), this pink prettiness gradually gives way to the new colour scheme with brown and beige consumables like ice cream, coffee, designer shoes, bags and more soft toys. In this section Ulman supposedly has the breast job. It terminates with the emotional crisis.

Following her emotional crisis of mid-August, there is a distinct turn towards domestic interests, an image of her in a classic yoga mediation pose epitomizes her new incarnation as 'life goddess' (Figure 2.9). The product shots in this final section of the performance

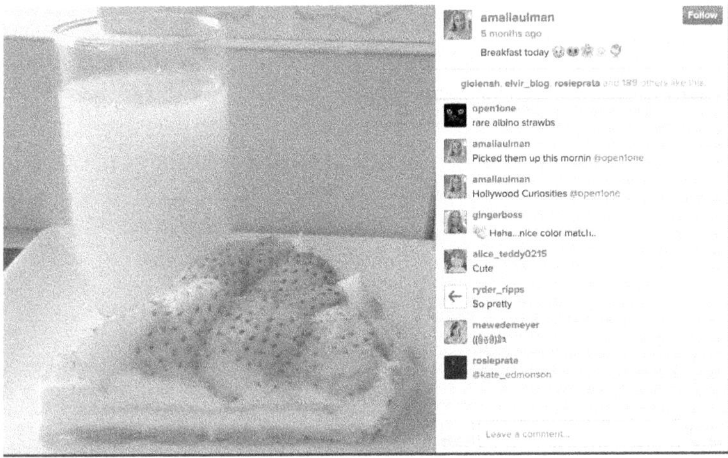

FIGURE 2.8 *Amalia Ulman,* Excellences & Perfections *(Instagram Update, 23 May 2014), courtesy: The Artist.*

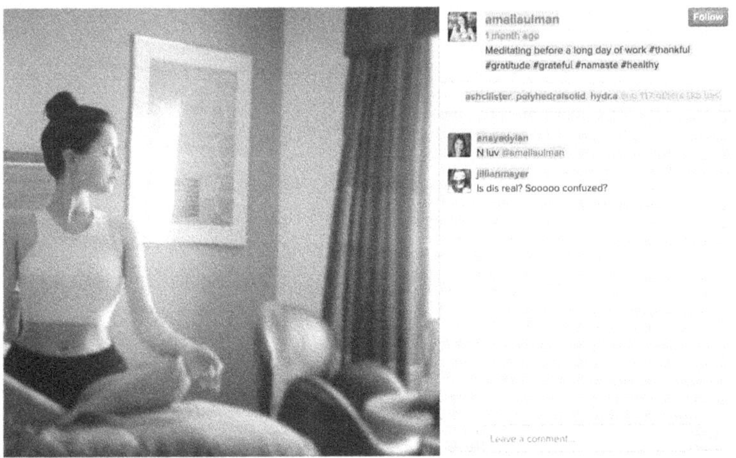

FIGURE 2.9 *Amalia Ulman,* Excellences & Perfections *(Instagram Update, 2 September 2014), courtesy: The Artist.*

have the slick look and careful framing of commercial photography, the out-of-focus prettiness gives way to a preponderance of clear shots of healthy food spreads. Throughout the work, there is in fact an intermingling of professional images and supposedly self-generated content, but the slickness of certain images is more apparent in the later healing phase of her narrative. In all three sections, selfies often taken in a mirror, sit alongside other portraits taken by others including professional images where she appears to be working as a model. There are also many uncredited images that she presents as her choices rather than necessarily of her making – the kind of sharing of content typical of Facebook rather than Instagram.

5 Performativity, masquerade and the work of gender

The analysis of her work predicably has emphasized narcissism, consumerism and self-commodification. For example, one article posed the question: 'Selfies in the name of art: progressive or narcissistic?'[69] Ulman's frequent use of the selfie opens her to the charge of narcissism, while apparently displaying the kind of self-obsession more typical of a teenager. According to social media commentator Alicia Eler: 'The selfie is both an adolescent and celebrity social phenomena.' She argues that these two groups in particular 'have an intense focus on self-appearance, and how they are perceived by others'.[70] The intense focus on appearance and the regard of others has traditionally, of course, also been gendered as feminine.

While the adolescent tone is particularly evident in the 'cute girl' phase of the project, the emulation of social media celebrity is continuous. Rhizome's artistic director Michael Connor describes how Ulman replicates those kinds of aspirational profiles, creating a potent mix of excess and believability:

Through judicious use of sets, props, and locations, *Excellences & Perfections* evoked a consumerist fantasy lifestyle. Ulman's Instagram account is a parade of carefully arranged flowers and expensive lingerie and highly groomed interiors and perfectly plated brunches. These images are excessive, but also believable – because they're so familiar. For many privileged users, social media is a way of selling one's lifestyle, of building one's brand. And Ulman went to great lengths to replicate the narrative conventions of these privileged feeds, from her use of captions and hashtags (#simple, #cutegasm), to the pace and timing of uploads, to the discerning inclusion of 'authentic' intimate or emotional content (a photo of a lover or a moment of despair).[71]

The celebrity culture of people who are famous for being famous, typified by the Kardashians and other lesser-known self-branding mortals, is clearly the backdrop for *Excellences & Perfections*. Given the prevalence of self-marketing and the extreme versions of femininity routinely promoted on Instagram as well as other digital platforms, is Ulman's work an exaggeration of feminine stereotypes? Certainly, her various self-images do not have the mocking quality of artists like Wilke, nor the easily recognized artificiality of Sherman's bygone fashions. On the surface, Ulman's images of the self do not display the requisite distance between the stereotype and its copy that we have come to expect from feminist work. And perhaps that is the whole point; in this way Ulman immerses herself and the viewer in various genres of stereotypical femininity far more successfully than Wilke.

Another key way in which this work has been framed is via the very familiar idea that gender is a performance – or at least femininity is a performance. Describing her aims for *Excellences & Perfections*, Ulman said, 'I wanted to prove that femininity is a construction, and not something biological or inherent to any woman. Women understood the performance much faster than men. They were like, "We get it – and it's very funny". She continues, 'The joke was admitting how much work goes into being a woman and how being a woman is not a natural thing. It's something you learn.'[72]

Here, Ulman echoes Simone de Beauvoir's famous adage written in 1949: 'One is not born, but rather becomes, a woman.'[73] Or going back further, we could see Ulman's work as part of the acknowledgement of the supreme artificiality of femininity discussed in Joan Riviere's 1929 essay 'Womanliness as Masquerade', which concludes with the startling observation that there is no difference between the performance of femininity and genuine womanliness.[74] So what is Ulman adding to this very familiar idea? Why has her work been lauded as the first Instagram masterpiece and as an art world sensation?[75]

Clearly, Ulman is remaking a classic rather than breaking radical new ground here and that is part of why the work was so deeply resonant. She is generating online content that could be placed in the lineage of the women's pictures of the 1940s, the romantic weepies that specifically targeted a female audience. In other words, while her audience included men, it is addressed principally to the pleasures and interests of women: as she said women 'get it' – femininity is a labour, but perhaps a labour of love. There were also female followers who clearly didn't 'get it' and just wanted grooming tips and recommendations. One persistent follower Gabrielle Matelson is clearly keen to emulate Ulman's dyed hair colour. On two occasions Ulman replies to her hair queries.[76]

Ulman also acknowledges the eruption of anger when the fictional nature of the project was revealed:

> With *Excellences and Perfections*, people got so mad at me for using fiction. That was the main critique: 'It wasn't the truth? How dare you! You lied to people!' Well, that's because you should learn that everyone is lying online. I'm not the first one! There are so many girls that go to hotels to take a better selfie, or another expensive place. If they're trying to be a social climber or whatever, that's what they do. It's normal. It's becoming more and more normal to be conscious of those things. It's funny how people still take it with this value of truth.[77]

The audience is clearly a key part of *Excellences & Perfections* as the careful archiving of their comments up to the reveal indicates. Followers, in fact, are turned into unwitting participants when the work is archived. Along with the women who got it, there were fans, jokers, critics, trolls, haters and the occasional follower trying to catch her out. Ulman frequently appears to be bravely dealing with trolls and negativity. A caption from a post on 9 July 2014 says, 'dun care bout all ur negativity'.[78] She clearly had the troll audience in mind in terms of narrative content, as she puts it, 'the sadder the girl, the happier the troll'.[79] The project then is not just about femininity, it is about the way it is received on social media – the project is a perfect snapshot of some of the swarm-like behaviours Web 2 has unleashed.

Audience commentary also pinpoints the moments of artificiality that prefigure the final reveal. For example, on 23 June 2014 an exchange between Ulman and a follower uncovers the artifice of an image of Ulman looking at her phone (Figure 2.10). The caption of the post suggests Ulman is on her own waiting for someone, but the image belies that – it is not a selfie. When asked if she has 'an Instagram butler', she replies that she is joking and he/she has caught her out.[80] Distancing techniques, then, were in the project in real time, often in the text/image interactions, but also in the images such as the cute girl image with nipples exposed that I mentioned earlier.

Are these glimmers of distancing how Ulman's performance of self-fashioning can be read critically? Or to put this another way, how does the project interrogate obsessive self-fashioning, rather than simply showing it? Each time I have presented this material as a paper, the audience has overwhelming felt there was no criticality that they could discern in the self-fashioning on display. Certainly, *Excellences & Perfections* is not a classic critique of feminine self-fashioning in the manner of first-generation feminist artists, like Annette Messager. Messager's accumulation of images of women undergoing beauty treatments in *Voluntary Torture* (1972) gains its critical purchase through the sheer number of images of strange

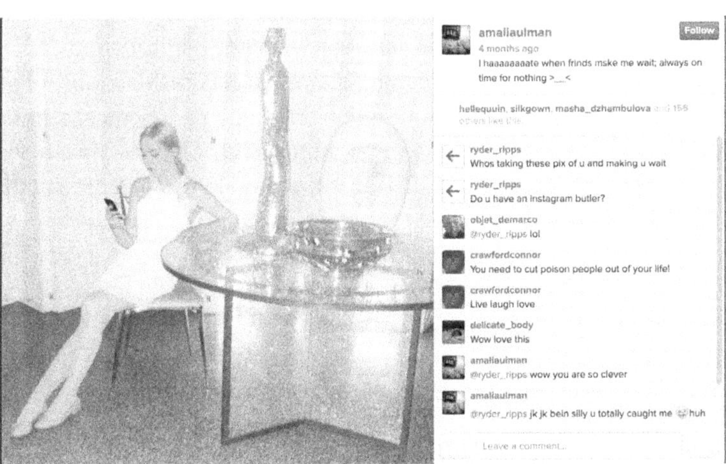

FIGURE 2.10 *Amalia Ulman,* Excellences & Perfections *(Instagram Update, 23 June 2014) (always on time for nothing), courtesy: The Artist.*

procedures framed by a title that mocks the activities depicted. Most importantly, Messager's attitude is presented unambiguously and simultaneously with the images.

In contrast, *Excellences & Perfections* is a much more 'open text' to use Umberto Eco's famous term.[81] It is a well-crafted fiction that enables identification as much as trolling. For the many women who 'get it' it is funny, perhaps teetering on the edge of parody, for others it reveals its high art credentials but not with any great fanfare. Ulman herself underscores the absence of parody and criticality:

> There's a difference between humor and parody . . . . People denounce my performance and say it's like, you're laughing at basic bitches. But, you know, I'm also a little bit of a basic bitch – I'm laughing at myself a little bit. I'm also all these things – the cat lady, the crazy female artist, the feminist, and I'm the conservative woman who goes to work every day. And I'm tapping into all these things. I don't stand on the outside and just judge.[82]

The unveiling of the performance however does shift the presentation of femininity, not to the more familiar feminist modes of parody and judgement, but certainly producing a kind of critical distance. Viewed from the angle of post-reveal we can see unveiled what Mary Ann Doane calls the 'flaunting of femininity', that is, *Excellences & Perfections* puts on display three very distinct and different forms of feminine masquerade.[83] When flaunted in this fashion, according to Doane, oppressive norms of femininity become like masks to be worn or held at a distance. In other words, they become visible and optional. Female agency, for Doane, is located in the gap created by such perceptions. The reveal then enables a flip from immersion to distance. What happens, though, if the distance produced is now too far away from the image? By this I mean that the paradoxical 'too early, too late' temporality of *Excellences & Perfections* is repeated spatially: too close, too far.

In this way, the masquerade of femininity takes on a new contradictory form. Looking at the images in *Excellences & Perfections*, stereotypes are indulged and proximity to the image is embraced. Rather than breaking up the love affair between women and the image, which Mary Anne Doane perceived as a necessary step away from feminine stereotypes, Ulman seems to amplify that romance. And then with the reveal, femininity becomes total artifice – we believe nothing of what we see. My sense is that this contradictory spatial and temporal structure is what produces anger as much as humour. Depending on the audience's capacity to tolerate ambiguity and incongruity, the work may anger or amuse, horrify or delight. For those of us that find it humorous, it is perhaps because it speaks to the guilty pleasures of commodified Western femininity. Ulman's performance reflects the contradictory nature of our accommodations of the interminable task of femininity within a feminist sensibility. Normative femininity and feminism often do not sit easily together, or in the same time and space – perhaps what this fiction shows is simply the truth of that proposition.

3

Cool intimacy
Pairs, couples and duos

In a catalogue for an exhibition titled *Health and Happiness in Twentieth-Century Avant-garde Art*, American art historian Donald Kuspit remarked that the themes of health and happiness are not generally associated with avant-garde art.[1] Instead, the avant-garde is typically oriented towards youth, rebellion and destruction, rather than the quieter pleasures of happiness. Such an orientation suggests an individualistic combative masculinist approach to art and life, very far from the traditionally feminine occupations of building and maintaining familial relationships, tending and mending the social fabric, as well as the sappier chick lit ends of this relational domain: love, intimacy, romance. These typically feminine roles and concerns are not particularly evident in late-modern or contemporary art practice, except insofar as relational art might be said to be concerned with human relations.[2] Romantic relations, needless to say, have not been a prominent part of the relational art remit, that is, not until Nat Randall and Anna Breckon's extraordinarily powerful participatory artwork, *The Second Woman* (2016).

The Second Woman is the exemplary contemporary two-person performance I examine in this chapter. This performance transforms the impersonal technique of seriality associated with minimalist and conceptual art, to produce a strikingly unsentimental picture of romance. In fact, this two-person participatory performance, framed by a queer eye, uses repetition to make heterosexual romance appear very strange. One hundred mostly male volunteers-cum-participants perform the same scene one after another with Randall or one of her delegates. In the five Australian performances Randall has starred, but since 2018 *The Second Woman* has also been performed by others. In Taiwan, Zhu Zhi Ying was in the lead role in a Chinese language production, and most recently in 2019 in New York actor Ali Shawkat replaced Randall. In New York, the performance was promoted by the catchy and pithy slogan that sums up the key parameters of the work: 'One woman. 100 men. 24 hours.'[3] Framed in this way, the pairing of one woman with 100 different men over 24 hours suggests a female rival to the conquests of infamous male philanderers, real and fictional: Don Giovanni and Casanova. This reversal of power, with a woman commanding a series of men, is key to the way *The Second Woman* reframes heterosexual romance.

While romance is an important genre in many other art forms – film, literature, opera – in post-1960s visual art it is not a prominent theme. *The Second Woman* thus takes an appreciable risk in framing an endurance performance around a romantic relationship, albeit with a critical eye. The two-person work is nonetheless the ideal structure to examine basic human relations because in philosophy, psychology and psychoanalysis the pair, couple or dyad is the principal focus for accounts of intersubjectivity. Philosophically, the relationship between two subjects is usually framed asymmetrically: self and other, master and slave, or less hierarchically I and Thou. That structure presupposes a singular subject, the 'I' or self, that is then set in relation to another. Traditionally, of course, the second subject, the other in the dyad or dialectic, is indeed secondary, thereby becoming the familiar figure of disenfranchisement analysed in much feminist and postcolonial criticism. The privileging of the singular self falls away with most of the two-person works I consider – they model interdependence and equality in intriguing and unprecedented ways.

This chapter considers how the two-person performance negotiates both intimacy and the form of the couple. Given that two-person works in body art and performance often involve actual couples, impersonal techniques of distancing abound. If in one-person works the self is presented with minimal autobiographical elaboration, in two-person works intimacy is the personal dimension that is simultaneously conjured and negated.

Philosopher Christopher Lauer defines intimacy as fundamentally a type of recognition, suggesting mutual recognition is at the heart of intimacy, enabling each person in a relationship to feel seen, known or understood in their particularity.[4] While the philosophy of recognition might stress the interdependence of self and other, Lauer frames intimacy as more slippery, contradictory and ambiguous: it demands what cannot be delivered, what he calls 'a closeness beyond closeness'. For him, intimacy involves our innermost nature, what he posits as dividing us from others – 'one's deepest nature, that which is very personal or private'. However, he argues that when 'we strive for intimacy in a relationship, we strive for a dissolution of this division'.[5] While the contradiction he constructs here seems overstated – our inner lives are hardly unique or incommunicable – the tension between connection and individuation in proximate relationships is an issue that frequently arises in two-person performances. Such works create occasions to think about our connections to, and disconnections from, others.

The chapter surveys a variety of two-person works. In the first part, I examine non-romantic pairs and duos and their performances, acts and actions, which take three main forms. The first variant is when one part of the pair is the artist who engages or teams up with participants; the second is when a pair of artists collaborates, like Linda Montano and Tehching Hsieh. The third variation is when artists construct pieces for pairs of participants to enact, such as the works of Lygia Clark and Franz Erhard Walther. The second part of the chapter considers the emotionally cool presentations of mainly heterosexual relationships, focusing in particular on the work of Ulay and Abramović, and Sophie Calle and her unnamed male lovers. The final part of the chapter examines *The Second Woman* and its contribution to the contradictory condition of cool intimacy.

1 Relations

In contrast to single-person performances, works with two bodies, however they are configured, create an intersubjective relation, even when formal or sculptural investigation seems to be the principal concern. For example, stripped back art practices of early performance art often unleashed corporeal magnetism, that is forces of attraction and repulsion, empathy and shame, whether they intended to or not. Such an elementary force is certainly at work in some of Marina Abramović's basic training exercises involving two bodies.

I experienced the power of one of her very simple two-person interactions in 2013 at the forum for the performance art project, 13 Rooms at Pier 2/3 Walsh Bay in Sydney, curated by Hans Ulrich Obrist and Klaus Biesenbach. The exercise, led by an instructor from the Marina Abramović Institute, entailed standing up and looking deeply into the eyes of the person beside you. From memory, it was supposed to be someone you didn't know. I think this conjoined gaze only lasted for four or five minutes but it seemed like much, much longer.[6] To me, the action felt curiously both embarrassing and invasive, as though such prolonged visual contact should be reserved only for lovers or mothers and babies. As a component of Abramović's method – her accumulated techniques for exploring the links between mind and body drawn from forty years of performance art research – no doubt this simple action is designed to provoke these kinds of complex emotional responses.

Certainly, Abramović discusses the emotional reactions triggered by the direct gaze in relation to her 2010 two-person performance, *The Artist Is Present*, at the Museum of Modern Art in New York (Figure 3.1). At the core of this endurance performance (of roughly 700 hours) staged in the public space of the museum was a mutual gaze: each visitor or participant sat opposite Abramović for a period of time principally determined by the visitor. In an interview about the work, she emphasizes the inward turn the action promoted:

when you enter the square of light and you sit on that chair, you're an individual, and as an individual you are kind of isolated. And you're in a very interesting situation because you're observed by the group (the people waiting to sit), you're observed by me, and you're observing me – so it's like triple observation. But then, very soon while you're having this gaze and looking at me, you start having this invert and you start looking at yourself. So I am just a trigger, I am just a mirror and actually they become aware of their own life, of their own vulnerability, of their own pain, of everything

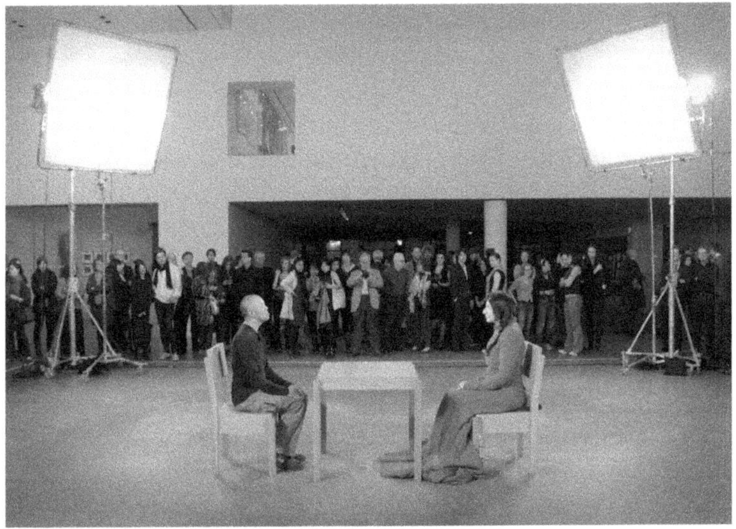

FIGURE 3.1 *Marina Abramović,* The Artist Is Present, *2010, Courtesy: Marina Abramović Archives © Marina Abramovic/VG Bild-Kunst. Copyright Agency, 2020.*

– and that brings the crying. [They are] really crying about their own self, and that is an extremely emotional moment.[7]

That such a simple action could have such profound effects is intriguing, but perhaps not surprising to anyone aware of the way silence and inaction operate in practices like meditation. Presumably, the mutual gaze sufficiently anchors the participant in time and space, creating a relatively passive state, which enables things (thoughts, feelings) to emerge that might otherwise be repressed, unnoticed in the busyness of life or perhaps more actively, actually defended against. The literalist scenario of two bodies facing each other, with no script or prescribed content, presumably makes space for the emergence of the visitor's subjectivity. Aesthetic subtraction here enables the emergence of the bare life of the body, suggesting a kind of latent volatility that can be subdued or amplified.

It is interesting to consider whether the audience watching this performance contributes to the intensity of the interlocked gazes. Or whether like couples using public space for an uncomfortable conversation, there is something about the knowledge of observation that contains emotions, insists on decorum and diffuses intensity. Abramović describes the audience, and even her presence, as receding when the person turns inward, but Abramović and the audience are of course still present, even if not the focus of attention. They serve as a relatively impersonal holding environment for both theatrical release and the containment of emotions.

The emerging genre of one-on-one performances that pairs one performer with one participant in this fashion more usually does not admit an audience. Thus, the transaction between performer and participant remains private and thereby more open to risk and uncertainty about format and roles. Certainly, I have signed up for a number of one-on-one performances with some trepidation, not knowing what to expect. One of the most memorable, however, is Norwegian artist Mette Edvardsen's poetically titled work *Time Has Fallen Asleep in the Afternoon Sunshine: A Collection of Living Books* (2010), which I experienced at the Biennale of Sydney in 2016. When booking a timeslot, the participant needed to choose a book. I chose Herman Melville's short story 'Bartleby'. The performance was held at a public library in Newtown, an inner-city suburb of Sydney. There were instructions outside the library to commence at the circulation desk; from there I was able to borrow my 'living book'. She (the living book) took me to a quiet unpopulated part of the library and recited from memory a large chunk of Melville's short story (Figure 3.2).

The performance provides an interesting experience of shifting roles in relation to reading, in particular active and passive positions are refigured in complicated ways. For example, the normal activity of reading was ceded to the living book, but the more passive role of observation as part of a crowd gave way to the active listening required when you are the only audience member.

The work recalls the childhood pleasures of being read to: the bedtime readings of early childhood before surrendering to sleep. Although, of course, the living book isn't reading and is able to return your gaze. Victoria Pérez Royo captures the effects of this animation of the book very well:

> some of the conditions of traditional reading are preserved: a quiet
> place is offered in which concentration is possible. The reader

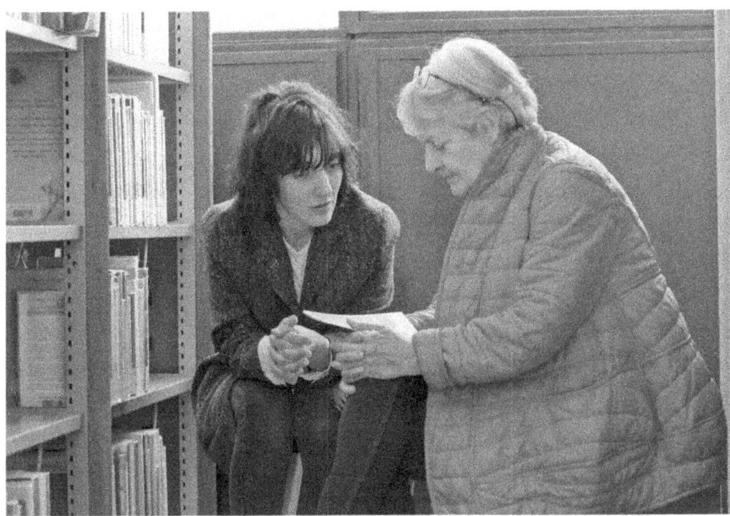

FIGURE 3.2 *Mette Edvardsen*, Time Has Fallen Asleep in the Afternoon Sunshine: A Collection of Living Books, *2010. Photo: Document Photography – Sydney Biennale (Sydney). Courtesy of the artist.*

decides the moment to start reading, provided the book is not already *borrowed*. But in the displacement and reconception of reading that this project proposes, new conditions arise: the book is not in the hands of the reader, but in front of her. The reading is constituted by the meeting of two people, by the co-presence of performer-spectator that characterizes the performing arts, in contrast to the solitude of a usual literary reception. Besides, the moment of encounter is stronger here than in the case of the spectator being comfortably positioned in a row of seating, because the situation proposed in *Time has fallen asleep in the afternoon sunshine* is intimate: the book has a voice and also a body. The spectator is not safe in the unidirectionality of her gaze, but is also subject to the gaze the book returns.[8]

Intriguingly, the project summary used to promote the performance for the Kunstenfestivaldesarts in Brussels took little account of this complex interpersonal dynamic. The performance takes place, it states, with 'disarming naturalness and without the intermediary of a physical object'. The description continues 'the living books remind us that learning a text "by heart" is an act of love that mobilizes memory as much as forgetfulness. It is the direct transmission of this process that makes the encounter so very moving.'[9] Being the recipient of this act of love is indeed moving; however, the affects involved are more complicated than this description would suggest. The emphasis on directness and the removal of the physical intermediary underscores the intimacy of the encounter but ignores the mediation of the living book. The delight of being told a story, which is the core of this experience, is complicated because of the delivery by a stranger to whom one owes one's attention. So while there were gains from a recital, for example, I was struck by how much more alert I was to the beauty of the prose when I was hearing rather than reading the text, there were also losses: a stranger, unlike an indulgent parent or a book, requires social effort and can elicit shyness triggered by the affect of shame. The encounter thus combines two of the most other-oriented feelings: love and shame. It is the combination of these two affects that enables cool intimacy: the gift of reading tempered by the self-conscious unbuffered encounter with a stranger.

When artists engage with each other in performance their coupling can allow the audience to shift back into the indulgent position of viewer or voyeur. The apotheosis of the collaborating pair must surely be Tehching Hsieh's *Art/Life: One Year Performance (Rope)* 1983–4 where he was tied to fellow artist Linda Montano from 4 July 1983 to 4 July 1984. The rules of this extreme durational performance were established at the outset and were certified by witnesses: the artists were required to always be in the same room, to remain joined by the 8-foot rope tied around their waists, and yet never to touch. The rope was attached by sailor's knots that were sealed with lead and signed by two witnesses – the intact seals at the close of the project served as confirmation of its truthful enactment.[10]

Sleeping together in the same room was relatively easily accomplished by single beds; showering, according to Thomas McEvilley, was exempted from the same room rule and one presumes that included visits to the toilet.[11] The pair taped their conversations but these more personal relics of the performance are not available for public scrutiny. The work thus documents the voluntary surrender of the artists' privacy, and yet preserves their privacy by shielding the core of the interpersonal experience. As Alex and Allyson Grey remark: 'it is one of the most highly publicized works of performance art' and yet 'it retains an impenetrable privacy. No one will ever know "what it was like" but the artists themselves.'[12] The main documentation of the work accessible to the public are the many photographs: the couple in their separate beds, the couple in the street, the couple at their separate desks. When shown full frontal, which was a common compositional stance they used for photographic documentation, their expressions are mostly neutral, betraying nothing of their feelings or their attitude to each other (Figure 3.3). The presentation of the work is thus deliberately deadpan and unsensational – devoid of 'personal clutter' to cite a structuralist filmmaker's distaste for that dimension of Carolee Schneemann's practice.[13]

The roping together of the two artists' bodies is usually discussed as an endurance task rather than as something disturbing, potentially embarrassing and deeply intimate. As Frazer Ward explains, the tenor of Hsieh's practice is 'anti-psychological and anti-subjective', thereby discouraging an inquiry into the experience of extended proximity.[14] Hsieh considered the work to be a 'formal exercise', as Karen

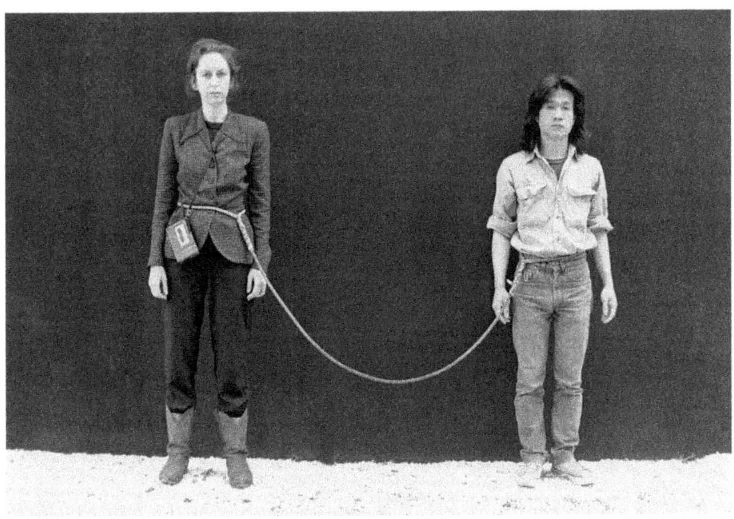

FIGURE 3.3 Art/Life One Year Performance 1983-1984. *Life Image* © 1984 *Tehching Hsieh, Linda Montano. Courtesy the artists.*

Gonzalez Rice puts it, and actively resisted what she calls 'personal, social and political interpretations' of the piece.[15] Hsieh refers to this work in a very literalist manner as simply about 'passing time'.[16] In other words, his commentary avoids the personal and downplays the psychological side of the work, showing no interest in the emotional dimension of such extended intimacy with someone, who at the outset of the project he barely knew.

Indeed, in the many interviews with the artists about this fascinating experiment with attachment and co-existence, one rarely gets a strong sense of how they navigated their extended period of intimacy. Hsieh refers only to the 'struggle' of being joined together and always in close proximity, giving little of the flavour of his personal experience.[17] Lara Shalson notes that Hsieh even denied that he and Montano formed a couple; instead he insisted on their separateness. He refers to the format as 'two people equal before the law of the work'.[18] This model of equality and co-existence is intriguing given that authorship of the work is usually attributed solely to him. That said, in interviews Hsieh does demonstrate an acute awareness of their differences both as artists and as people, and apart from his refusal to allow Montano to contribute to his carpentry activities, does not seem overly sexist.[19]

In contrast, Montano describes her position in much less individualistic, almost autonomic, terms. In an interview conducted while the work was still in train, she articulates her dispassionate method for endurance: 'once you give the mind a command, then you watch the body carry out the process.'[20] Her detachment, so much in evidence here, is significantly amplified in a later interview where her stance verges on self-abnegation: 'By staying tied to Tehching Hsieh in his *Art/Life: One Year Performance*, I died a little each day, learning humility and collaboration.'[21] Her commentary on the performance, while acknowledging the psychological dimension, is bent on the renunciation of feeling. For her, the performance is a kind of abreaction: enabling her to purge the emotions that were stirred up:

> Besides training the mind, the piece raises so many emotions to the surface that the soap opera quality eventually gets boring. I feel as if I've dredged up ancient rages and frustrations this year

and although I'm glad that I went through with them, I now feel that holding any emotional state for too long is actually an obsolete strategy. On the other hand, because I believe that everything we do is art – fighting, eating, sleeping – then even the negativities are raised to the dignity of art. As a result I now feel much more comfortable with the negative. It's all part of the same picture.[22]

Montano aims for cool intimacy that dissipates rather than amplifying feeling, while in contrast Hsieh has that orientation at the outset.

Fast-forward ten years and the format of the confined couple is made into a very public spectacle that turns a critical eye on audience voyeurism, ignorance and the objectification of others. The collaboration between artists Coco Fusco and Guillermo Gómez-Peña, *Couple in the Cage: Two Undiscovered Amerindians Visit the West* (1992–3), as the title indicates, framed the two artists as specimens in a cage representing a newly discovered fictious tribe, the Guatinaui. The performance took place in various cultural institutions (museums and art galleries) and public plazas around the world; venues included Covent Garden in London, Chicago's Field Museum of Natural History, Walker Art Center in Minneapolis and the Australian Museum in Sydney. The couple was presented in the manner of zoo animals, circus freaks or nineteenth-century anthropological displays.

In tenor, the work is fairly typical of 1990s ideology critique where the excesses of our racist past are rehashed by repeating shameful practices of human objectification and degradation, sometimes where those acts occurred in previous centuries. The performance was leavened, in this instance, by Fusco and Gómez-Peña's very camp interpretations of Amerindian dress and their absurd presentation of Guatinaui traditional stories and practices (watching TV, making voodoo dolls). The Guatinaui stories were performed by Gómez-Peña for a fee in gibberish with the occasional English word. This humorous presentation of the couple and their intimate daily life is a key part of the cooling of this potentially volatile work about human displays.

While the anthropological or biological idea of a couple was clearly in play here, the focus, at least retrospectively, was on the audience's reactions. In the documentary about the work, an astonishingly large part of the audience take the performance at face value.[23] Their reactions ranged from dismay and outrage to blithe evasion of expected ethical responsibilities to others. The documentary seemed intent upon revealing this shocking level of ignorance and gullibility, as well as unwitting displays of inhumanity – much of the audience appear to be devoid of compassion and untroubled by human exhibits. What is missed when the attention is focused on the audience is the underlying idea that justifies such a display, namely that one couple (in this case, a man and a woman) is representative of a race or nation. That biological shorthand for 'the species' or 'the people' is surely also operative in Tehching Hsieh's collaboration with Montano. Reproductive pairs in an experimental situation have a tendency to inflate into this larger impersonal narrative of bodies: examples, specimens, cases.

The gendered nature of the pair is less important for the two-person works of Lygia Clark and Franz Erhard Walter. Their two-person participatory works of the 1960s and 1970s, the sculptural equivalents of event scores, create couples in uncomfortable proximity, often by binding them together.[24] Brazilian Lygia Clark and German artist Franz Erhardt Walther worked at approximately the same time in the mid- to late 1960s. Clark was living in Brazil when she began to use bodies as the support for her aesthetic propositions. Walther begins to work with the binding of bodies and fabric when he was a student in Dusseldorf in the early 1960s and continues this practice while formulating his major work, *Werksatz* (First Work Set), which he compiled over a six-year period, 1963–9. Significantly, in these artists' works there is no visible emotional display, which is not to say they are without feeling but simply to signal the impersonal mode that takes the heat out of the bare life of bodies.

A number of works by Clark use the couple: *Dialogue of Hands* (1966), *The I and the You* (1967), *Dialogue Goggles* (1968), *Biological Architecture: Egg-shroud* (1968) and *Living Structures: Dialogues* (1969). These works bring together participants in a variety of ways: to complete an action in the case of *Biological Architecture*, while the remaining four works all tie or bind two people together at different points of the body (abdomen, wrist, leg, head) suggesting both a shackle, a forced confrontation and the possibility of collaboration or gestural dialogue, as the titles direct. What might be called the dangers of intimacy (vulnerability, intrusion, loss of freedom) are also evoked by this binding together.

Of the works that involve couples, the two that create the greatest intimacy, *The I and the You* and *Dialogue Goggles*, disrupt or mute connection through blinding the participants or mediating the gaze through goggles and the distraction of a swivelling mirror. These two works clearly enable a kind of intense but diffuse proximity. *The I and the You* is the only work by Clark that explicitly refers to gender. It is comprised of two suits, each with seven zip pockets that the couple are invited to explore. Inside the openings are substances that are loosely gendered – rough for men, smooth for women – so that the man discovers masculine textures inside the woman's suit and the woman similarly discovers feminine qualities or textures inside the man's suit. The process of exploration reveals to each participant the self in the other. When the participant is within the suit, materials do not register objectively but are apprehended as a series of qualities that might pertain to many things – bristly, rough, silky, wet-like. This fragmentary perception is amplified by the incapacity to see what is being felt.

Ariella Budick describes Clark's later works as involving 'messily hippie improvisation' and perhaps in these works with pairs that characterization is most apt.[25] These works often have the look or feel of a hippie encounter, like the dreamy faces absorbed in mutual touch in *Dialogue of Hands* or the staging of a new dawn in *Biological Architecture: Egg-shroud*. *Biological Architecture: Egg-shroud*, with its evocation of birth and death, acts out these seminal moments of existence through the simple means of plastic sheets (Figure 3.4). The two participants face one another; each person puts his or her feet into small net bags sewn into a large rectangular sheet of plastic. They are instructed to wrap the body of the other with the sheet. One life breaks through the shell; the other is shrouded by it. Despite the volatility of acting out life and death moments, the requirement to act or to play a role perhaps lessens the intensity of contact between the two participants; action lessens introspection as surely as the blocking tactics of *The I and the You* diffuse intimacy.

Vulnerability and openness are also qualities of Walther's work with pairs, particularly his fabric pieces that require two bodies. In his series of fabric constructions for bodies, the *First Work Set*, there are fifty-eight pieces or elements as he called them, fourteen of which involve couples. He attributes the openness or incompleteness of

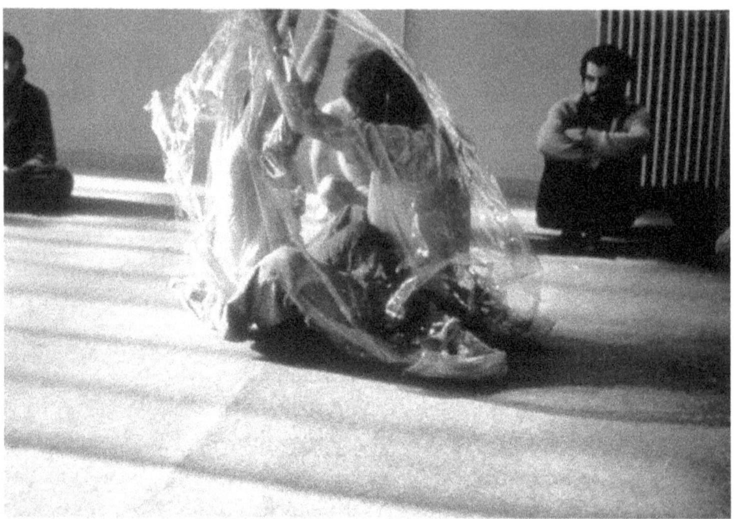

FIGURE 3.4 *Lygia Clark*, Biological Architecture – Egg-Shroud, *1968. Photographer: Unknown. Courtesy of 'The World of Lygia Clark' Cultural Association.*

his work to his childhood experience of the uncertainty of wartime Germany – he was born in 1939.[26] While his initial description of the works as 'instruments for processes' tends to minimize the role of the body and the relationships between bodies, his works nonetheless call up ideas of precarity, intimacy and confrontation just like Clark's, albeit in a much more deadpan, non-expressive manner.[27]

In *30 Closeness* (1967) and *31 For Two* (1967) participants are yoked very closely together by a length of fabric. The pieces determine the distance between bodies. In the case of *For Two*, a rectangle of fabric is pierced by two circles that allow the heads of the two participants to face one another (Figure 3.5). In *Closeness* a rectangle of fabric is surmounted by two loops of material for the two heads, drawing the couple together in extremely close proximity (Figure 3.6). In both cases, there is very little room for the participants to experiment, despite the fact that fabric is a reasonably flexible material. The participants are then positioned, or it would not be too strong to say that they are forced, to look at one another. *Closeness* is the most confronting pairing with the two facing bodies both touching the fabric plane that hangs between them while also keeping them apart.

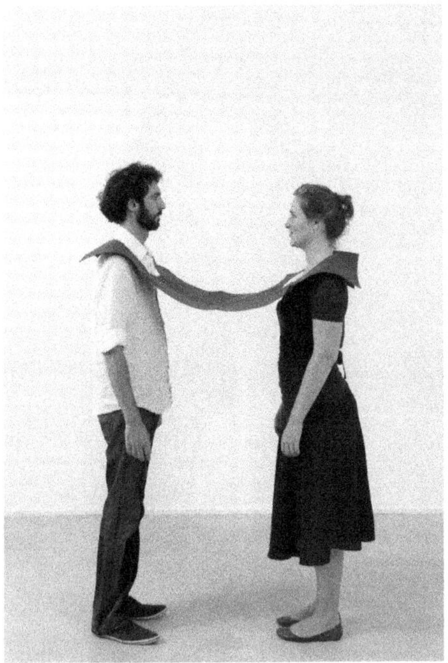

FIGURE 3.5 *Franz Erhard Walther,* Für Zwei (Connection (head)). Single Element n°31 of 1.Werksatz element n°31 of 1.Werksatz, *1967, 47 × 124 cm. Photo François Doury. Courtesy Peter Freeman, Inc.*

Most pairs in the *Work Set* are positioned much further apart. For example, in the twelve other works involving couples, there are mostly quite considerable distances between bodies. The distances make one think of alienation, or contact that is strained or tenuous, in marked contrast to these two elements where the couples are, if anything, too close.

In the early photo-documentation of the elements a stark formality and pictorial austerity is emphasized that matches how Walther writes about this series in a deadpan, unemotional fashion. The openness he ascribes to the work is perhaps meant primarily as a contrast to closed, autonomous or completed works of art. The elements are certainly not open to a very wide range of uses; mostly they can only be used in one predetermined way. The body or bodies enact that one way, rather than choosing it. Curiously, he talks about 'possible ways of interacting' with the pieces, as if there were a range of configurations.

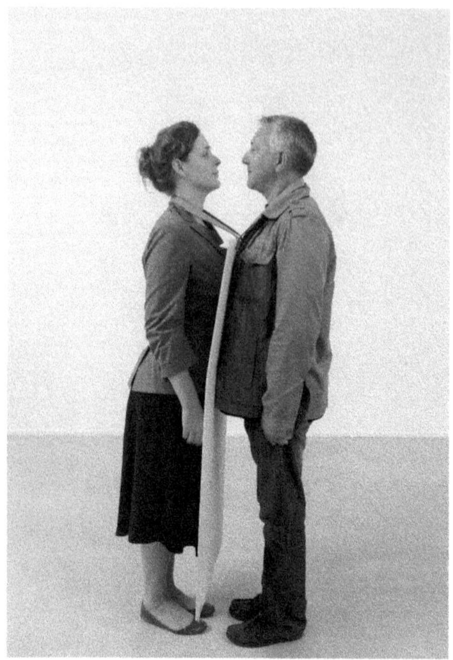

FIGURE 3.6 *Franz Erhard Walther,* Nähe (Connection - separation (head-body)) Single Element n°30 of 1.Werksatz single element n°30 of 1.Werksatz, *1967, white fabric: 119 × 59.5 cm leather tape: 68 × 3 cm. Photo François Doury. Courtesy Private collection, Brazil.*

Following a typical anti-intentionalist strategy, he also suggests use is 'determined by the instrument' rather than the artist.[28] Irrespective of how authorship is conceptualized, his 'sculptural situations' are visually compelling arrangements of bodies and instruments in space, for a viewer at least, if not the participants.[29] The photographs call up a sense of frailty, almost melancholy, as if the arrangements represent a stripped down sociality where mute confrontation, orchestrated by the work and its pliable geometry, is at the core of human relations. The construction of such situations where nothing much happens recalls the kind of reduction of action, purpose and meaning associated with Samuel Beckett's theatre of the absurd.

Curiously, both artists documented their works in natural settings, but neither talks about the most desirable way to encounter them. In the case of Clark, I have not read an account that clearly identifies who she thought would use *Dialogue of Hands*, *Dialogue Goggles* or *The I and the You*, or in what kind of context. Only her propositions enacted at the Sorbonne in Paris had clearly identified student participants.

Walther's discussions of gallery presentation are a bit more revealing. Initially, he did not expect to be able to exhibit his fabric forms and talks of limited interest from his fellow students when he was a student at Dusseldorf.[30] In 1966 when exhibition possibilities were presented to him, he chose to show participants how to interact with the *Work Set*.[31] For example, for Harold Szeeman's landmark exhibition *When Attitude Becomes Form* (1969) at Bern Kunsthalle and Jennifer Licht's show *Spaces* (1969–70) at the Museum of Modern Art in New York, Walther was in the gallery demonstrating how to interact with his instruments. However, he says very little about what he thinks the interactions might mean for the participants, or whether in fact the gallery is a sympathetic context. His feeling, consistently expressed, that the works should not have an audience, other than the participants, certainly suggests the gallery is not the ideal arena. In contemporary exhibitions, such as the Thirtieth Bienal of São Paulo in 2012, I have seen his work being demonstrated by gallery staff rather than freely available for experimentation, which underscores the formality of the pieces and removes the possibility of chance encounters.

In a similar fashion, Clark's work is now usually displayed with specially trained invigilators who help audience members experiment with the materials. Given the intimate situations created by both artists, and their roles as pioneers of participatory art, their minimal attention to the nature of the participants and the ideal place of participation is a curious oversight. Did either envisage total strangers might collaborate to animate the works? In photographs of contemporary enactments of Walther's *For Two*, amusement seems to be the most common reaction to being forced into intimate contact. Humour frequently operates as a distancing mechanism, a natural corollary of embarrassment.

I assume such reactions are not part of how he conceived the activation of his work; certainly there is nothing in his writing to suggest he anticipated that reaction. But when you strip bodies back to mere material, the range of reactions to that attempted reduction is bound to be more diverse and unpredictable, at least at the beginning of that art's reception. Clark's more psychologically attuned works have distinct points of contact, thereby more effectively channelling the tactile relations enacted into something more subtle and communicative. The vocabulary of contact and gesture she elaborates makes possible a kind of dialogue.

In Walther's works the participants are given little guidance on how to understand their immersion and contribution to the work of art. One wonders if he is staging a kind of inaction, passivity or loss of agency and position, in contrast to the contrived experiment with freedom that characterizes Clark's work. Her work, along with other vanguard artistic practices of the 1960s in Brazil, has been called an 'experimental exercise of freedom' by Brazilian critic Mário Pedrosa.[32] The phrase conjures with the idea of the liberation of the aesthetic, along with notions of openness, action and participation. If her experiments are about a carefully curtailed intensity, Walther's are more about dissociation, muteness, social awkwardness, forced intimacy and proximity.

Awkwardness and humour would cut across the intense inwardness Abramović describes as an effect of the two-person work. Self-consciousness keeps the participant in the here and now, rather than allowing the kind of psychic clearing that could lead to tears. That these earlier experiments with the couple proceeded so very differently to Abramović's endurance performance suggests different models of intimacy are in operation – dialogical, estranged and reflexive. Dialogue or connection can be via speech, movement, touch or the gaze such as we see in Clark's propositions. Disconnection or estrangement could be triggered by feelings of impingement, shame, shyness and even humour – Walther's work demonstrates this style of engagement. The reflexive response to intimacy is the curious withdrawal into the self that Abramović describes in relation to *The Artist Is Present*, where the connection to the other enables an engagement with less accessible parts of the self.

2　Relationships

The mutual gaze at the heart of *The Artist Is Present* was previously used in Abramović's collaborative work, *Nightsea Crossing* (performed twenty-two times between 1981 and 1987) with her then-partner

Ulay (Uwe Laysiepen). The artists sat at either end of a long table; they faced one another in silence and without moving for seven hours. Abramović claims that the work unleashed other dimensions of consciousness: 'It meant crossing the ocean of the unconscious. For hours and hours we didn't do anything except sit at a table and look at each other. It opened the doors to perception to us and we were surfing different mental states.'[33] While Abramović uses the idea of the unconscious here, the work also partakes of spiritual traditions of self-transcendence. As Lynn McCreedie explains, the work is: 'their tribute to the cultures – Indian, Tibetan, Australian Aboriginal – in which ceremonies and meditation techniques had been developed to take the practitioner close to the state of death'.[34] Mary Richards interprets their practice using Leo Bersani's idea of 'self-shattering': ego dissolution that she argues is in the service of communion.[35] The link to André Green's notion of death narcissism discussed in Chapter 1 is most evident in this desire to lose the self that Bersani describes as 'the pleasure of a kind of self-obliteration' 'a spatial, anonymous narcissism'.[36] But while the egoistic self is certainly negated by the meditative practice, it is not so clear that communion with the other is the result. From Abramović's description, the connection to the other enables what she describes as inner surfing, a drifting off made possible by reflexive intimacy. In short, the couple format creates a closed circuit that facilitates an inward turn.

Other works from the period of their relationship (1975–88) conjure more obviously with couple-related themes like trust, dependence and empathy. One performance in particular from what has become known as the Relations Series involves profound mirroring – it is titled *Talking about Similarity* (1976). In this work, Ulay sews his mouth shut and Abramović has to answer questions posed by the audience as if she were him. The performance ends when she answers on her own behalf. The performance curiously relies upon their romantic connection, while also steadfastly leaving it out of account. Her task of empathic understanding sits oddly beside her seeming indifference to his suffering following the masochistic act of muting and self-censorship.[37]

The kind of identification with Ulay required of Abramović – to speak from his position – demonstrates the type of empathy referred to as the 'Platinum Rule'.[38] That is, she is *not* asked to consider what *she* would say in his position. That form of identification, which uses the feelings and desires of the self as the model of empathy, is often referred to as idiopathic. It involves projection. The shorthand for this so-called 'Golden Rule' is the biblical instruction 'do unto others as you would have them do unto you'. The stronger platinum position is to consider the perspective of the other, particularly when it does not correlate with one's own. Rephrasing the classic adage of projection, the instruction becomes 'Do unto others as they would have you do unto them'.[39] The perfect attunement in evidence here fails; or the work would never end. Mary Richards sees the work as about fused identity, which of course was something the couple played upon given their visual similarity.[40] They were literally fused together in a later work, *Relation in Time* (1977) where the two sat back to back for seventeen hours with their hair joined together and gradually unravelling.

There are, of course, other performing couples who are, or were, romantically involved: Gilbert and George, VALIE EXPORT and Peter Weibel, and Carolee Schneemann and James Tenney. The question of intimacy is barely raised in relation to the first two couples. In the case of London-based couple Gilbert and George, their presentation as 'living sculptures' clad in their instantly recognizable uniform of suit and tie, coupled with their highly formal manner, shifts the focus away from their private life. Their uniform operates as a kind of mask that conceals both their individuality and by extension their relation to each other.

EXPORT's collaborations with Weibel operate as a critique of typical heterosexual ways of being, rather than foregrounding their relationship; that is, he takes a servile or secondary role. For example, he appears in the subservient role of a dog on a leash in *Portfolio of Dogness* (1968). He is very explicit about his contribution, and the sexist framework that has been eschewed: 'The release of the woman from male servitude is carried to extremes in a playful and provocative way.'[41] Similarly, Weibel is her assistant in *Tap and Touch Cinema* (1968), announcing the availability of her tactile cinema. The work conducted in public spaces enabled male participants to touch but not to see EXPORT's naked breasts concealed behind a box-like structure with a makeshift curtain. Weibel appears with a megaphone as the spruiker for her performance, rather than a central performer himself. In both works, their personal relationship is secondary to the exploration of feminist concepts of agency. In other words, EXPORT's negation of typical forms of male power and dominance (both actual and ocular) made use of her actual intimate relationship – an impersonal social critique borrowed material from the personal domain.

In contrast to the gender role reversal of EXPORT and Weibel, Schneemann's documentation of her sexual relationship with her partner aims for equality. In her highly erotic film *Fuses* (1964) she wanted to show sex as an intimate act and in terms of a 'lived sense of equity'.[42] She frames *Fuses* as in conversation with Stan Brakhage's film *Window Water Baby Moving* of 1959, which documented the birth of his child. She felt that despite the fact that Jane and Stan passed the camera back and forth, the birth was claimed for the masculine eye: 'the male eye replicated or possessed the vagina's primacy of giving birth'; the camera, as it were, became the primary aperture, rather than the woman's body.[43] In *Fuses* there is a constant shifting between male and female bodies to cut across such typical gendered positions. As Schneemann explains: 'I edited sequences so that whenever you were looking at the male genital it would dissolve into female and vice versa.'[44]

This dissolution of male and female, along with self and other, was at the core of the erotic experience for Schneemann. However, she felt there was no representation of sex that approached the manner in which she experienced it:

> I wanted to see if the experience of what I *saw* would have any correspondence to what I *felt* – the intimacy of the lovemaking . . . . And I wanted to put into that *materiality* of film the energies of the body, so that the film itself dissolves and recombines and is transparent and dense – like how one feels during lovemaking. . . . It is *different* from any pornographic work that you've ever seen – that's why people are still looking at it! And there's no objectification or fetishization of the woman.[45]

The film is indeed an extraordinary achievement in showing highly explicit images of sexual arousal and lovemaking in an avant-garde format that serves sexual equality. The unusual way in which it was made no doubt contributes to the unique vision of sexuality. For example, Schneemann did the filming even though she is a participant in the film. She used borrowed wind-up Bolex cameras that could film for thirty seconds. The wind-up mechanism meant that some element of chance entered into what was recorded – she notes that if the camera was on a chair or hanging from a lamp 'the merge of bodies might shift from the lens focus', or the camera 'would only capture my buttocks, or some area of all green'.[46]

She accepted what the camera captured rather than working to a set plan; chance is, of course, an excellent tactic of impersonality. The film was made over three years, so the sequences do not capture a single act, but the love life of her and her partner of ten years, the composer James Tenney. It is filmed in the house they shared with their cat Kitch as the only spectator and Schneemann conceived the film as from the cat's point of view.[47] The fragmentary sequences of film were further processed and 'collaged', as she put it, by adding layers of paint to the celluloid, burning it, baking it and collecting the dirt and cat hair that was in the studio.[48] The aroused bodies of Schneemann and Tenney are thus mediated by these layers and thereby distanced from us – therein lies the coolness of *Fuses*.

Despite the distancing mechanisms, *Fuses* is nonetheless erotic, arousing a mimetic reaction in the body of the viewer. Eliciting this kind of visceral reaction is surprisingly uncommon in body art. Masochistic art would be an obvious exception here, where the damage to the artist's body frequently calls up a feeling of vulnerability in the viewer's body. Likewise, erotic or pornographic images usually provoke a mimetic response in the viewer: watching the sexuality of others arouses the sexual response of the viewer. Watching someone vomit has this same visceral effect; British artist Stuart Brisley's vomit video *Arbeit Macht Frei* (1973) generates a queasy feeling if not the urge to vomit.

One can account for this peculiar capacity of bodies to resonate with others by referring to what psychoanalytic theorist Mikkel Borch-Jacobsen calls 'mimetic' bonding or identification; that is, an emotional bond that is characterized by incorporative bindings to the other.[49] This form of bonding, he argues, is prior to object love, that is, love of another; it is a feature of primary narcissism. This kind of primitive binding to the other accounts for affect contagion – panic would be a key example. Such bonds, then, allow feelings and bodily sensations to seemingly spring across bodies, revealing the porosity of self and other. And *Fuses* models this perviousness visually with filmic dissolving and the mutability of gender depiction.

Schneemann's celebration of sexuality and equality contrasts markedly with the depictions of transactional heterosexual sex by Abramović and Andrea Fraser. Abramović's role swap with a sex worker in Amsterdam *Role Exchange* (1975) is documented from the outside of the building. It records only that she was visited by three customers, but not the outcome of those encounters, which were shielded by a closed curtain – the usual signal that a transaction was in progress.

Andrea Fraser's controversial work *Untitled* 2003 is much more explicit (Figure 3.7). A single camera in the upper corner of a hotel room records her sexual encounter with a collector who was selected by Fraser's art dealer Friedrich Petzel.[50] An edition of five videos was produced of the encounter (he paid for and received one as arranged at the outset). *Untitled* is silent and runs for roughly an hour. Fraser describes the work as empowering:

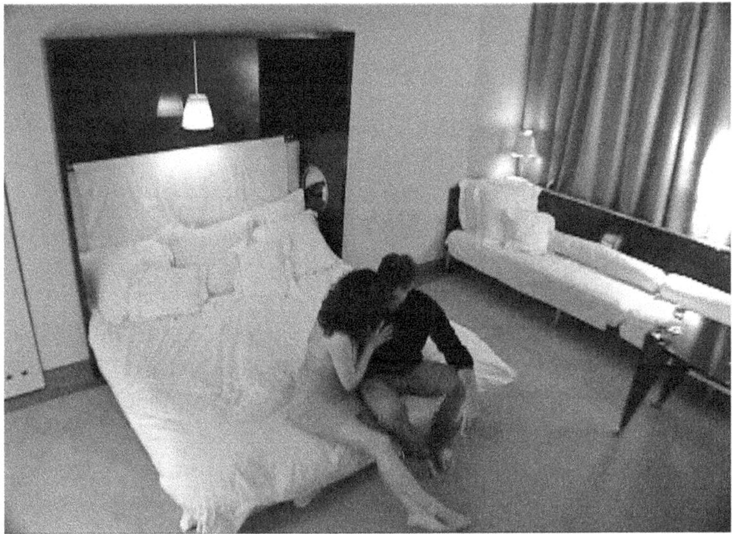

FIGURE 3.7 *Andrea Fraser,* Untitled, *2003, DVD, 60 minutes, no sound. Courtesy of the artist.*

> My own experience of doing the piece was really very empowering
> and quite in line with my understanding of my own feminism. It
> was my idea, it was my scenario, I was producing a piece that I
> would own, I was very much in control of the process. I never felt
> used by the collector. In fact, I was much more concerned about
> using him.[51]

Fraser's rhetoric here evokes a longstanding tradition of praising women artists who take up the active position in any polarized pairing. Control and choice, this tradition suggests, are all that is required for feminist empowerment. Yet raising the question of agency within the sexual, erotic and pornographic domains while a crucial part of emancipation also involves a much more complicated subject position inflected by desires and fantasies. In other words, enfranchisement in the sexual domain is not rational and orderly in the manner of rights and entitlements in the public sphere. Perhaps highlighting the limits of the vocabulary of liberation in these domains is the real achievement of Fraser's piece. Certainly, the conversion of sexual intimacy into a cool art transaction does not seem adequate to the task she assigns it.

More sympathetic readings frame the transaction through the mode of art production to which Fraser has most consistently contributed – institutional critique. Much of her work can be characterized as witty and sophisticated critiques of the institution of art and its rituals. What does this piece tell us about the institution of art? According to Susan Cahan, 'The relations between artist and collector have been stripped of material mediation. The social relation between Fraser and the collector *is* the work of art.'[52] The description could refer to Mette Edvardsen's work discussed earlier as well as innumerable other one-on-one performances. In a sense, *Untitled* and its reception reveal the astonishingly formalist means that are routinely used to describe body art and performance, even when the act in question is emotionally charged, deeply personal and more usually conducted in complete privacy. This ultra-cool interpretative framework attempts to render the excitement of sexual intimacy as just another mundane relation, supposedly elevating the sexual actions of the body to the status of art while also denigrating them to a commercial transaction between artist and collector. The impersonal presentation of sex, from a single fixed point of view akin to a security camera, is an extreme example of disconnected or estranged intimacy.

The French artist Sophie Calle adopts a similarly detached viewpoint to present the misadventures of her love life. The end or break-up of the couple features in two of her works: *Exquisite Pain* (2003) and *Take Care of Yourself* (2007). The failure of coupling, of course, better approximates the lack of happiness characteristic of the avant-garde. In each instance, her lover is completely absent from the piece, or perhaps more accurately, rendered as a kind of cipher that enables Calle's perspective (or her cronies') to remain in the forefront. In *Take Care of Yourself*, the email in which a lover callously dumps Calle, is the prompt for the work. That email is rigorously and humorously scrutinized by a band of avenging women.

In *Exquisite Pain* the countdown to the end of a relationship – with yet another callous cowardly man – overtakes her countdown to an anticipated reunion with said man. The project consists of two parts: 'before unhappiness' and 'after unhappiness'. The former documents her time in Japan using diary entries and deadpan snapshot style photographs that are stamped with the remaining days until the unhappiness of her break-up will arrive. The second part collects the painful memories or suffering of friends and strangers. Like Linda Montano she sought to use repetition to rid herself of painful emotions; her intention was to continue until she had 'worn out my own story through sheer repetition'.[53]

3 *The Second Woman*

The Second Woman follows the same kind of serial method that Calle deploys in *Take Care of Yourself*. Calle enlisted 107 women to interpret her break-up email; Nat Randall (or her substitute) repeats the same scene with 100 men who have responded to a call out. The premise of *The Second Woman* is quite simple. There is a script of roughly ten to fifteen minutes, which brings together a couple whom it is implied have recently had a fight, maybe even a break-up. The scene takes place inside a red cube enclosed by translucent fabric that enables the audience to see in but not the performers to see out; live recordings of the performance are shown in real time on an adjacent screen (Figure 3.8). The carefully constructed mise-en-scène delivers typical Brechtian distancing – we are made aware of watching a performance and the synchronous filming of it (Figure 3.9). That set-up provides a very cooling framework for the volatile scene.

As the programme notes indicate, the scene is inspired by John Cassavetes's *Opening Night* (1977), a film about a play called *The Second Woman*. In *Opening Night* the complex nesting of one drama inside another creates a slightly vertiginous quality, particularly as the main character of both film and play is unravelling (Myrtle and Virginia, respectively) and it's not entirely clear why. The dialogue of Randall and Breckon's *The Second Women* is strangely plucked from across the film, and while there are jumps in topic and unclear antecedents for some of the lines, overall the scene coheres.

The scene goes as follows. He arrives. They have a drink. Marty has brought take-away food, they sit down to eat and what seems like a well-rehearsed argument ensues about their relationship, her self-regard and his feelings for her. When he fails to respond to Virginia's prompt to say 'I love you', she registers her frustration and

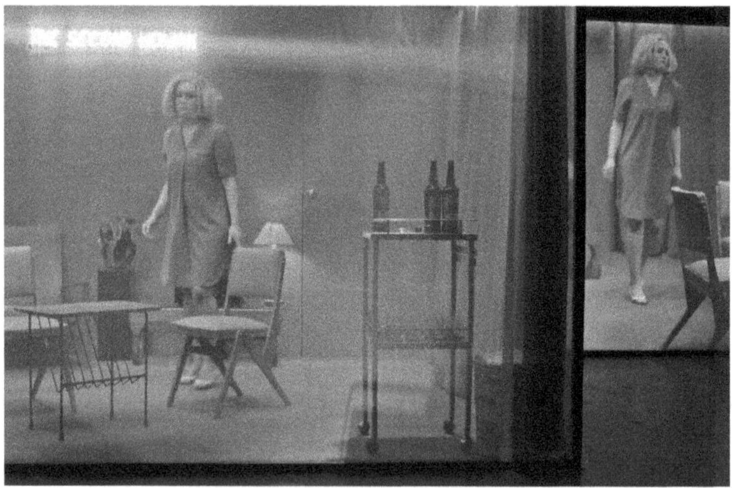

FIGURE 3.8 *Nat Randall and Anna Breckon,* The Second Woman, *with set design by Genevieve Murray, 2016, performed at Liveworks Sydney 2017. Photograph Heidrun Lohr. Courtesy of the artists.*

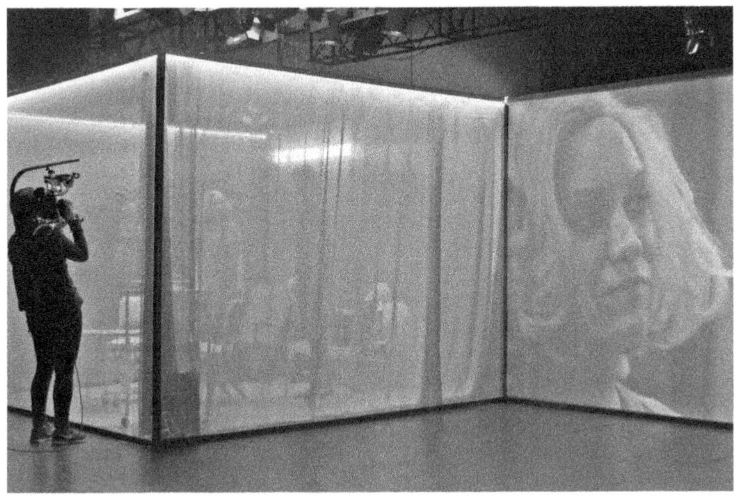

FIGURE 3.9 *Nat Randall and Anna Breckon,* The Second Woman, *with set design by Genevieve Murray, 2016, performed at Liveworks Sydney 2017. Photograph Heidrun Lohr. Courtesy of the artists.*

anger by throwing some of the take-away food at him, sometimes just a few noodles, on occasions most of the packet. That fighting component is transformed when she puts on some music; the mood changes and they dance together; or on occasions they don't, the resentment remains (Figure 3.10). The scene terminates with Virginia telling Marty she thinks he should leave; she then offers him $50, the fee previously promised for the performance. As he leaves, he has the last line, which is either 'I love you' or 'I never loved you'. There are two points in the scene for the male participant to exercise some agency: at the very beginning, when she asks him what he is thinking, and at the very end, with this choice of damage or repair. These details are not disclosed in the programme notes but various participants have now given away the contents of the script and the backstage instructions.[54]

On paper, as it were, it is hard to understand the incredibly compelling quality of the repeated scene. The same scene repeated 100 times could simply be boring. Yet nothing could be further from the truth. I witnessed roughly thirteen hours of the total of twenty-four at Perth Institute of Contemporary Art in March 2018 and could

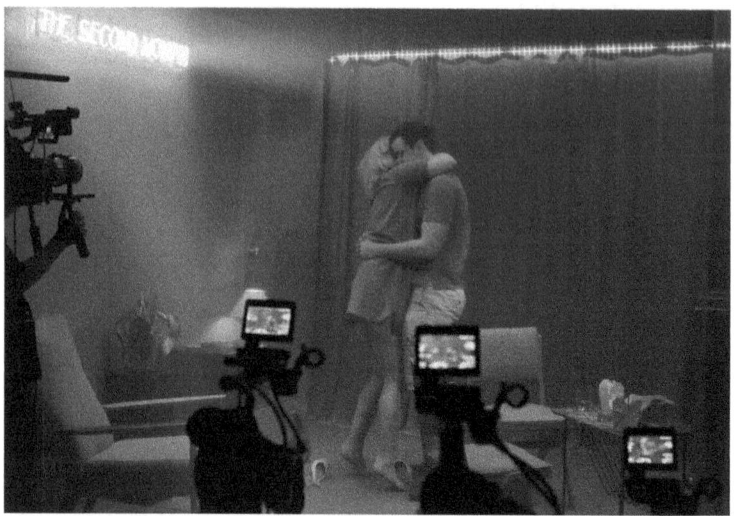

FIGURE 3.10 *Nat Randall and Anna Breckon,* The Second Woman, *with set design by Genevieve Murray, 2016, performed at Liveworks Sydney 2017. Photograph Heidrun Lohr. Courtesy of the artists.*

easily have stayed for more. The full house at virtually any hour of the day or night, and the perpetual queue, testified to this being a widely shared sentiment. So what were the sources of fascination and deep pleasure that made the work so engaging?

First off, there is the pleasure of repetition. We are all familiar with the childhood yearning for repeated pleasures – wanting to play the same game or hear the same story over and over again. In teen years, it might be listening to the same album on endless repeat. In other words, alongside bad repetition (boring, numbing, compulsive) and therapeutic repetition (the exhaustion of feeling described by Calle and Montano) there is a type of good repetition (comforting, familiar, reassuring) that this work clearly amplifies. Curiously, in the key articles on serial methods in art, there is no acknowledgement of the immense pleasures of repetition.[55] Serial methods, when deployed by conceptual artists, generally result in a numbing effect, ensuring any amassed information is drained of interest. In the case of *The Second Woman*, familiarity with the script certainly compounds the distancing effect of the mise-en-scène, but it also enables attention to the nuances of each encounter between Randall and the successive

'Martys'. Randall's capacity to engage and manage a great variety of men also becomes ever more powerfully felt as she is tested by some gross, and some small, departures from the script.

In the face of this complex weave of sameness and differences, the audience strangely coheres as a group; people talk between Martys (there's a short break between each performance Figure 3.11). There's an unusual impulse to share and discuss what has been seen, felt and enjoyed. It is as though the audience becomes a team sharing the bigger picture of the performance unknown to the successive men. This group formation isn't really discussed in the growing literature on the work; rather the treatment of masculinity has received the most critical examination. For example, commentators have remarked on the unravelling of masculinity, and even the script writers have indicated a central aim of the performance was to turn the tables on the various men participating.[56] As Teresa Tan reports, 'Randall and The Second Woman co-creator Anna Breckon carefully constructed the work to make the male performers interchangeable – playing on a long history of substitutable women in film.'[57] Breckon

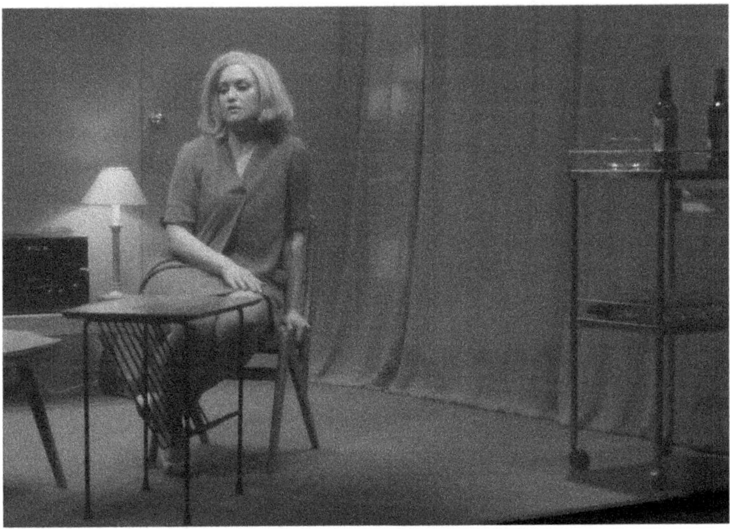

FIGURE 3.11 *Nat Randall and Anna Breckon,* The Second Woman, *with set design by Genevieve Murray, 2016, performed at Liveworks Sydney 2017. Photograph Heidrun Lohr. Courtesy of the artists.*

states: 'When each guy walks through, there's this shock about the substitutability of men . . . . In film history, it's normally been women that are substitutable and men who are unique and individual and have personalities. We invert that film history.'[58] Women, then, are impersonal replaceable bodies, men are particular and individual. In *The Second Woman*, it is certainly true that the point of identification is with Virginia, not with the male character – the usual point of identification in classic Hollywood cinema. The audience gasps each time a Marty says, 'I never loved you', and they laugh and wince when men try to take control of the scene, or make themselves more important, or refuse to follow the rules.[59]

Teresa Tan argues that a 'pattern' of masculine behaviour emerges from the repetition of the same scene. She cites Randall's remarks on what the serial method reveals: 'The thing about repetition is that it presents a generic quality of a particular mode of masculine emotion.' Randall explains further: 'The work is very much looking at gendered conventions of emotion, so really unpacking a performance of masculinity and femininity within a queer lens.'[60] That generic quality of masculine emotion is at once present and yet also hard to pinpoint given the large sample of men's emotional reactions on display. The desire to deduce a pattern from the diverse sample, however, is surely one of the sources of fascination. The audience is challenged to make sense of the series of similar but different encounters.

The amalgam of repetition, substitutability, sameness and difference calls up a very particular kind of seriality. Significantly for a feminist/queer production, it is what Juliet Mitchell, in her book *Siblings*, calls the 'law of the mother'. The phrase 'the law of the mother' is clearly modelled on French psychoanalyst Jacques Lacan's 'the law of the father' which marks the end of the enclosed dyad of mother and child and the opening out to the Symbolic, the so-called paternal world of language, sociality and culture. In contrast, the law of the mother is about the crucial role of recognition and the binding together of siblings to form a familial group with rivalry and love combined in a potent but workable mix. The mother's role, Mitchell argues, is to introduce seriality: siblings are recognized by the mother as different from each other, yet equal.[61] According to Mitchell, the 'law of the mother' assures the child 'there is room for you as well as me'.[62] The trauma of displacement by a younger sibling and attendant feelings of murderous jealousy are thereby tempered by the recognition that one is 'part of a series'.[63] The sibling becomes the template for subsequent relationships with peers, and even partnerships can be modelled along the lines of these lateral relations rather than the vertical axes of parents.

In *The Second Woman* the deployment of this kind of lateral seriality means that the tables are not quite turned on masculinity. Masculinity is certainly on display in a truly unprecedented manner, but there is room made for each participant and their variations from the script. If Randall were not so luminously present to each man, as well as to the audience, the examination of masculinity would not be so compelling. Her care and her neutrality let the men hang themselves if they have a mind to; she is not a co-conspirator.

The accommodation of different men, then, sets the work radically apart from the interchangeability of women that patriarchal visual culture fosters – consider the confusing array of blonde women in Hitchcock's films, or the women as 'mass ornament' in Busby Berkeley musicals, to give just a couple of examples. Instead of reducing men to their bodies or making them into an undifferentiated mass, each one appears as he chooses to present himself and is recognized as such. So while a very broad range of men can be Marty (they are substitutable in that sense), they are also present as individuals. The law of the mother delivers this very affirmative kind of sequence. In this way, the queer lens of *The Second Woman* employs a very different logic of relation. Such relations return us to the sociality of women with which I began, which can now be theorized as the cooperative lateral relations made possible by the law of the mother. Participatory art conjuring with this kind of sociability opens up the genre of relational art to new ethical and political possibilities.

4

'Collective effervescence'
Group formation from fusion to virtual togetherness

The disappearance of the conscious personality, the predominance of the unconscious personality, the turning by means of suggestion and contagion of feelings and ideas in an identical direction, the tendency to immediately transform the suggested ideas into acts; these, we see, are the principal characteristics of the individual forming part of a crowd. He is no longer himself, but has become an automaton who has ceased to be guided by his will.[1]

– GUSTAVE LE BON

In Nato Thompson's landmark exhibition of 2012 on the social turn in contemporary art, *Living as Form: Socially Engaged Art from 1991-2011*, he includes the joyful response to Barack Obama's electoral victory by Harlem's African American community alongside projects orchestrated by artists and art collectives. The celebration is described in the exhibition catalogue as almost a 'choreographed' response, suggesting an intentional mass movement of bodies, or a synchronized wave of feeling.[2] Thompson acknowledges that the inclusion of this event significantly stretches the parameters of socially engaged art, given that there was no 'singular author or organization' responsible for the 'spontaneous eruptions of joy and street parading'.[3]

In the catalogue, curiously this event is presented just like the other art projects: the title is simply listed as *Harlem, New York*, with 'Election Night' in the slot usually assigned to the artist, group or collective. The exhibition also included another mass event – the protests in Cairo associated with the Arab Spring. Thompson explains that protests in Tunisia and Egypt have become models of spontaneous popular action that express 'the collective desire to contest power'.[4] *Tahrir Square, Cairo Egypt*, 2011 is the Egyptian example included in the catalogue.[5] These inclusions produce an unusual continuity between art and life, well reflected in the clever title 'Living as form', which suggests life itself is sometimes shaped and art-like. As Thompson puts it: 'Just as video, painting, and clay are types of forms, people coming together possess forms as well.'[6] This chapter is about such forms: artworks where people come together (or are brought together) to form groups.

When coming together generates exuberant group behaviour it is described by sociologist Emile Durkheim as 'collective effervescence'.[7] This term brilliantly captures the sense of a groundswell or bubbling up of shared feeling and the buoyancy and animation that groups make possible. Durkheim argued that such group actions and feelings indicate when the 'strengthening influence of society makes itself felt'.[8] For him, the coming together generates and demonstrates great creativity as much as revolutionary spirit. Here he stands against the negative understanding of social coalescence, represented by Gustave Le Bon among many others, for whom the crowd is associated with a failure of individual will and a lack of thought.[9]

In terms of the impersonal theme that orients this book, the subsumption of individuals into the group is, of course, one of the typical ways in which impersonality is understood. Group identity is assumed to be impersonal, social and shared, no matter how it is formed, whether via creed, country, colour, class or culture – to use Kwame Anthony Appiah's enumeration of the main categories of social convergence and belonging.[10] Transient groups formed in relation to an issue or an event, such as the protests and celebrations identified by Thompson, would even more starkly illustrate the impersonal theme because the points of connection between members of the group are contingent and situational.

As one might expect, socially engaged art has de-emphasized personal expression. Distributed or shared authorship with networks, collectives or communities is preferred over the traditional creations of the solo artist. Indeed, Claire Bishop begins her seminal book on participatory art, *Artificial Hells: Participatory Art and the Politics of Spectatorship* (2012), by questioning precisely this current doxa about the supposed moral superiority of works produced collectively or at least without singular authorship.[11] She argues we need a more nuanced account of collaborative authorship, which entails thinking beyond the 'false polarity of "bad" singular authorship and "good" collective authorship'.[12]

A work of art produced by a number of bodies is, of course, a routine proposition in dance and music and there are many specialized terms to describe the various group formations: the *corps de ballet*, a dance troupe, an ensemble, a company, orchestra or band. While there have been collectives in the visual arts and collective productions, these are not an absolute requirement as they are in some other arts. Perhaps, then, what the visual arts uniquely contributes here is the facility to 'make the group strange' and thereby make it newly visible as a meaningful or significant artistic form.

How do we think about the integration of individuals into a group? The chapter considers some of the ways in which bodies are assembled to form an image of collectivity or community. Specifically, I am interested in works that show us society's 'strengthening influence' to cite Durkheim, and which, most importantly, forge a kind of social bond that enables the formation of a 'we'. By way of contrast, I also consider group works that fail to convert a physical bond into a social bond and thus do not form a 'we'. The final section of the chapter examines newly emerging forms of group identity: the virtual group or gathering made possible by digital culture. I look closely at Angelica Mesiti's four-channel video *Citizens Band* (2012), a work that brings together four immigrants and their distinct musical and performative traditions to form a virtual musical group or ensemble. They are another group that does not form a 'we' in the conventional sense, yet the blending together of their performances across time and space suggests a different model of contemporary belonging.

1 The terms of engagement: Group, collective, community

In art history and theory, curiously the term 'group' is not much used to describe the social arrangements and forms made possible by performance, participatory and relational art practices. Yet the group, according to sociologist Georg Simmel, is the unit of measure between the whole of society and the individual, making it the most appropriate term for the forms of coming together these works enact.[13] Allied terms that describe various types and sizes of group formation include assembly, community, network, a fraternity, a collective, the crowd, the multitude, perhaps even the people and the many. However, in the literature about relational and socially engaged art the terms most consistently used to describe artworks involving gatherings are 'community', 'collective', 'collectivism' and 'collaboration'.

This trend can be seen in the titles of key publications, for example: Blake Stimson and Gregory Sholette's edited collection *Collectivism after Modernism: The Art of Social Imagination after 1945* (2007); Grant Kester's two books on the social turn in art *Conversation Pieces: Community and Communication in Modern Art* (2004) and *The One and the Many: Contemporary Collaborative Art in a Global Context* (2011); as well as his recent collection edited with Bill Kelley, *Collective Situations: Readings in Contemporary Latin American Art 1995-2010* (2017).[14] Similarly, the recent Centre Pompidou show *Cosmopolis #1: On Collective Intelligence* (2017), curated by Kathryn Weir (with associate curators Caroline Ferreira, Charlène Dinhut, Ilaria Conti and Ellie Buttrose), sought to examine the current drive to 'create collectively'.[15] The 'collective intelligence' flagged in the exhibition title deliberately shifts away from the negative assumption that group production leads to intellectual diminution.

Of these terms, collectivism has the most chequered history. It has suggested both a utopian ideal as well as the forced conformity evident in communist regimes such as the USSR and the People's Republic of China. As Stimson and Sholette indicate, the collectivist dream darkens after the Second World War becoming associated with 'gray on gray, beehive-like representations' underpinned by 'a loss of individual will'.[16] This cold bureaucratic version of impersonality, where individuality is ignored or suppressed, surfaces in some group works, as we will see shortly. That suppression contrasts with the intertwining of personal and impersonal tendencies that I have been tracking in this book. Continuing in that vein, my preference is for group works where that coldness is countered, or kept at bay, and an enlivening social bond is represented or felt.

In contrast to the ambivalent connotations of collectivism, phrases like 'collective intelligence', and terms like 'community' and 'collaboration', suggest the harmonious coming together of people, and ideally, their fruitful cooperation. In classical sociology, the term 'community' is usually contrasted with society – *gemeinschaft* (community) versus *gesellschaft* (society) to use the original German terms. The distinction was first made by Schleiermacher, but is commonly ascribed to German sociologist Ferdinand Tönnies. He contrasts the social bonds underpinning these groups as: 'real and organic life' (community) versus 'ideational mechanical formation' (society).[17] Richard Sennett glosses this idea of community as aligned with the intimacy of the small-scale and characterized by mutual bonds, personal connections and feelings of togetherness. Sennett's preference, however, is for the modern impersonal rule-governed domain of society where we encounter strangers and people unlike ourselves.[18] These two meanings of social relatedness are crucial for considering group works in the visual arts and the kinds of co-operation, if any, that are developed by them.

Cooperation characterizes the group dynamic of only one type of group, according to psychoanalyst Wilfred Bion. It is the modus operandi of what he calls the 'sophisticated group' or 'work group', that is, a group in touch with reality and ruled by a 'rational or scientific approach to a problem'.[19] Cooperation, not groupthink, is crucial for Bion's account of the rational work group. He argues that '[e]very group, however casual meets to "do" something'. In that activity, he continues, 'they co-operate'.[20] The 'work group' is inflected and constituted by this conscious joint purpose. For him, however, the 'work group' emerges against the background of what he suggests are the more common 'basic assumption groups'. The latter have all the hallmarks of regressive behaviour; they come together in what he calls 'valency' rather than cooperation, that is they spontaneously and instinctively converge in relation to three basic assumptions.[21] The 'dependence' group comes together to seek the security provided by a leader; the 'fight-flight' group unifies against a common enemy or danger; and the 'pairing' group provides the context for sexual pairing.[22] These assumptions, as should be clear from the descriptions, are not oriented to development, learning or problem solving. Under the sway of the basic assumptions, the individual can sink into 'the herd', as Bion puts it, discovering the quality he acerbically calls 'groupishness'.[23] Bion's contrast between the impetus of work and the operation of the basic assumptions for group formation enables some of the mechanisms of positive and negative coalescence to come more clearly into view.[24]

Philosopher Axel Honneth's recent writing on the group – his essay titled 'The I in We: Recognition as a Driving Force of Group Formation' – takes a more positive approach to the function of the group, arguing that psychoanalysis fails to acknowledge that 'involvement in social groups strengthens the ego'.[25] As his title indicates, recognition plays this strengthening role. For him, it is 'individuals' dependency on experiences of social recognition' that explains the desire for group membership.[26] The group affirms the individual in three key ways, according to Honneth. He reveals that what might be regarded as simply self-relations are actually dependent upon group, familial or peer recognition. These self-relations are: self-esteem, self-confidence and self-respect. His assertion is that there is a continued need for external affirmation for at least two of these relations, namely self-esteem and self-confidence. The autonomy of the self that is so central to traditional Western thinking on subjectivity is undercut by this emphasis on the constitutive role of the social group for the sense of self.[27] So, for example, he argues that self-esteem relies on others' 'lifelong affirmation', particularly their recognition of one's valuable talents and skills.[28] For him, this form of recognition is the most significant factor for group formation today.

Similarly, self-confidence requires subjects to 'receive constant, reliable affection' which they encounter in relationships of love and friendship.[29] These principally dyadic relationships, he states, are not groups 'in the strict sense of the term'.[30] Nonetheless, it is this self-other relation that is most closely related to the negative group formations of crowd, horde and herd. The merged emotional tie of infancy between parent and child is reframed by Honneth. He argues the recognition afforded by adult love and friendship is 'modelled on the structure of early symbiosis'.[31] For self-confidence, then, there needs to be constant 'repetition of symbiosis-like experiences of recognition' across the life course.[32]

Self-respect is the only relation that does not demand constant repetition. For him, the detachment of the individual from the peer group is a developmental accomplishment of adolescence. The approval of the peer group in effect lessens at this point in the life course. The simple assumption of the role of the citizen, then, permanently establishes a feeling of self-respect, he argues.[33] He concludes by stating:

> Neither self-respect nor self-esteem can be maintained without the supportive experience of practising shared values in the group. Therefore, far from constituting a threat to personal identity, groups are, to take a phrase from Adorno, a primary 'source of humanity'.[34]

As this conclusion indicates, Honneth's account stresses not just the fortifying aspect of the group but its necessity for individual flourishing. The negativity of the group is acknowledged, but largely minimized.[35]

In the art historical literature to date there has been no engagement with the complex literature on groups. And as the attention to community, cooperation and collaboration might indicate, there is a definite preference for terms with positive connotations, the more negative terms for group formation – like mob, mass, gang, rabble, horde, pack, herd and crowd – tend to be excluded from the discussion. Although, early participatory performances like Yoko Ono's *Cut Piece* (1964) and Marina Abramović's *Rhythm 0* (1974) unleashed audience aggression, making that reaction a crucial part of the works' reception and interpretation. While these two pieces are often read in terms of vulnerability and elective passivity, they also powerfully highlight group aggression in the reception of performance art. It is worth briefly outlining the nature of that reception as aggression and regression are an important aspect of the way groups are theorized.

In *Cut Piece*, Ono invited the audience to cut away her clothing with a pair of scissors supplied for that purpose. At Carnegie Hall in New York, she sat impassively on stage making herself vulnerable to whatever action ensued. The audience members who came on stage to participate displayed a range of behaviours from respectful to aggressive and objectifying. While an audience is not usually thought of as a group (their joint purpose for gathering has little to do with each other) when they become participants in a work of art they meet together for a shared task. This very small shift is evidently sufficient to encourage negative group-like behaviours, such as the lowering of inhibitions, increased boldness and anti-social aggression. Licence is tacitly given for a break in the usual standards and constraints on audience behaviour (respect for the performers and others through silence and stillness). The result is a curious release of individuals from the audience social contract. Yet release from one kind of group membership makes possible the power of another – the lawlessness of mob rule.

Abramović similarly made herself vulnerable to the actions of the audience, but in her case, there was a wider range of objects that they could use to interact with her. On a table were placed seventy-two objects including honey, a gun loaded with one bullet, a scalpel, bread, grapes. Abramović reported at the conclusion of the performance:

> The experience I learned was that . . . if you leave decision to the public, you can be killed . . . . I felt really violated: they cut up my clothes, stuck rose thorns in my stomach, one person aimed the gun at my head, and another took it away. It created an aggressive atmosphere. After exactly 6 hours, as planned, I stood up and started walking toward the public. Everyone ran away, escaping an actual confrontation.[36]

Abramović's summary of audience aggression towards her, followed by their shamed retreat, captures the peculiar group behaviour unleashed by the open-ended task of interaction. Le Bon explains this kind of behaviour as the result of instinctual drives being given free play. He writes: 'In the life of the isolated individual it would be dangerous for him to gratify these instincts, while his absorption in an irresponsible crowd, in which in consequence he is assured of impunity, gives him entire liberty to follow them.'[37] The aggressive atmosphere of the group, to use Abramović's terms, allowed the lowering of inhibitions and the assumed impunity more typical of an anonymous crowd.

2 Fused bodies

With these various accounts of the group in mind, let me turn now to art practices that purposefully join bodies together. This section considers extreme forms of bodily connection that literally tie or bind bodies together. There are many more examples of this genre of body art than I am examining here, for example, Cecilia Vicuña's *Clit Nest* (2019), Justene Williams's *A Sonorous Body* (2017), Josephine Cachemaille's *FEEL UP: Collective Body Blanket* (2016), the Kingpins's *Polyphonic Ring Cycle* (2009) and some of the elements from Franz Erhard Walther's *Werksatz*, to name just a few. All bind or join bodies together with material or materials. Rather than being comprehensive, my selection aims to highlight works that attempt to conjure sociality through binding bodies together.

Perhaps one of the most vivid images of bodily fusion is Brazilian artist Lygia Pape's *Divisor* (Divider) (1968) which assembles bodies together into a mobile monochrome (Figure 4.1). The work is comprised of a large square of white fabric, 30 metres × 30 metres, with slits positioned equidistant apart to form a grid through which the participants put their heads. The work only comes to life when it is animated by a group of participants; their bodies are an essential part of the work. Pape conceived *Divider* as an 'authorless work' – a collective work that could be made without her being present.[38] In other words, like a conceptual art instruction piece, or an event score, the final realization of the work does not rest solely with the artist.

According to curator Iris Candela, *Divider* was originally devised by Pape in 1967 to be performed inside the gallery but then she offered it to a group of children from Chácara de Cabeça, one of Rio de Janeiro's many favelas or shanty towns.[39] The following year she organized a series of performances of the work. The only specific

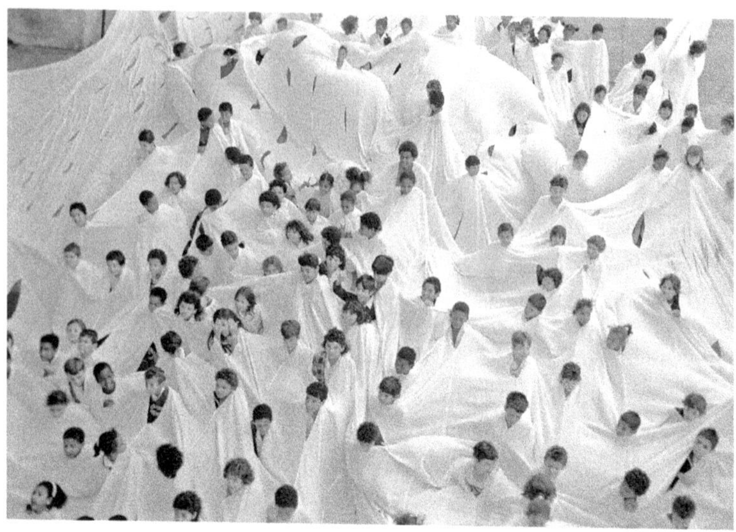

FIGURE 4.1 *Lygia Pape,* Divisor, *1968. Performance at Museu de Arte Moderna, Rio de Janeiro, 1990. Photo: Paula Pape © Projeto Lygia Pape.*

location Candela mentions is Aterro do Flamengo, the garden adjacent to Museu de Arte Moderna in Rio de Janeiro designed by legendary Brazilian landscape architect Roberto Burle Marx.

Most recently in 2017, the work was paraded through the streets of New York as part of Pape's survey show at The Met Breuer. An intern described her experience of the work, outlining in particular how that experience varied depending on the person's location within the divider. She writes:

> Within the shared performance of *Divisor*, each participant had their own experience. While my position on the edge of the canvas afforded me a view of the street and a sense of my surroundings, my neighbor closer to the middle of the cloth had completely surrendered herself to the guidance of our fellow participants.[40]

This account of the differentiated experiences of the work illuminates the gradations of agency, trust and capitulation that are part of the performance. Participation delivers a nuanced picture of the 'we' that is formed and performed by the task.

The participant's experience was certainly carefully considered by Pape. However, she emphasized the disjuncture between the head and the rest of the body that the work effects: 'You feel your body without a head, or without arms and legs.'[41] This division between the head and the rest of the body was intended to be amplified by hot air blown below the sheet, while freezing cold air would have suffused the area above the sheet. Guy Brett indicates that she did not have sufficient resources to add the temperature variations to the work.[42]

Viewing *Divider* from the outside, the participants appear like anonymous impersonal dark dots punctuating the sheet. It is not immediately obvious that their experiences vary according to location. Instead, the work initially suggests an image of social conformity 'the gray on gray of collectivism' identified by Stimson and Sholette. But it is also an image of solidarity, particularly when the *Divider* is processed through public space and takes on the appearance of a coordinated march. Critics' accounts of the work viewed from outside, emphasize the unusual blending together of these negative and positive connotations of the group. For example, Candela interprets the work as 'a metaphor or memorial not only for the "collective body" of a community but also for the subjugated masses affected by Operation Condor'.[43] The year of its making, 1968, marked the beginning of the US-backed Operation Condor: a campaign of political repression and state terror across the Southern Cone of South American intended to eradicate left-wing sympathizers and influences.

The fabrication of the work during the dictatorship period in Brazil (1964–85) certainly adds a political edge to this collective action. In that context, a work suggesting the biopower of public assembly calls up Brazilian critic Mario Pedrosa's vivid description of the type of optimistic forward-looking art made under conditions of political repression. He called such works an 'experimental exercise of freedom'.[44] I briefly mentioned his idea in Chapter 2 in relation to the work of Lygia Clark. In the case of *Divider*, collective movement, action and agency are imagined when fertile conditions for their realization were not present. Yet, as Candela points out, the optimism of community is interlined with an image of mass subjugation; the participants once enclosed within the grid-like structure are anonymized and severely restricted in movement and action.

In a similar vein, Brett calls *Divider* an ambivalent vision of assembly because of the toggling between being together and apart, or as he puts it, the work speaks of both 'community' and 'atomisation'.[45] He cites Pape to explain each state. Atomization is portrayed in largely negative terms by her: the 'massing together of man, each inside his own pigeonhole'.[46] In contrast, the production of community catches up individual movements into a joined radiant energy, suggestive of collective effervescence: 'the plane is alive through their individual movements. Energy spreads over the whole of this primordial plane of light.'[47] The ambivalent image of social fusion enables a complicated account of the group: the participants clearly cooperate to animate the divider, albeit they are massed together, confined and anonymized. The loss of individuality is in the service of the 'we' of the social group. The self dissolves into the 'we' as the price paid for connectivity and collectivity. The perennial tension between the individual and society that Simmel characterizes as a battle for individuality and independence against 'the weight' of history, heritage and culture is one reading of the work.[48] Or following Honneth, that fusion and dissolution of the self in community can be seen as part of self-constitution – the symbiosis-like experience that is necessary for self-confidence.

The British artist Lucy Orta also joins bodies together to form grids, or on occasions, lines of interconnected bodies. While she was trained in fashion and textiles her work is classified as design art, a designation that acknowledges the cross-over between art and design and the interrogation of these frequently polarized terms. Collaboration with her artist husband Jorge Orta propelled her from producing fashion items for the luxury market to making clothing that operates as a means of assembly. The most striking of these works for my purposes are her series of performances and installations called *Nexus Architecture* (1998–2010) (Figure 4.2). The performances involve the public display of bodies clad in boiler suits joined together by fabric umbilical cords that fan out from each quarter of the body like spokes. The basic format clearly reprises Lygia Clark's participatory work *The I and the You* (1967), which similarly used all-encompassing boiler suits equipped with a cord to join participants together at the navel (Figure 4.3). Likewise, Orta's term 'body architecture', immediately calls up Clark's idea of 'biological architecture'.

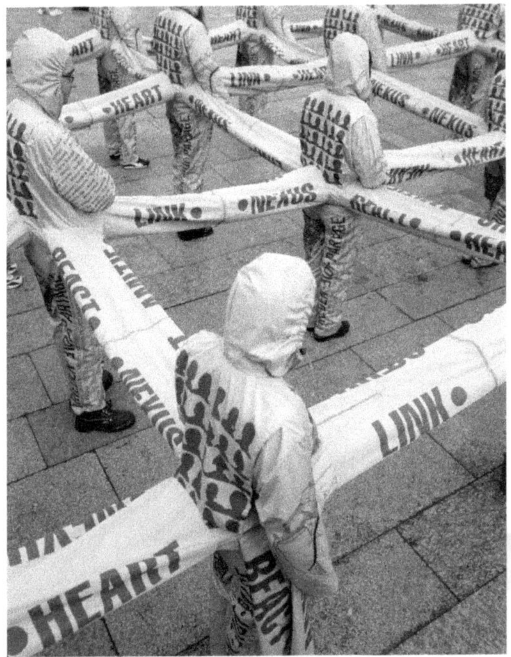

FIGURE 4.2 *Lucy + Jorge Orta,* Nexus Architecture x 50 Intervention Köln, *2001. Original Lambda colour photograph, laminated. Framed 157 × 127 cm. Photo: Peter Guenzel. Courtesy of the artists.*

Clark's biological architecture works, made in Paris in the late 1960s, like *Nexus Architecture*, stress interconnection: 'man', she wrote, is 'becoming the living structure of a cellular architecture, the mesh of an infinite tissue'.[49] This phrasing strongly evokes the work of French philosopher Maurice Merleau-Ponty. The participant in her work becomes a 'fold' in the 'flesh of the world' to use his terms; that is, the body is continuous with the world – part of its tissue – and yet individuated, a cell or fold within it.[50] The 'cell' or single body enjoins others to form a living architecture.

In one such action, Clark used the simplest of means (a plastic sheet with bags sewn to the ends) to stimulate the formation of architecture. First, she proposed experimentation with the meagre materials, and then the assembly of two, three or more people through invitation.[51] Her description emphasizes the transience of

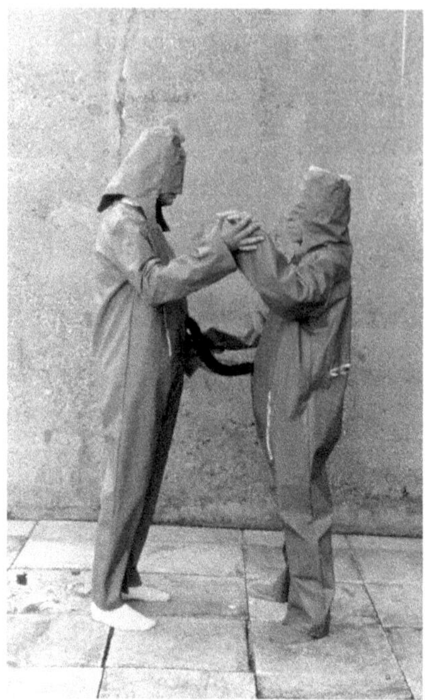

FIGURE 4.3 *Lygia Clark,* The I and the You, *1967. Photographer: Unknown. Courtesy of 'The World of Lygia Clark' Cultural Association.*

the resulting architecture: there is a multiplication of connected cells followed by dissolution:

> The environment only exists in the sense that there is this collective expression. It is created by the gestures of participants, in which each person takes a sheet of plastic and in turn produces a cell which involves this or that participant, and so on. Through each of these gestures a living biological architecture is born, which when finished the experience is dissolved.[52]

With touch and gesture as the communicative means, a temporary environment of bodies is elaborated. 'Tactile communications', as she puts it, creates 'poetic shelter in which inhabiting is equivalent to communicating'.[53] The work demonstrates a kind of 'bodily writing', to use choreographer Susan Leigh Foster's expression coined to give agency, intention and meaning to the moving body and to contest the opposition between thinking and action.[54] Here movement enables the co-assembly of the group and their surroundings – together they form biological architecture.

At times, that architecture is like an intimate embrace, at others a channel of exploration. For example, in *Biological Architectures I* (1969) bodies are first meshed with the plastic sheet, hands and feet go into the attached nylon sacks, then inside that shelter each participant tries to wrap the other's body in the sheet.[55] The ensuing tangle makes the support structure difficult to separate from flesh. An image documenting the action captures the moment of wrapping (Figure 4.4): the six bodies fill the frame enmeshed in the simple materials, their downcast eyes suggest deep concentration, the three faces we can see register pleasure. One woman looks ecstatic as if she has been taken out of herself; it is an intriguing image of the

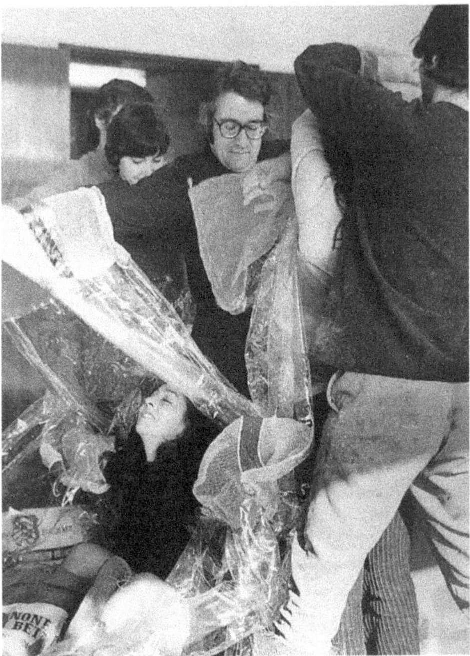

FIGURE 4.4 *Lygia Clark*, Biological Architectures I, *1969. Photographer: Unknown. Courtesy of 'The World of Lygia Clark' Cultural Association.*

individual/group dynamic. Her loss of ego enables her to be at 'one with other subjects', to use Honneth's phrasing, or perhaps it is the other way around: being at one with others enables the loss of ego.[56]

Another work in this series, *Biological Architectures II* (1969) uses the same sheet and pocket arrangement to create a tunnel. A blindfolded pair, lying on their backs, approach from opposite ends, endeavouring to recognize each other through touch when they meet in the middle. Photographic documentation of this work shows joyful expressions as participants make their way out of this partly human passageway.

These works were generally not witnessed by anyone but the participants; the encounters are only accessible through documentation. Guy Brett describes these experiments with great precision: 'The notion of a structural support and of space was woven together with an experimental and unpredictable exploration of the psychology of people.'[57] The result of this structural development, he argues, was a softening of individuation in order to create deeper connections: 'the interaction of individuals in the collective became ever less delineated, more fluid, marked by deeper and previously untouched levels of interiority.'[58] These works are highly unusual in their capacity to recognize and affirm the I in the 'we' and to touch deeper levels, while also marking the diminution of the ego. The form of recognition most closely follows Honneth's account of the early symbiosis necessary for self-confidence – the mode of affirmation is elemental and tactile.

Lucy and Jorge Orta's *Nexus Architecture* is a more public affair: the performances are mostly ephemeral 'interventions' in public space, to use her term; the installation versions are shown in galleries.[59] The series was thus primarily made to be seen and exhibited rather than experienced by wearers; certainly, there is no commentary about the participants' experience from the inside. Although on occasions the participants are broadly identified: architectural students animated a segment of sixteen suits in the opening weeks of the Venice Biennale (1995), teenagers from an orphanage took part in the Global March Against Child Labour (1998), and for the Second Johannesburg Biennale (1999) a group of migrant women fabricated the suits in vibrant African textiles and formed a human chain on the streets of Johannesburg.[60]

In her explanation of her aims, it is the social link between people that Lucy Orta emphasizes as the core idea of this series of works. She writes:

> in . . . my ongoing *Nexus Architecture*, clothing becomes the medium through which social links and bonds are made manifest, both literally and metaphorically. The links of zippers and channels, while enhancing the uniformity of the workers' overalls, create androgynous shapes that defy classification by the usual social markers and attempt to give form to the social, not the individual body.[61]

Orta creates a social body out of many bodies, significantly reducing the individuality of the participants. Seen in motion, this social body presents a compelling and fluent image of synchronization, the connected bodies move as one.[62] The soft umbilical cords falling from the waist of the costumes make the bodies' interdependency seems less regimented than Pape's *Divider* but the looser connections between bodies also diminishes the idea of a collective will animating movement. *Divider* needed bodies in order to exist: together the group occupied the seriated holes, together they moved the large canvas. In contrast, the bodies turn out to be unnecessary for *Nexus Architecture*, hence the work is in fact repeatedly exhibited without them. This practice inadvertently signals that the costume is the core part of the work: the grid of suspended empty boiler suits is sufficient to convey the idea of a collective or social body.

What does this empty version of sociality connote? For me, it is symptomatic of a more general trend in contemporary art to invoke social relations and social engagement without a clear idea of what that qualification means. Indeed, the degradation of the meaning of sociality seems to be magnified in the literature on Orta where the tendency is to elide the distinction between physical and social links. This conflation can be seen in the critics' repeated assumption that a physical link is sufficient to suppose a social link. Urban theorist Paul Virilio is a typical example. He writes: 'Each individual keeps an eye on, and protects, the other. One individual's life depends on the life of the other. In Lucy's work, the warmth of one gives warmth to the other. The physical link weaves a social link.'[63] Similarly, fashion theorist Joanne Entwistle has argued: 'Instead of differences, we are offered a powerful vision of possible, momentary collectives or networks of being whose connections are rendered visible and visceral in time and space.'[64] The connections are certainly physical and visible, but their conversion to a social or collective bond is less than clear. In sum, *Nexus Architecture* has a tautological character: coming together is in the service of coming together, there is no real reflection on forces of adhesion or bonding.

Orta was, of course, a favoured practitioner in the theorization of relational art practices by French curator Nicolas Bourriaud. And her work exemplifies the vague ethics and politics of his brand of relational art: artworks circle a well-known problem but with no obvious position, analysis or depth of understanding. That problem, in Orta's case, is the erosion of social bonds. The idea that social bonds have been weakened is a fairly widespread diagnosis of our times, often seen as flowing from the market-driven culture of neoliberalism and the rampant individualism it has unleashed. According to Bourriaud, the aesthetic response to the attenuation or severance of social bonds is an upsurge of small gestures that mend, repair and reconnect. There is no larger political agenda that orients action or gives it meaning. He states: 'Artistic activity, for its part, strives to achieve modest connections, open[s] up (One or two) obstructed passages, and connect[s] levels of reality kept apart from one another.'[65] Such art, he argues, offers 'small services' which aim to repair 'the weaknesses in the social bond'.[66] This description of relational art is very frequently cited in the literature on contemporary art. For example, French philosopher Jacques Rancière, in an article that identifies key tendencies in contemporary art, argues that relational art (as characterized by Bourriaud) addresses the 'lack of connections' in contemporary society.[67]

Orta's highly abstract image of connection combines a curious almost survivalist urge for protection from an unspecified impending emergency with nostalgic longing for the collective body or commonwealth of the social contract. In this way, her collective bodies sit awkwardly between a lost utopian moment of modernist collectivism and a futurist dystopian vision of conjoined anonymous protest and emergency.

3 Huddle, pile, clump: Loose associations

The next three works I want to consider also form collective bodies but through a looser means of assembly. The first is *Huddle* (1961), an iconic group work by choreographer and dancer Simone Forti (Figure 4.5). It is what she called a 'dance construction', a term that captures its categorical slipperiness situated part way between sculpture and performance. The work consists of between six and nine participants who respond to a set of instructions devised by Forti. The instructions are very simple; according to Forti, the group needs 'to bond together in a tight mass while remaining standing and to take turns climbing over the top of the mass'.[68] The duration of the piece is set by her at ten minutes and she indicates that a suitable place for its execution allows the audience to walk around the mass of bodies. The work is thus about the visibility of the mass and its activities as much as the teamwork of the participants.

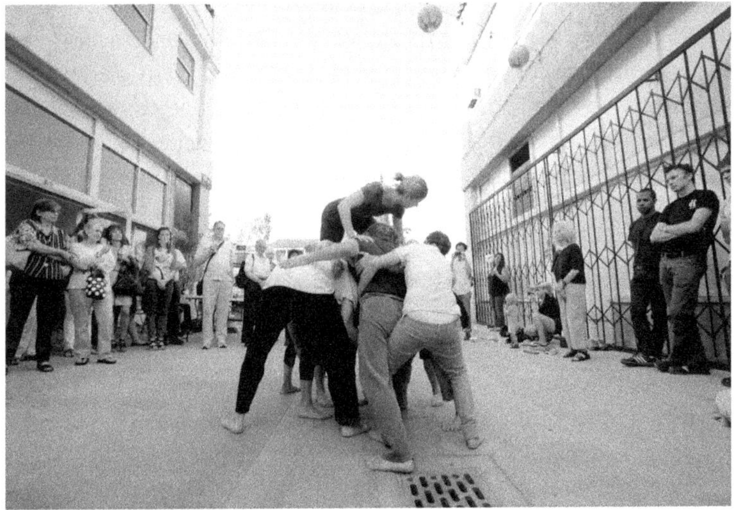

FIGURE 4.5 *Simone Forti.* Huddle *from Dance Constructions. 1961. Performance: 10 minutes. The Museum of Modern Art, New York. Committee on Media and Performance Art Funds. © 2020 The Museum of Modern Art, New York. Performed at The Box, Los Angeles 2009 Image: © 2021 The Box.*

Huddle is an evocative title, at once a straightforward sporting term but also a grouping with a distinct affective tone outside of that context: it suggests the need to cleave to others. The latter sense of the term is relied upon in the poem by Emma Lazarus that appears on the Statute of Liberty: 'Give me your tired, your poor. Your huddled masses yearning to breathe free.' The conjunction of the term 'huddle' with 'mass' in the American context must surely recall this kind of precarity and vulnerability that Lazarus qua the nation promises to embrace and shelter.

The idea of interdependence is certainly a key feature of the work noted by many critics. Forti herself describes the cooperative requirements of the situation with great concision: 'The performers are just doing what they need to do to climb or to sustain each other climbing.'[69] While *Huddle* sounds like a relatively simple almost deadpan instruction piece, its performance makes possible intriguing kinds of interactions. In her commentary on *Huddle*, art historian Meredith Morse teases out the social consequences of the piece. Those performing the work, she reports, experienced a 'receptiveness of self to others, opened by the kinesthetic relation'.[70] Here Foster's 'bodily writing' is acutely present: movement and touch enable corporeal dialogue and a kind of ethics of care. Participants register those meanings of the work very clearly: one participant said that the work made them aware of the 'relationship between the group and the individual'. Another described the intense proximity: 'You are breathing someone else's breath and you can hear all their sounds.'[71] This intimate grouping also involved restrictions. As Forti puts it, the 'task limits each huddler's activities to these modes, while he/she makes the myriad adjustments, decisions, actions that fulfil the task'.[72] The participants are bound by a kind of social contract insofar as they submit to the rules of the work and they form a very intimate 'work group', to use Bion's terms, established by touch and intense proximity.

The format of Forti's *Huddle* is echoed in Zhang Huan's *To Add One Meter to an Anonymous Mountain* (1995). Both are made of bodies brought directly together, without any kind of mediating armature, in order to form a shape: an igloo-like form in the case of Huddle, a pyramid in the case of *To Add One Meter to an Anonymous Mountain* (Figure 4.6). Huan's work also has a simple instruction at its core:

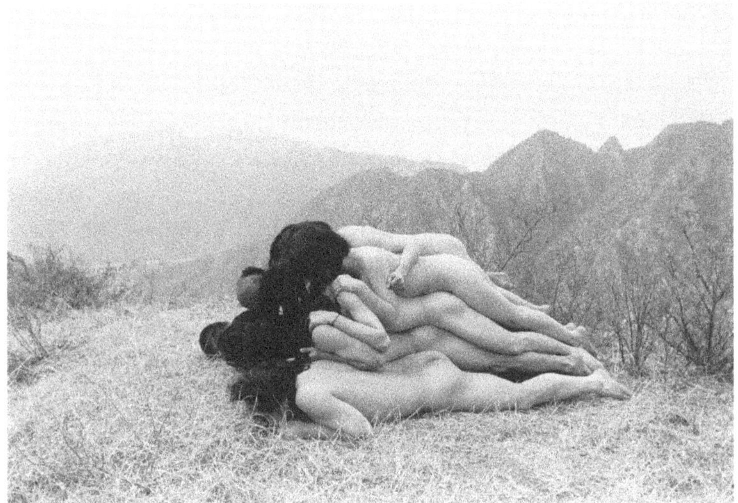

FIGURE 4.6 *Zhang Huan*, To Add One Meter to an Anonymous Mountain, *1995. Performance, Beijing, China © Zhang Huan Studio, courtesy Pace Gallery.*

ten bodies (two women and eight men) are used to fulfil the task indicated in the title. The recording of the one-off performance shows the ten participants, artists from Beijing's East Village, arriving at the summit of a mountain, taking off their clothes, forming an orderly queue before lying down one by one, at first on the ground, and then on top of one another to make the requisite form – a metre high pile of bodies.

While the completion of the task is a collective action, the social dimension of the task is not emphasized. Each phase moves quickly and without hesitation or negotiation, the anonymous bodies are treated rather like brute material, that is sorted by weight and assembled like a building material. Huan has described the work in a manner that has little to do with the actual physical formation. He says: 'It is about humility. Climb this mountain and you will find an even bigger mountain in front of you. It's about changing the natural state of things, about the idea of possibilities.'[73] Given the pointlessness of the task, the ideas of alteration and new horizons of possibility are both extremely unlikely readings of the work. Like Orta's reprise of Lygia Clark, here too there is a return to the forms of pioneering body art, but the tensions and relations between individual and group are excised, leaving just the impersonal literalism.

There are a number of performances that conjure more deliberately with this kind of impersonal massing together of bodies. For example, Tania Bruguera's *Tatlin's Whispers #5* (2008) where the unknowing audience in the Tate Turbine Hall was herded together by two mounted policemen using typical crowd control measures. According to Bruguera, the audience is led to speculate about the purpose of these extreme measures of state control.[74] Their uniform subjection to state power is assumed to be explicable through reference to states of exception types of current events. The impersonal mass in Francis Alÿs's *When Faith Moves Mountains* (2002) assembles around a sand dune; 500 participants, like a row of indistinguishable ants, shovel sand a few inches. Like Huan's work, the mass performance is argued to function metaphorically; staged outside Lima in Peru, it supposedly signifies the way 'minimal reforms are achieved through massive collective efforts'.[75] The logic only holds if reforms are absurd and futile.

Annika Ström's *Seven Women Standing in the Way* (2011–ongoing) also works with very minimal means and the looser huddle format (Figure 4.7). The work has been performed at various art spaces around the world and as the title indicates it consists of seven women standing in the way.[76] The women, who are all in their sixties, stand together in a conversational clump that creates a barrier at the entrance to an art space; they chat and drink and appear completely oblivious to the efforts of others to gain entry. Ström indicates that when it was first performed in Berlin the women stood out from the cool younger crowd, but when staged in Norway in small towns, visitors were often the same age as the seven women.[77] Usually, the women's age and gender should render them socially invisible; as artist Hito Steyerl has famously noted, being a woman over fifty is the best way to attain invisibility.[78] Despite or perhaps because of their supposed social invisibility, they should be attuned to the needs and desires of others. Instead, these seven women demonstrate a totally anti-social stance to others, subverting the expectation that women's mode of being in the world should be considerate and spatially contracted.

In the era of social distancing, their defiant occupation of space is both uncomfortable to watch and yet highly amusing. The women behave like the oblivious men charted by Casey Miller in her walks

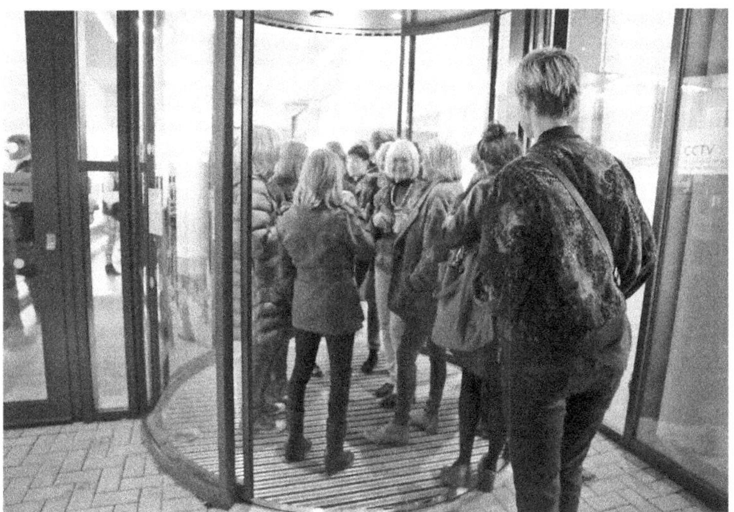

FIGURE 4.7 *Annika Ström's* Seven Women Standing in the Way *(2011–ongoing) at Focal Point Gallery in* duh? Art & Stupidity *curated by Paul Clinton/Anna Gritz 2015, Southend by Sea, UK. Courtesy of the artist.*

around Los Angeles with her partner during lockdown. Miller documents the many American men who refused to move out of the way for them, even when it is a requirement of the state to maintain a safe 1.5-metre distance from others.[79] Miller, of course, is simply applying to the current situation a longstanding feminist analysis of male versus female spatiality. In Ström's work, those gendered expectations about spatial behaviour are humorously inverted. Women come together in a circle of solidarity, taking up public space in a manner more befitting of an inconsiderate manspreader. They are a very interesting case: a group that clearly coheres to form a very convivial 'we', but in a way that is simultaneously anti-social and yet incisively illuminates gendered social norms.

4 The swarm and *Citizens Band*

The last work I want to consider is the four-channel video installation *Citizens Band* (2012) by the Australian artist (and former member of the Kingpins) Angelica Mesiti. It constructs a band or group that does not physically come together. While the four band members never share the same space in real life, they share an immigrant experience. They have moved to the West from Sudan, Algeria, Mongolia and Cameroon. The performers now live in Brisbane, Sydney and Paris, thereby bridging two geographical locations significant to the artist: her country of origin, Australia, and her current place of residence in France. The performers were recorded in their home locations and then 'brought together', as it were, in the space of the work. It is the unusual group formation that particularly interests me here – the band personifies the strange together-apartness of the virtual world. More on this shortly.

The video installation is comprised of four screens arranged to form a square, each screen is surrounded by blank wall space that serves to firmly demarcate one screen from the next. Each member of the band appears on their own separate screen and each is also separated from the others temporally: they appear one after another. The audience is positioned in the centre of the darkened space enclosed by the large screens. They must shift their attention from screen to screen as the performers appear and disappear. The screen fades to black after each performance and there is a pause before the next person appears out of the dark.

The performers' confinement in separate cinematic cells serves to emphasize their isolation, adding to the poignancy of the piece, particularly as within the frame there is also little or no interaction with others. Only at the very end of the work are the performers united aurally through the blending together of the sounds of their separate performances. On the artist's website this blending is described in rather negative terms as 'a cacophony . . . produced by playing the four soundtracks together'.[80] At that point, all four screens are suffused with swirling blurred colour that seems to runs through the four cells finally breaching their boundaries. As the videos are usually shown on a loop, the work then returns to the first performer with these colourful sections creating bookends of aural unity.

The first performer is a Cameroonian woman, Loïs Geraldine Zongo, who is shown standing in water up to her waist in what appears to be a completely deserted public swimming pool in Paris.[81] She is performing a percussive water sequence (Figure 4.8). The drumming

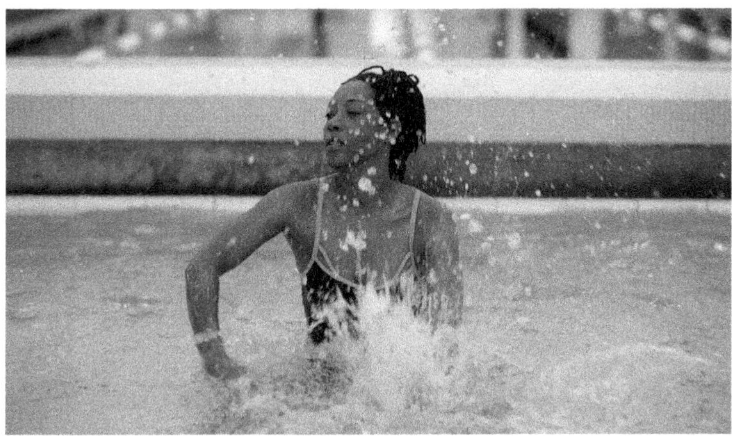

FIGURE 4.8 *Angelica Mesiti*, Citizens Band, *2012 (still). Four-channel High Definition video, 16:9, colour, sound, 21 minutes 25 seconds. © Angelica Mesiti. Courtesy the artist and Anna Schwartz Gallery.*

technique is called *akutuk* which, according to curator Bree Richards, produces 'beats using the dunk, cup and splash sounds created with her hands'.[82] Her black swimming costume with its brilliant blue straps and bindings chimes with the artificial blue of the chlorinated pool. Her light and airy water beats are complemented by the more conventional rounded and resonant sounds of drumming.

The second performer is a blind busker on the Paris Metro, Mohammed Lamourie from Algeria (Figure 4.9). He sings a folk ballad while playing a Casio keyboard tucked under his chin. Richards notes that he blends together 'sweet pure tones, murmuring humming and the rhythms of *Raï* music – a hybrid musical form that has been censored in Algeria'.[83] Without understanding the meaning of the ballad, there is nonetheless a feeling of sorrow and longing communicated by his performance. It has enormous poignancy that is entirely separate from his blindness, his need to beg in this fashion, and the indifference of the surrounding commuters, who barely register his presence or react to the simple beauty of the ballad. The incredibly moving quality of the performance is partly due to the quality of the song and Mohammed's wavering clear voice, but it is also the presence of the extended keyboard introduction suggestive of an unhurried performance, in no way compromised by the difficult

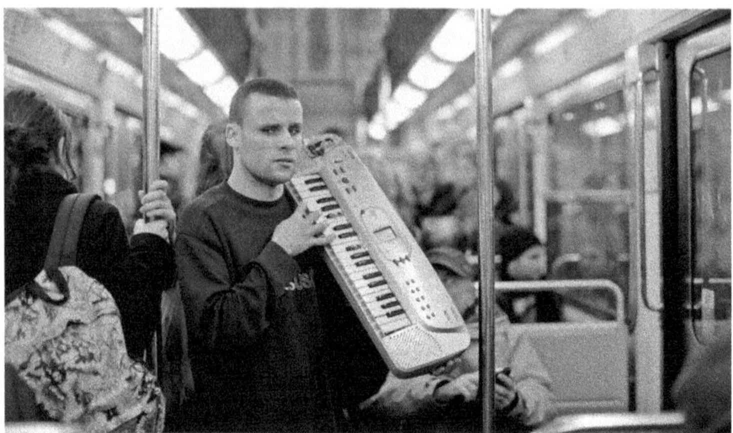

FIGURE 4.9 *Angelica Mesiti,* Citizens Band, *2012 (still). Four-channel High Definition video, 16:9, colour, sound, 21 minutes 25 seconds.* © *Angelica Mesiti. Courtesy the artist and Anna Schwartz Gallery.*

conditions of its delivery. It is as though despite the indifferent audience he continues to demonstrate fidelity to performance ideals beyond the mercantile.

The third performer is also a busker, Bukhchuluun Ganburged (Bukhu) who is from Mongolia (Figure 4.10). He plays the Mongolian *morin khuur* (horse head fiddle) and throat sings on a street corner in Newtown, an inner-city suburb of Sydney. His throat singing is an unearthly sound, and incredibly evocative like the hypnotic drones of Gregorian or Tibetan chants. Despite his placement in public space outside the instantly recognizable stripes of a 7/11, he is presented as an isolated figure sitting on a humble folding portable stool. Finally, Sudanese-born Asim Goreshi appears in his taxi in Brisbane whistling to himself in the dark (Figure 4.11). Richards indicates he too draws on specific musical traditions he is 'riffing on sacred Sufi Melodies'.[84] His whistling is exquisite and languorous, an unlikely sound to be found in a car at night. His eyes are closed as if he is carried away by the music to other times and places.

All four performers, then, are lone displaced figures working with distinctive musical traditions, the sounds of which are brought together to form a discordant band of citizens. The phrasing 'citizens band' calls up the idea of amateur or community contributions to

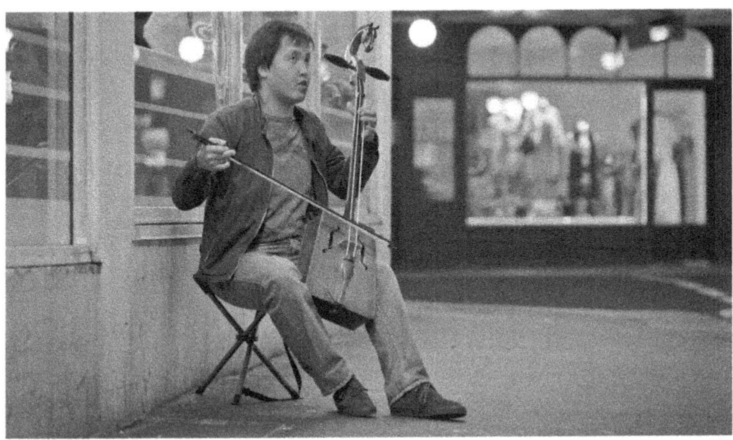

FIGURE 4.10 *Angelica Mesiti*, Citizens Band, *2012 (still). Four-channel High Definition video, 16:9, colour, sound, 21 minutes 25 seconds. © Angelica Mesiti. Courtesy the artist and Anna Schwartz Gallery.*

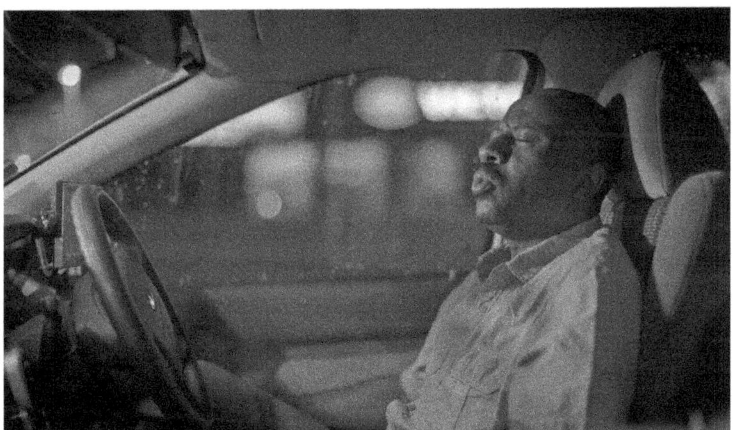

FIGURE 4.11 *Angelica Mesiti*, Citizens Band, *2012 (still). Four-channel High Definition video, 16:9, colour, sound, 21 minutes 25 seconds. © Angelica Mesiti. Courtesy the artist and Anna Schwartz Gallery.*

more highly professionalized fields, like citizen science where the public participates in research. Here it is community music that is evoked, shared musical cultures that the immigrant performers bring to their new places of residence or citizenship.

The word 'citizen' is an interesting choice of terms here. In Honneth's account of the self's relationship to others, only the self-respect of the citizen requires no further acts of recognition, it is given once and for all. These performers, then, have reached the age of majority and have taken up their rights and responsibilities in a new land. Bringing the state and official forms of belonging into play downplays the precarity of the two buskers – all four citizens are equal before the law. To frame these performers as citizens thus stresses social inclusion while the work itself stresses disconnection.

It is interesting to compare *Citizens Band* with other works where performers are dispersed and yet form a group. For example, the fan videos of Candice Breitz gather together different performers who never actually meet. She has made a series of multi-channel works that virtually assemble a group of fans of various pop stars (Michael Jackson, Madonna, Bob Marley, John Lennon) who sing a well-known hit together. These amateur singers are sometimes assembled into a grid of head shots; at other times they are shown almost full-length and side by side, with black backgrounds to visually unify the group into an ensemble. The focus in these works is not so much on their separation from each other on discrete monitors, cells or panels but on the fandom that joins them together in song. In contrast, in *Citizens Band* the performers' singularity is underscored; their specific locations apart from one another is as important as their formation into a virtual band.

Communication across distance is at the core of Trisha Brown's *Roof Piece* (1973) which also constructs a group from spatially dispersed participants. The work took place in an urban environment across a ten-block area in Soho in New York. The twelve dancers, clad in bright red to accentuate visibility, were stationed on the flat lower Manhattan roof tops in among the characteristic water towers (Figure 4.12). The performance started at Brown's building in Wooster Street and consisted of relayed sequences of improvised movements, which were supposed to be copied from performer to performer. Inevitably, the sequences transmuted as they were repeated from one end of the course to the other – the termination point was Robert Rauschenberg's building in Lafayette Street.[85] Here communication was body to body, organic and small-scale, like Tönnies's *gemeinschaft*, rather than being broadcast to the potentially

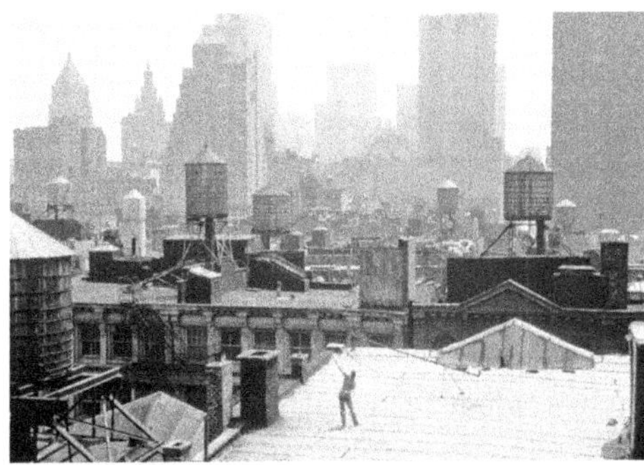

FIGURE 4.12 *Peter Moore,* Trisha Brown's 'Roof Piece', NYC, 1973, *1973, colour photograph from hi-res scan. Mounted: 12 × 18 × 1/2 in. (30.5 × 45.7 × 1.3 cm) © 2020 Barbara Moore / Licensed by VAGA at Artists Rights Society (ARS), NY, Courtesy Paula Cooper Gallery, New York.*

limitless audience of modern society. Yet *Roof Piece* also shows the breakdown of such an ideal of community and communication in the modern city; bodies try and fail to faithfully transmit a sequence of movements. *Citizens Band* deepens and furthers this unravelling of the organic community.

The band members' highly attenuated connections to each other, their homelands and their surroundings recall the tenor of philosophical discussions of community in the late twentieth century that similarly emphasized anomie and disconnection. I am thinking here of work by continental philosophers such as Jean-Luc Nancy's *The Inoperative Community*, Maurice Blanchot's *The Unavowed Community*, Alphonso Lingis's *The Community of Those Who Have Nothing in Common* and Giorgio Agamben's *The Coming Community*.[86] As Ian James adroitly summarizes, the position of Blanchot and Nancy converges around the '"nothing" of community' – the gaping space or absence of community left by the withdrawal of a 'transcendent principle', whether divine, imperial or monarchical, which would legitimize political organization.[87] This widespread pessimism about community was partly triggered by the failure of communism.

In the contemporary world the concern with disconnection has only amplified but now it is overlaid with the rhetoric of telepresence.

Technologies of connection abound, yet paradoxically as German philosopher Byung-Chul Han argues, they isolate. As he puts it: 'Electronic media such as radio *assemble* human beings. In contrast, digital media *isolate* them.'[88] His provocative argument is that the digital revolution has unleashed a new type of negative group: the swarm, a 'fleeting and unstable' form comprised of digital individuals 'gathering without assembly'.[89] He disputes the possibility of communal or collective action attributed to the multitude by Michael Hardt and Antonio Negri.[90] Curiously, Le Bon's mindless crowd is preferred to the swarm. In Han's view, the crowd coheres and has a voice, whereas the swarm is a group of individuals creating what he calls a 'shitstorm' or scandal. He argues, 'For a crowd to emerge, a chance gathering of human beings is not enough. It takes a soul, a common spirit, to fuse people into a crowd. The digital swarm lacks the soul or spirit of the masses. Individuals who come together as a swarm do not develop a *we*.'[91]

While the citizens band in Mesiti's work is not a swarm, it is nonetheless an example of a coming together that does not form a conventional 'we'. The citizens remain individuals who are gathered together but without the force of an assembly. Perhaps what Mesiti's work brings to this formulation of digital citizenry is a more positive conception of such groups. The band does not fuse together to cause a shitstorm, rather they live peaceful lives in parallel. In other words, they model non-intrusive co-existence, the kind of impersonal urban life that Richard Sennett has praised as necessary for the public culture of cities.[92] Mesiti's distinct group of citizens brilliantly models this cosmopolitan mode of coming together where individuals remain unknown to each other – anonymous and distant – and yet their music blends together. This conception of the group that comes together while remaining apart preserves distant urbanity in digital togetherness.

This impersonal kind of sociality is crucial for modern democracies: people contribute their skills and knowledge to the common good without necessarily knowing those who benefit, or those with whom they indirectly cooperate. Rather than a social bond, this form of togetherness is modelled along the lines of the social contract that peaceably binds citizens together around shared moral and political obligations. Intriguingly within this broader view of society, Mesiti inserts a kind of community of listeners. In an interview with Bree Richards she reports: 'Creating a community within the installation, between performers on screen and the audience, is something I am always thinking about.'[93] She makes this comment after explaining her involvement with collectives and her rejection of the idea of 'the singular artist working in isolation'. Here, we come full circle and return to where I began: the enormously productive power of the questioning of conventional ideas of authorship. Mesiti's careful construction of nested groups – band, community and digital society – is a wonderful by-product of the urge for self-effacement.

Conclusion

A typology of bodily configurations (one, two and many bodies), and their main relations (self-display, intimacy, social connection), has been the organizing framework of this book. To conclude I want to consider a work that complicates this typology by combining all three configurations. The work I have in mind is the last performance work I encountered on 13 March 2020 just before the Covid-19 shutdown in Australia.[1] It is a delegated performance by Cuban artist Tania Bruguera titled *UNNAMED* (2020) which was part of the twenty-second Biennale of Sydney. *UNNAMED* is an intimate work involving touch and close proximity in the two-person moment of its delivery and thus very powerfully raises the issue of the uncertain future of this genre of art in the post-pandemic world.

I'm not by nature or inclination a writer who is particularly adept at predicting the next big thing or legislating what forms future art should take, so I will use this provocation to look backwards rather than forwards, following the lead of my New Zealand colleague, curator and writer Robert Leonard. In a blog post for City Gallery in Wellington, he suggested that the meaning of some art works has dramatically shifted in the age of Covid-19. In response to this insight, in the midst of the pandemic in April 2020 he asked friends and colleagues to choose art works that they felt were radically reframed by the present moment. As he put it: 'They say art can change the way we look at the world, but the world can also change the way we look at art.'[2] Bruguera's *UNNAMED* is without doubt in this latter category.

UNNAMED was staged in what is called the Turbine Hall, an old industrial building of cathedral-like proportions on the lower apron at Cockatoo Island in the western reaches of Sydney Harbour. Previously a place of internment for convicts in the nineteenth century and then a major ship-building and repair facility in the twentieth century, the island has become a favourite off-site location for the biennale since 2008. Placed in the middle of one of the many cavernous sections of the Turbine Hall and surrounded by the rusted detritus of a bygone industrial age, *UNNAMED* was subtly set apart from its surroundings by an inconspicuous slightly raised pale dais. Dramatically lit from above, the setting consisted of a spare arrangement of furniture, suggestive of a makeshift clinic. In the centre was a portable massage table and stool, to the left a raised metal tray and a small storage cabinet, to the right was a modest wooden two drawer filing system left partly opened to reveal lines of stacked cards. On the cards were the stories, neatly typed and formatted, of 753 people who died defending the environment between 2015 and 2018.[3] The information – which is of course incomplete, it only includes reported deaths – was provided by Global Witness, an international NGO that according to the biennale catalogue 'investigates resource-related corruption and associated environmental and human right abuses'.[4] The 753 people were assassinated for defending their local environments against both state and corporate interests. Staged directly after an Australian summer dominated by reports of bushfires all along the eastern seaboard, the commemoration of lives lost in this fashion had an added relevance and poignancy.

The mode of presentation of the subject matter, however, did not exemplify or amplify the mood of these tragic and terrible stories. The visual presentation of the work was unsentimental and unsensational; the texts were factual in tone, just like neutral news reporting. In other words, the presentation of callous and calculated murder to protect the vested interests of the state or venal private enterprise was completely deadpan; anger and outrage, which would certainly be entirely justified emotions to accompany the revelation of this knowledge, were not a constitutive part of the work. Similarly, Bruguera's thoughts and feelings on the fact of ongoing 'ecocide' were certainly not incorporated into the fabric of the work. The tone instead was deliberately objective, cool and dispassionate, or impersonal to use the term I have been using throughout this book to characterize the afterlife of conceptual art strategies and aesthetics.

During the opening week of the biennale, the performance was conducted intermittently so that the file cards could be inspected in the absence of participants. The presence of a person in the space signalled the availability of the one-on-one experience. The performance proper, then, begins when a participant agrees to the conditions of the work and chooses a card from the filing cabinet. It turns out that the person in the space is a professional tattooist, who manages the whole transaction. When I participated in the performance, there was a very warm, friendly and reassuring woman called Lu, a local Sydney tattooist who runs a private studio called Tatu Lu Tattoos. She copied the name on the card onto a piece of paper and handed the card back to me after I climbed onto the massage table. She then prepared my arm to receive what is called an invisible tattoo. In other words, no ink is involved; marks on the skin are produced by minor abrasion. The participant chooses not only the card but also the placement of the tattoo; most people in the documentation for this work that I have seen chose their arm, but other parts of the body could be used. In the catalogue, a previous work, *Impermanent Revolution* (2009), using the same technique shows invisible tattoos inscribed, or being inscribed, on the participants' backs.

The name on the card is tapped out in capital letters onto the body of the participant with closely spaced small dots using a pointed bamboo stick. Meanwhile the participant reads out aloud the name on the card and then the short account of the circumstances of his or her death. Sometimes the performance involved just the two participants – tattooist and the person receiving the tattoo – at others there was an audience for the performance as the whole action was conducted without any kind of screening or attempt to make the procedure private.

Depending on the sensitivity of the skin, the tapping resulted in different bodily reactions. The skin of my friend flared up into a very angry red welt, spelling out UNIDENTIFIED – she chose an unidentified rural worker. I chose Elisa Badayos; she was killed on 28 November 2017 in the Philippines. A member of a human rights group, she was shot while on a fact-finding mission over a land dispute.[5] My tattoo was a slightly raised pink welt clearly spelling out her name; it completely disappeared after a couple of days.

The work begins and ends with the name of this one individual. Bruguera's catalogue entry for the biennale catalogue emphasizes the importance of this singularity: 'Participants have a selected name inscribed onto their bodies to personalize the data and to contrast the magnitude of these issues with the individual solitary reaction to them; you are only one person, only one member of the public, only human.'[6] The tactic of personalizing our relationship to complex political, social and historical issues by providing a singular focus, or point of identification, is the mainstay of historical drama as well as a tactic sometimes used in museums. For example, when I visited the US Holocaust Memorial Museum in Washington DC in 2000, I was confronted by two large bins of passports at the entrance, one labelled for men, the other for women. I was instructed to select a passport to guide me through the museum. The particular individual life narrative charted in the passport is thereby overlaid onto the broader chronology of the Holocaust told across the many rooms in the museum. The comprehensibility of one life is set against the enormity of the Holocaust.

UNNAMED has two 'one person' moments, neither of which is about the investigation of the self. As the preceding description indicates, one slides into and implicates the other: the solitary defender, it is implied, is just like you 'one member of the public'. The first moment is the life commemorated: the activist or defender of the environment whose name is taken from the drawer and who provides a way to personalize and personify environmental destruction, resistance and, in some instances, state-sanctioned murder. We learn of the state of our world and the destructive exploitation of finite resources one person at a time. The second 'one person' moment is when that individual name is temporarily carried on the skin of the participant, making the participant into the medium of the work. In other words, the participant becomes the canvas for this act of commemoration. Like a living sculpture, to use the apt term of Gilbert and George, the participant moves through private and possibly public space for two or more days carrying the defender's name on their skin and thereby becoming an integral, albeit dispersed, part of Bruguera's work.

It is a quite startling use of the one-person genre. Autobiography is nowhere in sight; gender is immaterial. Indeed, none of the typical markers of group identity matter much here: sex, gender, ethnicity, race, class, nationality, religion. Instead, the idea of the solitary person, first the defender, then the participant, underscores the importance of individual action. It is the deed of the individual not the doer's personal identity that is the focus. The feeling of helplessness that might be our typical reaction to a global crisis, over which we feel we have little or no control, is counteracted by the idea that individual actions matter; individual lives matter.

And the actions of the individual here are not about the self; they are informed and directed by collective interests – the common good that underpins and should be served by the social contract. Again, the catalogue captures this sentiment perfectly:

> In a way, these land and environment defenders are the people that are fighting our fight, fighting for all of us. When we see the numbers – almost 200 people died every year in different parts of the world – then we understand not only how we are all interconnected, but also that we are all responsible.[7]

The stress on interconnection is extremely prescient; while the work was made about the environment, the idea of connectivity also holds for how we have been forced to think during a pandemic. This aspect of the work has amplified in importance. Yet thinking of this conjunction, I am also reminded of an early meme which very powerfully brought the two issues together: 'Climate change needs to hire Corona Virus's publicist.' The urgency about the pandemic needs to be transposed to climate change. Perhaps this could be a consequence of our new global awareness. Certainly, the need to think about our interconnectedness, and our responsibility to each other, has never in my lifetime been spelt out so explicitly. The pandemic catchphrase 'we are all in it together', inaccurate as it may be in addressing the very different individual experiences resulting from economic inequalities, nonetheless describes these current circumstances in which the individual is required to act in the interests of the collective. Practising social distancing and other mechanisms of transmission minimization, we know, are in order to protect others as much as the self. It is this important shared reality that *UNNAMED* is very adept in addressing. The work binds the individual, whether defender or participant, into the group through the idea of an important and pressing environmental issue facing us all. The social dimension of *UNNAMED* is thus very powerfully evoked.

Alongside the individual and the group dynamic there are also two 'two person' moments. The intimate procedure of the tattoo involves two people, and the relationship of the participant with the defender becomes a kind of hypothetical pairing. The first pair involves a body-to-body transaction in real time and space; it is an intimate but distanced professional encounter like patient and doctor or any other cosmetic or therapeutic procedure we routinely undertake where touch is involved (dental work, haircuts, manicures, facials, massage). The sensitivity about touch in such circumstances and in greetings and salutations (hugging, shaking hands, kissing) will no doubt stay with us for some time. We will probably not feel comfortable, as the phrasing goes, participating in one-on-one performances like *UNNAMED* for some time.

Looking now at the component of the performance that involves touch, it seems risky, maybe even gratuitous. The artist's delegation of the performance to the tattooist becomes infinitely more complicated and ethically fraught. What assurance or protection is now owed by the artist to worker? And shifting across to the participant, what assurance would be required to comply with Covid-19 safety procedures? Would I submit to this now? And most importantly for thinking about the future of this work: How necessary is this visceral way of involving the participant? The second pairing I mentioned earlier, that of participant and defender, attempts to explain the need for this real corporeal involvement. The catalogue reports that the inscription directly on the skin 'forces empathy and remembrance'.[8] Does it really? Can empathy be forced? I suspect not. But do I feel things more deeply when my arm is being gently but just a bit painfully hammered? I'm not sure that I do feel more; but it is possible. I think the ritual of the performance does, however, help us to remember, to pay attention. Intriguingly, the catalogue entry frames and justifies the painful action as an antidote to the compassion fatigue associated with constantly watching distant suffering:

> Their names and the story that is shared with us breaks down the indifference to disaster brought up by news media and cuts through our inability to comprehend mass devastation. . . . The name, marked onto our bodies, helps us to understand. 751 stories are presented in UNNAMED as antidotes to indifference, feelings of insignificance and inaction.[9]

What enables the cut through or psychic clearing that facilitates such attention? Curiously, masochistic practices have previously been reported as facilitating precisely this cut through to the reality of suffering. For example, the performance in a private residence titled *Nourriture, actualités télévisées, feu* (1971) by French artist Gina Pane focused attention on the then-current political situation despite involving a sequence of progressively violent acts against herself. In the first act of three, Pane shoved raw meat into her mouth, then spat it out. Then she watched the television news with a bright light shining directly in her face and finally she put out small fires using her bare hands and feet. Pane reported that her actions facilitated the audience's attention to the news. She reports that they said they had not felt or heard the news before – they realized that there was a war going on and unemployment. She diagnoses their state of mind as being 'anaesthetized in the face of world news'.[10] It is curious that her actions had the effect of making the news real, rather than drawing attention to her. Her suffering is, as it were, for the audience; her passion sets off our compassion (suffering with). Is the mild pain of the invisible tattoo in *UNNAMED* performing a similar function of linking suffering and compassion? The minor pain we experience is clearly intended to connect us to other forms of suffering. If this is the case, how can this visceral identification operate in the virtual world we may be inhabiting for some time to come?

I realize that I am concluding with rather more questions than I am answering. And not only have I upset the taxonomy that I have been elaborating, but I have also thrown doubt on the future viability of many of these forms of body art and performance. Some works, however, might just come into their own in an era of social distancing. I was very struck by Robert Leonard's brilliant choice of Franz Erhard Walther as an artist whose work looks different now. It is worth citing in full:

I'd like to propose German artist Franz Erhard Walther as a poster boy for social distancing. Since the 1960s, he's been making minimalist-looking fabric objects for gallery goers to occupy and articulate. With their openings, fastenings, and straps, they are less sculptures than activities – performance scores. His body bags regiment populations into lines, shapes, patterns, tableaux, while his wall-mounted works hybridize clothing and architecture. Restricting yet benign, and often rather cosy, they suggest social structures, permutations of independence and interdependence – snapshots of group dynamics. But his work is never an orgy. He doesn't press bodies together, demanding respectful distance, equal personal space. Indeed, his works are all about getting together without touching. Now, with the pandemic, much of it looks like experiments in repressive-for-your-own-good social-distancing technology.[11]

Leonard's wry interpretation draws out the humour in Walther's cool arrangements – Walther's group works are experiments in 'repressiv e-for-your-own-good-social-distancing technology' and 'never an orgy'. His analysis also highlights how much more acutely aware we have become of bodily arrangements and relations: Walther 'doesn't press bodies together'; his works are all about 'getting together without touching'. The lack of touch in Walther's works is now very evident; we really notice it. The pandemic has brought such issues into sharp focus, as Leonard's commentary brilliantly illuminates.

Although this is a very new circumstance, I nonetheless hope that I have been looking at body art and performance this way all along. Certainly, this kind of careful attunement to the way bodies are in the world, either singly, in couples or groups, has been a central concern of this book. The taxonomy I have developed, and its complication by works like Bruguera's, provides a framework for thinking about our relations – starting with a self-relation, moving outwards to the typical dyad of self and other, and then finally encompassing group belonging and the larger social sphere. Body art and performance, I have been arguing, enable us to see, and to reflect on these relations, as well as to imagine them all anew. Looked at in this way, this visceral style of art has much to tell us about living together both now and into the future.

Notes

Introduction

1 Adrian Martin, 'Film Review: Never Look Away – Unless It's Conceptual Art', 20 April 2019. https://www.screenhub.com.au/n ews-article/reviews/film/adrian-martin/film-review-never-look-away -unless-its-conceptual-art-258232.

2 Brecht cited in Walter Benjamin, 'The Author as Producer', trans. Edmund Jephcott, in *Art after Modernism: Rethinking Representation*, ed. Brian Wallis (New York: New Museum of Contemporary Art, 1984), 299.

3 Vladimir Tatlin, 'The Initiative Individual in the Creativity of the Collective', in *Art in Theory 1900-1990: An Anthology of Changing Ideas*, ed. Charles Harrison and Paul Wood (Oxford: Blackwell, 1992), 309.

4 Osip Brik, 'The So-Called "Formal Method"', in *Art in Theory*, 323.

5 David A. Siqueiros et al., 'A Declaration of Social, Political and Aesthetic Principles', in *Art in Theory*, 388.

6 Roland Barthes, 'The Death of the Author', in *Image–Music–Text*, trans. Stephen Heath (New York: Hill and Wang, 1977), 143.

7 Ibid., 146.

8 Ibid.

9 Ibid.

10 Ibid., 148.

11 Denise Riley, *Impersonal Passion: Language as Affect* (Durham: Duke University Press, 2005), 1.

12 Sharon Cameron, *Impersonality: Seven Essays* (Chicago: University of Chicago Press, 2007), ix.

13 Charles Taylor, *A Secular Age* (Cambridge, MA: Harvard University Press, 2007), 281.

14 Christopher Bollas, *The Shadow of the Object: Psychoanalysis of the Unthought Known* (New York: Columbia University Press, 1987), 32.

15 Yve-Alain Bois, 'The Difficult Task of Erasing Oneself: Non-Composition in Twentieth-Century Art', *Institute for Advanced Study*, 7 March 2007. https://video.ias.edu/The-Difficult-Task-of-Erasing -Oneself.

16 See Yve-Alain Bois, 'Strzemiński and Kobro: In Search of Motivation', *Painting as Model* (Cambridge, MA: MIT Press, 1990), 121–55. See also Yve-Alain Bois, 'Chance Encounters: Kelly, Morellet, Cage', *The Anarchy of Silence: John Cage and Experimental Art*, exh. cat. (Barcelona: Museu d'art Contemporani de Barcelona, 2010), 188–203. Bois writes, 'the reason both Morellet and Cage resorted to chance is that it is one of the most efficient ways of producing non-intentional results and of absenting the self. There might be different motives of this desire for impersonality, each field (music, painting) carrying different baggage of tradition' (192). See also Yve-Alain Bois, *Ellsworth Kelly: Catalogue Raisonné of Paintings, Reliefs, and Sculpture, Volume One, 1940–1953* (Paris: Cahiers d'Art, 2015). Of Kelly he writes: 'If you started out by erasing yourself, your personality, your genius, and so on, if you started out by pretending you were not there, nobody would be able to come and say that Picasso did it better. If there was one thing Picasso did not know how to do, it was how to erase himself, how not to invent, how not to compose' (11).

17 Bois, 'Chance Encounters: Kelly, Morellet, Cage', 192.

18 T. S. Eliot, 'Tradition and the Individual Talent', in *Selected Essays*, 2nd edn (London: Faber and Faber, 1934), 21.

19 The impersonal urge is often presumed to be in opposition to the expression of emotions; Eliot shows how emotion and impersonality can be reconciled. In my previous books, I address affect in art history in greater detail. See Susan Best, *Visualizing Feeling: Affect and the Feminine Avant-garde* (London: I B Tauris, 2010); Susan Best, *Reparative Aesthetics: Witnessing in Contemporary Art Photography* (London: Bloomsbury, 2016).

20 T. S. Eliot, 'Tradition and Individual Talent', 22.

21 T. S. Eliot, 'Hamlet', in *Selected Essays*, 145.

22 Tim Dean, 'T. S. Eliot: Famous Clairvoyante', in *Gender, Desire, and Sexuality in T. S. Eliot*, ed. Cassandra Laity and Nancy K. Gish (Cambridge: Cambridge University Press, 2004), 48.

23 Ibid., 49.

24 Ibid., 51.

25 Ibid., 46–8.

26 Iris Murdoch, 'On "God" and "Good"', in *The Sovereignty of Good* (London: Routledge, 1970), 63.

27 Ibid., 64, 51.

28 Ibid., 63.

29 Lucy Lippard and John Chandler, 'The Dematerialisation of Art', in *Changing: Essays in Art Criticism* (New York: Dutton, 1971), 253.

30 Sigrid Gareis, Georg Schöllhammer and Peter Weibel, 'Introduction: Event – Trace – Context. On the Relevance of Historical Performance in the Exhibition Space', in *Moments: Eine Geschichte der Performance n 10 Akten*, exh. cat. (Karlsruhe: ZKM, 2012), 354.

31 Peter Weibel, 'The Performative Turn in the Exhibition Space', in *Moments*, 357.

32 André Lepecki, 'Zones of Resonance: Mutual Formations in Dance and the Visual Arts Since the 1960s', in *Move. Choreographing You: Art and Dance Since the 1960s*, exh. cat. (London: Hayward Publishing, 2011), 155.

33 Claire Bishop, 'Performance Art vs Dance: Professionalism, De-Skilling, and Linguistic Virtuosity', in *Is the Living Body the Last Thing Left Alive? The New Performance Turn, Its Histories and Its Institution*, ed. Cosmin Costinas and Ana Janevski (Berlin: Sternberg Press, 2017), 40–5.

34 Peter Osborne, *Anywhere or Not at All: Philosophy of Contemporary Art* (London: Verso, 2013).

35 Catherine Wood also uses a typology to consider post-1950s performance art. She organizes her book using 'I: the individual', 'We: the social' and 'It: the object'. See Catherine Wood, *Performance in Contemporary Art* (London: Tate Publishing, 2018).

Chapter 1

1 Carl Andre, *Cuts: Texts 1959–2004*, ed. James Meyer (Cambridge, MA: MIT Press, 2005), 291.

2 Ibid.

3 Frank Stella in Bruce Glaser, 'Questions to Stella and Judd' (1966), in *Minimal Art: A Critical Anthology*, ed. Gregory Battcock (Berkeley: University of California Press, 1968), 158.

4 Carl Andre, 'Preface to Stripe Painting' (1959), in *Theories and Documents of Contemporary Art: A Sourcebook of Artists'*

Writings, ed. Kristine Stiles and Peter Selz (Berkeley: University of California Press, 1996), 124.

5   In 1992 in a letter to James Meyer, Mel Bochner makes a similar admission: 'The use of self-generating procedures to make art was a liberation from the limitations of my ego. It represented an escape from individualism by the objectification of process. I remember believing that it may be the means of achieving Flaubert's dream of the annihilation of the author. On that point however, I was probably mistaken.' Mel Bochner cited in James Meyer, 'The Minimal Unconscious', *October* 130 (Fall 2009): 150.

6   Yve-Alain Bois, 'Ellsworth Kelly's Dream of Impersonality', 2013. https://www.ias.edu/ideas/2013/bois-ellsworth-kelly.

7   Ibid.

8   Liz Kotz, *Words to Be Looked At: Language in 1960s Art* (Cambridge, MA: MIT Press, 2007), 2.

9   Ibid., 254.

10 Sally Banes, *Democracy's Body: Judson Dance Theatre, 1962-1964* (Durham: Duke University Press), 40.

11 Harold Rosenberg cited in Howard Singerman, *Art Subjects: Making Artists in the American University* (Berkeley: University of California Press, 1999), 174.

12 Yvonne Rainer, 'A Quasi Survey of Some "Minimalist" Tendencies in the Quantitatively Minimal Dance Activity Midst the Plethora, or an Analysis of Trio A', in *Minimal Art*, 267.

13 Yvonne Rainer, 'A Manifesto Reconsidered', 2008, Serpentine Gallery, London. http://intermsofperformance.site/interviews/yvonne-rainer (accessed 15 August 2019).

14 Elise Archias describes Rainer's work as dealing with 'period questions of expression'. See her insightful discussion of 'modernist impersonality' in Martha Graham and Rainer, Elise Archias, *The Concrete Body: Yvonne Rainer, Carolee Schneemann, Vito Acconci* (New Haven and London: Yale University Press, 2016), 40–52.

15 A-effects aim not to put the audience in a 'trance'. Bertold Brecht, 'A Short Organum for the Theatre', in *Brecht on Theatre: The Development of an Aesthetic*, trans. John Willett (New York: Hill and Wang, 1978), 193; being 'entangled' is discussed as well as the 'hypnotic experience in the theatre' in Brecht, 'The German Drama: Pre-Hitler', in *Brecht on Theatre*, 78.

16 Rainer, 'A Quasi Survey', 267.

17 Ibid., 267.

18 Ibid.

19 Ibid.

20 Ibid., 269.

21 Carrie Lambert, 'On Being Moved: Rainer and the Aesthetics of Empathy', in *Yvonne Rainer: Radical Juxtapositions 1961-2002*, exh. cat. (Philadelphia: University of the Arts, 2002), 46.

22 Rainer, 'A Manifesto Reconsidered'.

23 Carrie Lambert-Beatty, *Being Watched: Yvonne Rainer and the 1960s* (Cambridge, MA: MIT Press, 2008), 133–4.

24 Mel Bochner, 'Serial Art, Systems, Solipsism', in *Minimal Art*, 100.

25 Sol LeWitt, 'Serial Project No.1 (ABCD)' (1966), in *Minimalism*, ed. James Meyer (London: Phaidon, 2000), 226.

26 Bochner, 'Serial Art, Systems, Solipsism', 100.

27 Ibid., 101.

28 J. R. Weinberg cited in Ibid., 100.

29 A. J. Ayer cited in Ibid., 92.

30 Ibid.

31 Ibid., 101.

32 Robert Morris, 'Note on Sculpture, Part 2', in *Continuous Project Altered Daily: The Writings of Robert Morris* (Cambridge, MA: MIT Press, 1995), 13.

33 Ibid.

34 Ibid., 15.

35 Eve Meltzer, *Systems We Have Loved: Conceptual Art, Affect, and the Antihumanist Turn* (Chicago: Chicago University Press, 2012), 11.

36 Ibid., 19.

37 See Peter Osborne, 'Conceptual Art and/as Philosophy', in *Rewriting Conceptual* Art, ed. Michael Newman and Jon Bird (London: Reaktion, 1999), 47–65.

38 David Raskin, 'Judd's Moral Art', *Donald Judd*, exh. cat. (London: Tate Modern, 2004), 81–2.

39 Meltzer, *Systems We Have Loved*, 119–20.

40 Ibid., 120.

41 Panofsky cited in Ibid., 77.

42 Ibid.

43 Eva Hesse in Cindy Nemser, 'A Conversation with Eva Hesse' (1970), in *Eva Hesse*, ed. Mignon Nixon (Cambridge, MA: MIT Press, 2002), 24.

44 Ibid.

45 Ibid.

46 Ibid.

47 Anna C. Chave, 'Minimalism and Biography', *The Art Bulletin* 82 no. 1 (March 2000): 151.

48 Ibid., 149. She concedes the gendered nature of her intervention, 157.

49 Briony Fer, 'Bordering on Blank: Eva Hesse and Minimalism', in *On Abstract Art* (New Haven and London: Yale University Press, 1997), 130.

50 Ibid.

51 David Raskin, *Donald Judd* (New Haven: Yale University Press, 2010).

52 Ibid., 1, 19, 58, 79, 88.

53 Glaser, 'Questions to Stella and Judd', 161.

54 Donald Judd, 'Yale Lecture, September 20, 1983', *RES: Anthropology and Aesthetics* no. 7/8 (Spring–Autumn 1984): 153.

55 Ibid.

56 James Meyer cited in Jonathan Flatley, 'Allegories of Boredom', in *A Minimal Future? Art as Object 1958-1968*, ed. Ann Goldstein, exh. cat. (Los Angeles: The Museum of Contemporary Art, 2004), 50.

57 Ibid., 53.

58 Frances Colpitt, *Minimal Art: The Critical Perspective* (Seattle: University of Washington Press, 1993), 117.

59 Susan Best, *Visualizing Feeling: Affect and the Feminine Avant-garde* (London: I. B. Tauris, 2011), 41–3.

60 T. S. Eliot, 'Tradition and the Individual Talent', in *Selected Essays*, 2nd edn (London: Faber and Faber, 1934), 17, 18.

61 Meltzer, *Systems We Have Loved*, 10, 22–3, 175–6.

62 Rainer quoted in Meyer, 'The Minimal Unconscious', 152.

63 Benjamin Buchloh, 'Robert Watts: Animate Objects, Inanimate Subjects', in *Neo-Avantgarde and Culture Industry: Essays on European and American Art from 1955 to 1975* (Cambridge, MA: MIT Press, 2000), 532.

64 Yve-Alain Bois, 'The Difficult Task of Erasing Oneself: Non-Composition in Twentieth-Century Art', *Institute for Advanced Study*, 7 March 2007. https://video.ias.edu/The-Difficult-Task-of-Erasing-Oneself.

65 Ibid.

66 In a seminar at the University of Sydney in May 2013, Ruth Leys and Michael Fried indicated that they both formulated their work as a response to anti-intentionalism. See Ruth Leys, 'The Turn to Affect: A Critique', *Critical Inquiry* 37 no. 3 (Spring 2011): 434–72. In the article, she indicates how the position she is articulating on anti-intentionalism is shared by her husband Michael Fried. She writes: 'In art criticism the same issue has been a focus of debate ever since Michael Fried, in "Art and Objecthood," defended high modernism against minimalism (or, as he also called it, literalism) on the grounds that the minimalist/literalist position made the viewer's subjective, present-tense experience stand in for – take the place of – the work itself (I am simplifying, of course).' 541 n. 31.

67 According to Judith Rodenbeck the 'effacement of self' is also a feature of Antonin Artaud's theatre. See Judith F. Rodenbeck, *Radical Prototypes; Allan Kaprow and the Invention of Happenings* (Cambridge, MA: MIT Press, 2011), 151.

68 Stella in Glaser, 'Questions to Stella and Judd', 149.

69 Ibid., 150.

70 Wladyslaw Strzemiński, 'B = 2' *Blok* (1924), in *Between Worlds: A Sourcebook of Central European Avant-gardes 1910-1930*, ed. Timothy O. Benson and Éva Forgács (Cambridge, MA: MIT Press, 2002), 499.

71 Ibid., 502.

72 Yve-Alain Bois, 'Strzemiński and Kobro: In Search of Motivation', in *Painting as Model* (Cambridge, MA: MIT Press, 1990), 121–55.

73 Wladyslaw Strzemiński, 'Unism in Painting' (1928), in *Between Worlds: A Sourcebook*, 654.

74 Judd in Glaser, 'Questions to Stella and Judd', 155.

75 Morris, 'Note on Sculpture, Part 2', 15.

76 Katarzyna Kobro and Wladyslaw Strzemiński, 'Composition of Space: Calculations of Space-Time Rhythm', in *Constructivism in Poland 1923 to 1936*, exh. cat. (Cambridge: Kettle's Yard Gallery; Lodz: Muzeum Sztuki, n.d.), 38.

77 Ibid.

78 Maria Gough, 'Composition and Construction', in *The Artist as Producer: Russian Constructivism in Revolution* (Berkeley: University of California Press, 2005), 21–59.

79 Fried cited in Ibid., 47.

80 Ibid., 12.

81 Ibid., 93.

82 Ibid., 94.

83 Tarabukin cited in Ibid.

84 Donald Judd, 'Specific Objects' (1965), in *Art in Theory 1900–1990*, ed. Charles Harrison and Paul Wood (Oxford: Blackwell, 1992), 812.

85 Stella in Glaser, 'Questions to Stella and Judd', 150.

86 Wilhelm Worringer, *Abstraction and Empathy* (1908), trans. Michael Bullock (New York: International University Press, 1953), 14–17.

87 Lucy R. Lippard, 'Eccentric Abstraction', in *Changing: Essays in Art Criticism* (New York: Dutton, 1971), 100.

88 Ibid.

89 Kasimir Malevich, 'From Cubism and Futurism to Suprematism. The New Realism in Painting', trans. Xenia Glowacki-Prus and Arnold McMillin, in *Malevich on Suprematism. Six Essays: 1915 to 1926*, ed. Patricia Railing (Iowa City: University of Iowa Museum of Art, Fall 1999), 28.

90 Curiously, Malevich writes of the zero of form as though it represented himself or reflected upon him: 'I have transformed myself *in the zero of form* and dragged myself out of the *rubbish-filled* pool of academic art.' Ibid. And again in the same article: 'But I transformed myself in the zero of form and emerged from nothing to creation, that is, to Suprematism, to the new realism in painting – to non-objective creation.' Ibid., 39.

91 André Green, *Life Narcissism Death Narcissism*, trans. Andrew Weller (London: Free Association Books, 2001), xi, 9, 49.

92 J. Laplanche and J. B. Pontalis, *The Language of Psychoanalysis* (London: Karnac, 1988), 255.

93 See for example, Sigmund Freud, 'On Narcissism: An Introduction' (1914), in *On Metapsychology: The Theory of Psychoanalysis*, trans. J. Strachey (Harmondsworth: Penguin, 1984), 68.

94 Sigmund Freud, 'Beyond the Pleasure Principle' (1920), in *On Metapsychology*, 316.

95 Ibid., 275.

96 Ibid., 288.

97 Ibid., 308.

98 Green, *Life Narcissism*, 222.

99 Ibid., 17.

100 Ibid.

101 Mel Ramsden, *Null Piece*, 1969 reproduced in Ann Stephen, *1969: The Black Box of Conceptual Art*, exh. cat. (University Art Gallery, University of Sydney, 2013), 79.

102 Green, Life *Narcissism*, 10.

103 Andre, *Cuts*, 99.

104 Andre, *Cuts*, 92, 275.

105 Rosalind E. Krauss, 'LeWitt in Progress', in *The Originality of the Avant-Garde and Other Modernist Myths* (Cambridge, MA: MIT Press, 1989), 251, 252, 254.

106 Sol LeWitt cited in 'Sol LeWitt, *13/3* (1981), The Metropolitan Museum, New York. https://www.metmuseum.org/art/collection/search/482523 (accessed 20 August 2019).

107 Sol LeWitt text from announcement card for Sol LeWitt exhibition at Dwan Gallery, 1967, reproduced in Meltzer, *Systems We Have Loved*, 68.

108 Jonathan Flatley cited in Ibid., 62.

109 Yve-Alain Bois, 'Dumb', in *Eva Hesse Sculpture*, exh. cat. (New York: The Jewish Museum; London and New Haven: Yale University Press, 2006), 19.

110 William S. Wilson, 'Eva Hesse: On the Threshold of Illusions', in *Inside the Visible: An Elliptical Traverse of Twentieth Century Art, in, of and from the Feminine*, ed. Catherine de Zegher, exh. cat. (Boston: Institute of Contemporary Art; Kortrijk: Kanaal Art Foundation; Cambridge, MA: MIT Press, 1996), 430–1.

111 Ibid., 430.

112 Andre, *Cuts*, 150.

113 Ibid., 151.

114 Green, *Life Narcissism*, 222.

Chapter 2

1 Marcia Tucker, *Anti-Illusion: Procedures/ Materials*, exh. cat. (New York: Whitney Museum of American Art, 1969), 44.

2 Ibid., 33.

3 In the catalogue Tucker indicates the work was not in the show, Ibid., 44.

4 Tucker calls it *Performance Area*, later it is referred to as *Performance Corridor* 1969. See Stefan Neuner and Wolfram Pilchler, 'Through the Looking Glass. Reflections on Bruce Nauman's *Live-Taped Video Corridor*', in *Bruce Nauman: A Contemporary*, ed. Eva Ehninger and Martina Venanzoni with Stephen E. Hauser (Münchenstein: Laurenz Foundation Schaulager, 2018), 60.

5 Tucker, *Anti-Illusion*, 44.

6 Lea Vergine, 'Bodylanguage' (1974), in *The Artist's Body*, ed. Tracey Warr (London: Phaidon, 2000), 236.

7 Ulay cited in Lara Shalson, *Performing Endurance: Art and Politics Since 1960* (Cambridge: Cambridge University Press, 2018), 69.

8 Willoughby Sharp, 'Body Works: A Precritical, Non-definitive Survey of Very Recent Works Using the Human Body or Parts Thereof', *Avalanche*, no. 1 (Fall 1970): 14–17.

9 Ibid.

10 Ibid.

11 James Joyce cited in Ibid.

12 Jane M. Blocker, *What the Body Cost: Desire, History and Performance* (Minneapolis: Minnesota University Press, 2004), 32.

13 Amelia Jones, *Body Art: Performing the Subject* (Minneapolis: Minnesota University Press, 1998), 152.

14 Nancy K. Miller, 'Changing the Subject: Authorship, Writing, and the Reader', in *Feminist Studies/Critical Studies*, ed. Teresa de Lauretis (Bloomington: Indiana University Press, 1986), 106.

15 Nancy K. Miller, 'The Text's Heroine: A Feminist Critic and Her Fictions', *Diacritics* 12, no. 2 (1982): 53.

16 Xavier Le Roy, 'Self Unfinished – The Thing About … Art & Artists – Xavier Le Roy', 26 August 2017. https://www.youtube.com/watch?v=QjUDY_54eLM.

17 Xavier Le Roy, 'Self Unfinished' (1998), in *'Retrospective' By Xavier Le Roy*, ed. Bojana Cvejić, exh. cat. (Paris: Les presses du reel, 2014), 163, 166–7, 165.

18 François Piron in the *Journal des arts of Connivence*, 6th Biennale de Lyon, cited in Xavier Le Roy, 'Self Unfinished'. http://www.xavierleroy.com/page.php?sp=d22f5301fc93b61aedfc31f0c3c53a88e553d8be&lg=en (accessed 21 September 2019).

19 Yvonne Rainer email 1999, reproduced on the website of Xavier Le Roy. http://www.xavierleroy.com/page.php?sp=d22f5301fc93b61aedfc31f0c3c53a88e553d8be&lg=en (accessed 21 September 2019).

20 Barbara Smith cited in Amelia Jones, *Body Art*, 151.

21 Lucy Lippard, 'The Pains and Pleasures of Rebirth: European and American Women's Body Art' (1976), *The Pink Glass Swan: Selected Feminist Essays on Art* (New York: The New Press, 1995), 102.

22 Joan Jonas, 'Mirror Check, Interview with Joan Jonas for 14 Rooms'. https://www.dailymotion.com/video/x20nmo1 (accessed 1 September 2019).

23 Ibid.

24 Ibid.

25 Michael Fried, *Absorption and Theatricality: Painter and Beholder in the Age of Diderot* (Chicago: University of Chicago, 1988), 93.

26 Joan Jonas cited in Rachel Cooke, 'Joan Jonas: "You don't know what you are doing sometimes. You just begin"', *The Guardian*, 4 March 2018. https://www.theguardian.com/artanddesign/2018/mar/04/joan-jonas-video-art-pioneer-tate-modern-exhibition-interview.

27 Eleanor Antin, 'Notes on Transformation' (1974), in *Theories and Documents of Contemporary Art: A Sourcebook of Artists' Writings*, ed. Kristine Stiles and Peter Selz (Berkeley: University of California Press, 1996), 774.

28 Howard N. Fox, 'Waiting in the Wings: Desire and Destiny in the Art of Eleanor Antin', in *Eleanor Antin*, ed. Nola Butler, exh. cat. (Los Angeles: Los Angeles County Museum, 1999), 44.

29 Eleanor Antin cited in Ibid.

30 Abigail Solomon-Godeau, 'The Woman Who Never Was: Self-representation, Photography and First-Wave Feminist Art', in *WACK! Art and the Feminist Revolution*, ed. Lisa Gabrielle Mark, exh. cat. (Los Angeles: The Museum of Contemporary Art and Cambridge, MA: MIT Press, 2007), 339.

31 Ibid., 341.

32 Ibid., 345.

33 Ibid., 343.

34 Catherine Wagley, 'Funny and Unflinching – Eleanor Antin bares all at LACMA', 23 May 2019. https://www.apollo-magazine.com/eleanor-antin-times-arrow-lacma/.

35 In an artist's statement from 1981, Ana Mendieta wrote: 'I have been carrying out a dialogue between the landscape and the female body (based on my own silhouette). I believe this has been a direct result of my having been torn from my homeland (Cuba) during my adolescence. I am overwhelmed by the feeling of having been cast from the womb (nature). My art is the way I re-establish the bonds that unite me to the universe. It is a return to the maternal source.' Ana Mendieta cited in Petra Barreras Del Rio and John Perrault, *Ana Mendieta: A Retrospective,* exh. cat. (New York: New Museum of Contemporary Art, 1987), 10.

36 Jones, *Body Art*, 185.

37 Ibid., 173, 182.

38 Ibid., 182.

39 Ibid., 168, 174, 154, 152.

40 Ibid., 186.

41 Ibid.

42 Lippard cited in Ibid., 175.

43 T. Magazine, 'Mostly True', *The New York Times Style Magazine*, 13 February 2015. https://www.nytimes.com/2015/02/13/t-magazine /sarah-manguso-amalia-ulman-heidi-julavits-diary.html.

44 According to Monica Steinberg, many of Ulman's followers were fake. She was the beneficiary of artist Constant Dullaart acquisition of fake accounts directed to artists. Monica Steinberg, '(Im)Personal Matters: Intimate Strangers and Affective Market Economies', *Oxford Art Journal* 42, no. 1 (2019): 54.

45 The project is archived on the Rhizome website, dates of Instagram updates are mostly taken from this site: https://webenact.rhizome. org/excellences-and-perfections/20141014162333/http://instagram .com/amaliaulman. Confusingly the book published on the project by Prestel, on occasions, has different dates listed for updates. See Amalia Ulman, *Excellences & Perfections* (Munich, London, New York: Prestel, 2018). Dates for the reproduced images were supplied by Arcadia Missa Gallery, London.

46 One of my ex-students, artist Marilyn Schneider, was in this category. She was first introduced to Ulman's work by an exhibition *Hyper Spectral Display (.hsd)* curated by Eleanor Ivory Weber at 55 Sydenham Rd, Marrickville in the inner west of Sydney, 28 June– 14 July 2013. See exhibition catalogue here: http://www.55sydenha mrd.com/wp-content/uploads/2014/01/55_hsd.pdf. She then followed *Excellences & Perfections* on Instagram the following year.

47 Ulman, *Excellences & Perfections*, 234.

48 Gilda Williams, 'Amalia Ulman', *Artforum* 55 no. 5 (January 2017): 227.

49 Anna Soldner, 'Artist, Feminist, Immigrant: An Interview with Amalia Ulman', 30 April 2014. http://bullettmedia.com/article/amalia-ulman-interview/#article-carousel.

50 Ibid.

51 Ulman cited in Alicia Eler, 'Amalia Ulman's Instagram Performance Exposed the Flaws in Selfie Culture', *CNN Style*, 29 March 2018. https://edition.cnn.com/style/article/amalia-ulman-instagram-exce llences-perfections/index.html.

52 Nathan Jurgenson, *The Social Photo: On Photography and Social Media* (Verso: London, 2019).

53 Roland Barthes, 'Rhetoric of the Image', *Image/ Music/Text*, trans. Stephen Heath (New York: Hill and Wang, 1977), 44. I am using Thierry de Duve's more succinct translation of 'the here-now and the there-then'. See Thierry de Duve, 'Time Exposure and Snapshot: The Photograph as Paradox', *October* 5 (Summer 1978); 117.

54 T. Magazine, 'Mostly True'.

55 Rachel Small, 'Amalia Ulman', *Interview* magazine, 14 October 2015. https://www.interviewmagazine.com/art/amalia-ulman.

56 Ibid.

57 Angelique Chrisafis, 'He Loves Me Not', *The Guardian*, 16 June 2007. https://www.theguardian.com/world/2007/jun/16/artnews.art.

58 'First Look' press release, 7 August 2014. https://235bowery.s3 .amazonaws.com/pressreleases/79/2014.8.7.FIRSTLOOK_RELA UNCH_PRESSRELEASE_V4.pdf (accessed 2 September 2018).

59 Peggy Phelan, *Unmarked: The Politics of Performance* (New York and London: Routledge, 1993), 146.

60 Ibid.

61 Douglas Crimp, 'The Photographic Activity of Postmodernism', *October* 15 (Winter 1980): 91–101.

62 Ulman, *Excellences & Perfections*, 235.

63 Ibid., 237.

64 Ibid.

65 'First Look' press release, 7 August 2014.

66 Kimberley Henze, 'Interfacing Femininities: Performance, Critique and the Events of Photography in Amalia Ulman's Excellences & Perfections' (Masters diss, University of Northern Carolina, Chapel Hill, 2017), 25–6. https://doi.org/10.17615/2q9v-db56.

67 Amalia Ulman cited in Cadence Kinsey, 'The Instagram Artist Who Fooled Thousands', *BBC Culture*, 7 March 2016. http://www.bbc.com /culture/story/20160307-the-instagram-artist-who-fooled-thousands.

68 Ulman, *Excellences & Perfections*, 231.

69 Genevieve Dwyer, 'Selfies in the Name of Art: Progressive or Narcissistic?', 25 January 2016. https://www.sbs.com.au/topics/life/article/2016/01/25/selfies-name-art-progressive-or-narcissistic.

70 Alicia Eler, *The Selfie Generation: How Our Self-Images are Changing Our Notions of Privacy, Sex, Consent, and Culture* (New York: Skyhorse Publishing, 2017), 1.

71 Michael Connor, 'First Look: Amalia Ulman – Excellences & Perfections', 20 October 2014. http://rhizome.org/editorial/2014/oct/20/first-look-amalia-ulmanexcellences-perfections/.

72 Rachel Mantock, '"Being a Girl is not a Natural Thing" – Why this Instagram Hoaxer Faked her Cool-girl Selfies', *Gadgette*, 10 February 2016. https://www.gadgette.com/2016/02/10/amalia-ulman-instagram-hoax/.

73 Simone de Beauvoir, *The Second Sex*, trans. H. M. Parshley (New York: Vintage, 1973), 301.

74 Joan Riviere, 'Womanliness as Masquerade', *International Journal of Psychoanalysis* 10 (1929): 306.

75 Kinsey, 'The Internet Artist who Fooled Thousands'.

76 See Ulman, *Excellences & Perfections*, 4 June 2014, 232 and 22 June 2014, 233.

77 Small, 'Amalia Ulman'.

78 Ulman, *Excellences & Perfections*, 235.

79 Kinsey, 'The Internet Artist'.

80 Ulman, *Excellences & Perfections*, 233.

81 Umberto Eco, 'The Poetics of the Open Work', in *Participation: Documents of Contemporary Art*, ed. Claire Bishop (London: Whitechapel; Cambridge, MA: MIT Press, 2006), 20–40.

82 Nate Freeman, '"I'm Laughing at Myself a Little Bit": Amalia Ulman on Her Show in London, and Ending Her Instagram Performance', *ARTnews*, 4 October 2016. http://www.artnews.com/2016/10/04/im-laughing-at-myself-a-little-bit-amalia-ulman-on-her-show-in-london-and-ending-her-instagram-performance/.

83 Mary Ann Doane, 'Film and the Masquerade: Theorising the Female Spectator', *Screen* 23, nos. 3–4 (September/October 1982): 81.

Chapter 3

1 Donald Kuspit, 'Happiness, Health, and Related Anomalies of Avant-Garde Art', in *Health and Happiness in 20th-Century Avant-*

garde Art, exh. cat. (Binghamton: State University of New York at Binghamton University Art Museum, 1996), 8.

2 See Helena Reckitt for an account of the neglect of feminist art in the discourse around relational art. Helena Reckitt, 'Forgotten Relations: Feminist Artists and Relational Aesthetics', in *Politics in a Glass Case: Feminism, Exhibition Cultures and Curatorial Transgressions*, ed. Angela Dimitrakaki and Lara Perry (Liverpool: Liverpool University, 2013), 131–56.

3 'The Second Woman at BAM Fisher', *Broadway World*, 18 October 2018. https://www.broadwayworld.com/regional/The-Second-Wo man-318938.

4 Christopher Lauer, *Intimacy: A Dialectical Study* (London: Bloomsbury, 2016), 1.

5 Ibid., 4.

6 Reports from the extended method-training workshops suggest fifteen minutes is the normal duration for this activity. Jacqueline Elise, 'I Tried the "Abramović Method" (And I think I Passed Out)', *VICE*, 30 April 2015. http://thecreatorsproject.vice.com/blog/i-tried-th e-abramovic-method-and-i-think-i-passed-out.

7 Daniela Stigh and Zoë Jackon, 'Marina Abramovic: The Artist Speaks', *Inside/Out: A MOMA/MOMA PS1 Blog*, 3 June 2010. http: //www.moma.org/explore/inside_out/2010/06/03/marina-abramovic -the-artist-speaks.

8 Victoria Pérez Royo, 'Real Fictions: *Time has Fallen Asleep in the Afternoon Sun*', https://www.kfda.be/en/program/time-has-fallen-asl eep-in-the-afternoon-sunshine (accessed 27 November 2019).

9 Project description, Ibid. Mette Edvardsen indicated to me in an email that this phrase 'an act of love' comes from a review in the *Guardian*. See Lyn Gardner, 'Time has Fallen Asleep in the Afternoon Sunshine – review, Birmingham Central Library', *The Guardian*, Tuesday 3 April 2012. https://www.theguardian.com/stage /2012/apr/03/time-has-fallen-asleep-review.

10 Joan Kee, 'Orders of the Law in the *One Year Performances* of Tehching Hsieh', *American Art* 30 (Spring 2016): 82.

11 Thomas McEvilley, 'Tehching Hsieh, Linda Montano', *Artforum* 23, no. 3 (November 1984): 98.

12 Alex and Allyson Grey cited in Frazer Ward, *No Innocent Bystanders: Performance Art and Audience* (Hanover: Dartmouth College Press, 2012), 144.

13 Text from Carolee Schneemann's performance *Interior Scroll* (also from *Kitch's Last Meal*) that speaks back to a structuralist filmmaker who can't look at her work, see Thyrza Nichols Goodeve, '"The

Cat Is My Medium": Notes on the Writing and Art of Carolee Schneemann', *Art Journal Open* 74 (2015): 5–22. http://artjournal.co llegeart.org/?p=63819.

14   Ward, *No Innocent Bystanders*, 137.

15   Karen Gonzalez Rice, 'Linda Montano and the Tensions of Monasticism', in *Beyond Belief: Theoaesthetics or Just Old-Time Religion?* ed. Ronald R. Bernier (Eugene: Pickwick Publications, 2010), 39.

16   Hsieh cited in 'For Me It Is Freedom: Six Hours with Tehching Hsieh', *Marina Abramovic Institute*, 23 June 2016. https://mai.art/ content/2016/6/10/tehching-hsieh-for-me-it-is-freedom.

17   Linda Montano and Tehching Hsieh, 'One Year Art/Life Performance: Interview with Alex and Allyson Grey' (1984), in *Theories and Documents of Contemporary Art: A Sourcebook of Artists' Writings*, ed. Kristine Stiles and Peter Selz (Berkeley: University of California Press, 1996), 778.

18   Hsieh cited in Lara Shalson, *Performing Endurance: Art and Politics Since 1960* (Cambridge: Cambridge University Press, 2018), 135.

19   Karen Gonzalez Rice argues that conflicts stemmed from gender expectations. See Rice, 'Linda Montano', 39 fn 41.

20   Linda Montano cited in Rice, 'Linda Montano', 38.

21   Ibid., 40.

22   Montano and Hsieh, 'One Year Art/Life Performance', 780.

23   Coco Fusco and Paula Herdida, *The Couple in the Cage: A Guatinaui Odyssey*, Video. https://www.youtube.com/watch?v=qv26tDDsuA8 &feature=emb_logo (accessed 20 October 2019). The importance of reception is registered by the Wikipedia entry for this work which details the various travails experienced each time the work was performed 'The Couple in the Cage', *Wikipedia Entry*, https://en.wiki pedia.org/wiki/Couple_in_The_Cage:_Two_Undiscovered_Amerin dians_Visit_the_West (accessed 26 November 2019).

24   For a discussion of the event score see Liz Kotz, 'Post-Cagean Aesthetics and the Event Score', in *Words to Be Looked At: Language in 1960s Art* (Cambridge, MA: MIT Press, 2007), 59–98.

25   Ariella Budick, 'Lygia Clark, Museum of Modern Art, New York – Review', 14 May 2014. https://www.ft.com/content/c1eea3c8-d6cc -11e3-b95e-00144feabdc0.

26   Erik Verhagen, 'The Work Can Never Be Finished. An Interview with Franz Erhard Walther', in *Franz Erhard Walther: The Body Decides*, ed. Elena Filipovic (Brussels: WIELS Contemporary Art Centre; CAPC musée d'art contemporain de Bordeaux in Collaboration with The Franz Erhard Walter Foundation and Konig Books London, 2014), 49.

27 María Emilia Fernández indicates 'at some point' the *First Work Set* was also titled *Instruments for Processes*, María Emilia Fernández, 'At the Boundaries of Language: The Body Reads, The Body Translates', in *Franz Erhard Walther: Objects, to Use/Instruments for Processes. exh. booklet* (Mexico City: Fundación Jumex Arte Contemporáneo, 2018), 48–49.

28 Walther cited in Verhagen, 'The Work Can Never be Finished', 61; Walther cited in Elena Filipovic, 'Sculpture Not to Be Seen', *The Body Decides*, 28.

29 Walther in Verhagen, 'The Work Can Never be Finished', 61.

30 Ibid., 60.

31 Ibid.

32 See Rina Carvajal's explanation of Pedrosa's phrase in, 'The Experimental Exercise of Freedom', in *The Experimental Exercise of Freedom: Lygia Clark, Gego, Mathias Goeritz, Hélio Oiticica and Mira Schendel*, ed. Susan Martin and Alma Ruiz, exh. cat. (Los Angeles: Museum of Contemporary Art, 1999), 35–6.

33 Abramović cited in Mary Richards, *Marina Abramović*, 2nd edn (Abingdon: Routledge, 2019), 105.

34 Lynn MacRitchie, 'Marina Abramovic: Exchanging Energies', *Performance Research* 1 no. 2 (Summer 1996): 31.

35 Richards, *Marina Abramović*, 19–20.

36 Leo Bersani in Tim Dean, Hal Foster, Kaja Silverman and Leo Bersani, 'A Conversation with Leo Bersani', *October* 82 (Autumn 1997): 6.

37 On the issue of masochism in performance art see Kathy O'Dell, *Contract with the Skin: Masochism, Performance Art and the 1970s* (Minneapolis: University of Minnesota Press, 1998) and Renata Salecl, 'Cut in the Body: From Clitoridectomy to Body Art', *(Per)versions of Love and Hate* (London: Verso, 1998), 141–68.

38 Roman Krznaric, *Empathy: Why it matters, and how to get it* (London: Random House, 2014), 60–1.

39 Ibid., 59.

40 Richards, *Marina Abramović*, 22.

41 Weibel cited in Jessica Ullrich, 'Contact Zones – Where Dogs and Humans Meet: Dog-Human Metamorphoses in Contemporary Art', in *Animals and Their People: Connecting East and West in Critical Animal Studies*, ed. Anna Barcz, Dorota Łagodzka (Leiden and Boston: Brill, 2018), 64.

42 Carolee Schneemann in 'Interview with Kate Haug' (1977), in *Imaging her Erotics: Essays, Interviews, Projects* (Cambridge, MA: MIT Press, 2002), 23.

43 Ibid.

44 Ibid., 33.

45 Schneemann cited in David Levi Strauss, 'Love Rides Aristotle through the Audience: Body Image and Idea in the Work of Carolee Schneemann', in *Imaging Her Erotics*, 322–3.

46 Schneemann in 'Interview with Kate Haug', 23.

47 Carolee Schneemann, 'Notes on Fuses' (1971), in *Imaging her Erotics*, 45.

48 This is how the film is described on Schneemann's website http://www.caroleeschneemann.com/works.html (accessed 12 December 2019).

49 Mikkel Borch-Jacobsen, *The Emotional Tie: Psychoanalysis, Mimesis and Affect*, trans. Douglas Brick and others (Stanford: Stanford University Press, 1993), 13.

50 Guy Trebay, 'The Way We Live Now: 6-13-04: Encounter; Sex, Art and Videotape'. https://www.nytimes.com/2004/06/13/magazine /the-way-we-live-now-6-13-04-encounter-sex-art-and-videotape.h tml. According to Fraser, Trebay's article makes a number of claims about the work that are inaccurate: the price of the work, the stipulations about the sort of collector, and the quote he attributes to Fraser which implies she wanted the sexual transaction to be 'normal to the extent it could be'. Fraser reports that it was the sale of the edition that was framed in terms of normality, not the sexual act. Fraser email to the author.

51 Praxis, 'Andrea Fraser in Conversation', *Brooklyn Rail*, October 2004. https://brooklynrail.org/2004/10/art/andrea-fraser.

52 Susan E. Cahan, 'Regarding Andrea Fraser's *Untitled*', *Social Semiotics* 6, no. 1 (April 2006): 9.

53 Sophie Calle, *Exquisite Pain* (London: Thames and Hudson, 2004), 203.

54 See, for example, these two accounts of participating in the performance: Annamarie Jagose and Lee Wallace, 'The Second Woman: A 24-hour Lesson in the Gendered Performance of Intimacy', *The Conversation*, 28 February 2018. http://theconversati on.com/the-second-woman-a-24-hour-lesson-in-the-gendered-per formance-of-intimacy-90455; Sam Twyford-Moore, 'Nat Randall's The Second Woman', *The Saturday Paper* 189, 27 January to 2 February 2018, https://www.thesaturdaypaper.com.au/2018/01/27/ nat-randalls-the-second-woman/15169716005699.

55 See, for example, Mel Bochner, 'The Serial Attitude', *Artforum* vol. 6 no. 4 (December 1967): 28–33. Bochner's description of this attitude stresses a kind of impersonal, almost quasi-scientific, method where 'order takes precedent over execution' and a 'predetermined process' is followed until it exhausts. This impersonal attitude to seriality is stressed by Sol Le Witt, who states: 'The serial artist does not attempt to produce a beautiful or mysterious object but functions merely as a clerk cataloguing the results of the premise.' Sol Le Witt, 'Serial Project No.1 (ABCD)' (1966), in *Minimalism*, ed. James Meyer (London: Phaidon, 2000), 226.

56 For example, Annamarie Jagose writes masculinity 'folds under pressure', Jagose and Wallace, 'The Second Woman'. Similarly, Sammy Preston describes *The Second Woman* as 'an unravelling of gender projection, positioning, and performance', Preston, 'On this Weekend: A 24-hour Performance of a Single Scene', *Broadsheet*, 18 October 2017. https://www.broadsheet.com.au/sydney/art-and-design/weekend-24-hour-performance-single-scene.

57 Teresa Tan, 'The Second Woman: Performance Artist Stages 100 Intimate Moments with 100 Men in 24 Hours', *ABC*, 20 October 2017. http://www.abc.net.au/news/2017-10-20/the-sec ond-woman-nat-randall-stages-100-dates-with-100-men/9064390.

58 Breckon cited in Garry Maddox, 'Nat Randall's The Second Woman is a Marathon Theatre Show for Bachelorette fans', *Sydney Morning Herald*, 19 October 2017. https://www.smh.com.au/entertainment/the atre/nat-randalls-the-second-woman-is-a-marathon-theatre-show-for -bachelorette-fans-20171019-gz3ysq.html (accessed 20 June 2018).

59 Jane Howard captures the nature of the identification with Randall well, while also noting the doubling of performer and character: 'In the repeats, scenes increasingly become a dance between Randall the performance artist and Virginia the character; between the man as volunteer, and the man as romantic partner Marty. Through each scene, the pair negotiate, in the moment, a relationship both as actors and as a couple.' Jane Howard, 'Radical Capability: Endurance and mutation in *The Second Woman*', *Kill your Darlings*, 17 June 2016. https://www.killyourdarlings.com.au/2016/06/radica l-capability-endurance-and-mutation-in-the-second-woman/?doing _wp_cron=1529467530.0140869617462158203125.

60 Randall cited in Tan, 'The Second Woman'.

61 Juliet Mitchell, *Siblings: Sex and Violence* (Cambridge: Polity, 2003), 11.

62 Ibid., 44.

63 Ibid., 29.

Chapter 4

1 Gustave Le Bon, *The Crowd: A Study of the Popular Mind* (New York: Macmillan, 1896), 12–13.

2 'Election Night Harlem, New York, 2008', in *Living as Form: Socially Engaged Art from 1991-2011*, ed. Nato Thompson (New York: Creative Time Books; Cambridge, MA: MIT Press, 2012), 148.

3 Nato Thompson, 'Living as Form', in *Living as Form*, 28.

4 Ibid.

5 'Tahrir Square Cairo, Egypt, 2011', in *Living as Form*, 230.

6 Thompson, 'Living as Form', 22.

7 See Emile Durkheim, *The Elementary Forms of the Religious Life*, trans. Robert Nisbet, 2nd edn (London: Allen & Unwin, 1976). The phrase 'collective effervescence' is used in the chapter section summary, Chapter VII, 'Origins of these Beliefs', part III, xvi.

8 Ibid., 210.

9 See the discussion of Le Bon and others in The Frankfurt Institute for Social Research, 'Masses', *Aspects of Sociology*, trans. John Viertel (London: Heinemann Educational Books, 1973), 72–82.

10 Kwame Anthony Appiah, *The Lies that Bind: Rethinking Identity: Creed, Country, Colour, Class, Culture* (London: Profile Books 2018).

11 Claire Bishop, *Artificial Hells: Participatory Art and the Politics of Spectatorship* (London: Verso, 2012), 8.

12 Ibid.

13 Georg Simmel cited in *Aspects of Sociology*, 68.

14 Blake Stimson and Gregory Sholette, ed., *Collectivism after Modernism: The Art of Social Imagination after 1945* (Minneapolis: University of Minnesota Press, 2007); Grant H. Kester, *Conversation Pieces: Community and Communication in Modern Art* (Durham: Duke University Press, 2004); Grant H. Kester, *The One and the Many: Contemporary Collaborative Art in a Global Context* (Durham: Duke University Press, 2011); Bill Kelley Jr. and Grant H. Kester, eds., *Collective Situations: Readings in Contemporary Latin American Art, 1995-2010* (Durham: Duke University Press, 2017).

15 Press Release for Cosmopolis #1: Collective Intelligence, October 2017. www.centrepompidou.fr › content › version › file › Cosmopolis_ENG.

16 Blake Stimson and Gregory Sholette, 'Introduction: Periodizing Collectivism', in *Collectivism after Modernism*, 7.

17 Tönnies cited in The Frankfurt Institute for Social Research, 'Society', *Aspects of Sociology*, 35 fn 23.

18 Richard Sennett, *Together: The Rituals, Pleasures and Politics of Co-operation* (London: Penguin, 2012), 37–9.

19 W. R. Bion, *Experiences in Groups and Other Papers* (New York: Tavistock Publications, 1961), 98–9.

20 Ibid., 143.

21 Ibid., 116.

22 Ibid., 62–5.

23 Ibid., 89, 95.

24 Ibid., 89.

25 Axel Honneth, 'The I in We: Recognition as a Driving Force of Group Formation', in *The I in We: Studies in the Theory of Recognition*, trans. Joseph Ganahl (Cambridge: Polity, 2012), 203.

26 Ibid.

27 The challenge to the opposition of autonomy and dependence is of course an established theoretical point repeatedly made by feminist scholars of political and social theory throughout the 1980s and 1990s. See, for example, Carol Gilligan, *In a Different Voice* (Cambridge, MA: Harvard University Press, 1982) and Jessica Benjamin, *The Bonds of Love: Psychoanalysis, Feminism and the Problem of Domination* (New York: Pantheon, 1988), among innumerable others.

28 Honneth, 'The I in We', 207.

29 Ibid., 206.

30 Ibid.

31 Ibid.

32 Ibid.

33 Ibid.

34 Ibid., 214.

35 Honneth also steers away from the negative aspects of psychoanalysis in other chapters in the book. See Honneth's responses to Joel Whitebook, 'Facets of the Presocial Self: Rejoinder to Joel Whitebook', *The I in We*, 221 and 'The Work of Negativity: A Recognition-Theoretical Revision of Psychoanalysis', *The I in We*, 200.

36 Abramović cited in Kriss Ravetto-Biagioli, *Mythopoetic Cinema: On the Ruins of European Identity* (New York: Columbia University Press, 2017), 147.

37 Le Bon cited in The Frankfurt Institute for Social Research, *Aspects of Sociology*, 74.

38 Lygia Pape cited in Lygia Pape interviewed by Lúcia Carneiro and Ileana Pradilla, 'Birds of Marvelous Colors', in *Lygia Pape: A Multitude of Forms*, exh. cat. (New York: Metropolitan Museum of Art, 2017), 21.

39 Iria Candela, 'The Risk of Invention', in *Lygia Pape: A Multitude of Forms*, 10.

40 Veronica Brown, 'Being a Part of Living Art: Lygia Pape's *Divisor* (Divider)', 3 April 2017. https://www.metmuseum.org/blogs/met-live-arts/2017/divisor-lygia-pape.

41 Lygia Pape cited in Guy Brett, 'The Logic of the Web', *Lygia Pape: Gávea de Tocaia* (São Paulo: Cosac and Naify, 2000), 307.

42 Brett, 'The Logic of the Web', 307.

43 Candela, 'The Risk of Invention', 11.

44 See Rina Carvajal's explanation of Pedrosa's phrase in, 'The Experimental Exercise of Freedom', in *The Experimental Exercise of Freedom: Lygia Clark, Gego, Mathias Goeritz, Hélio Oiticica and Mira Schendel*, ed. Susan Martin and Alma Ruiz, exh. cat. (Los Angeles: Museum of Contemporary Art, 1999), 35–6.

45 Brett, 'The Logic of the Web', 307.

46 Pape in Brett, 'The Logic of the Web', 307.

47 Ibid.

48 Georg Simmel, 'Metropolis and Mental Life', in *The Blackwell City Reader*, ed. Gary Bridge and Sophie Watson (Malden: Blackwell, 2002), 11.

49 Lygia Clark, 'L'art c'est le corps' (1973), in *Lygia Clark*, ed. Manuel Borja-Villel, exh. cat. (Barcelona: Fundacio Antoni Tapies, 1998), 233.

50 Maurice Merleau-Ponty, *The Visible and the Invisible*, trans. Alphonso Lingis (Evanston: Northwestern University Press, 1968), 146.

51 Clark, 'The Body is the House', *Lygia Clark*, 247.

52 Ibid., 247.

53 Ibid., 248.

54 Susan Leigh Foster cited in Jenn Joy, *The Choreographic* (Cambridge, MA: MIT Press, 2014), 17. She contests and complicates the opposition between thinking and acting in Susan Leigh Foster, 'Choreographing History', in *The Routledge Dance Studies Reader*, edited by Jens Richard Giersdorf, and Yutian Wong (London: Routledge, 2018), 378–9.

55 Description of *Biological Architectures I* in *Lygia Clark*, 253.

56 Honneth, 'The I in We', 208.

57 Guy Brett, 'Lygia Clark: Six Cells', *Lygia Clark*, 27.

58 Ibid.

59 Lucy Orta, *Operational Aesthetics: The work of Lucy + Jorge Orta* (London: University of the Arts, 2011), 26.

60 Ibid., 28.

61 Lucy Orta, 'Questioning Identity', in *GSK Contemporary: Aware Art Fashion Identity*, exh. cat. (Bologna: Damiani editore via Zanardi, 2010), 36.

62 See the choreographed performance that took place in Valencia in 2002, 9 October 2014. https://www.youtube.com/watch?v=Te0 nIXDB-BI.

63 Paul Virilio cited in Orta, *Operational Aesthetics*, 26.

64 Joanne Entwistle cited in Orta, 'Questioning Identity', 36.

65 Nicolas Bourriaud, *Relational Aesthetics*, trans. S. Pleasance and F. Woods (Paris: Les Presses du Réel, 2002), 8.

66 Bourriaud cited in Jacques Rancière, 'Problems and Transformations in Critical Art', trans. C. Bishop and P. Lafuente, in *Participation*, ed. Claire Bishop (London: Whitechapel, 2006), 90.

67 Rancière, 'Problems and Transformations', 90.

68 Simone Forti, '*Huddle*: Artist's Statement' (2011), in *Simone Forti: Thinking with the Body*, ed. Sabine Breitwieser, exh. cat. (Salzburg: Museum der Moderne, 2014), 96.

69 Simone Forti cited in Meredith Morse *Soft is Fast: Simone Forti in the 1960s and After* (Cambridge, MA: MIT Press, 2016), 125.

70 Morse, *Soft is Fast*, 147.

71 Ibid.

72 Forti, '*Huddle*: Artist's Statement', 96.

73 Zhang Huan cited in 'Zhang Huan', The Art Story. https://www.the artstory.org/artist/zhang-huan/artworks/ (accessed 30 April 2020).

74 Tania Bruguera in 'The Artist as Activist: Tania Bruguera in Conversation with Clair Bishop', 6 April 2016. https://www.youtube. com/watch?v=4raYhes7Owl.

75 This is the description of the work on MOMA's website, 'Francis Alÿs, *When Faith Moves Mountains*, 2002'. https://www.moma.org/ collection/works/109922 (accessed 27 May 2020).

76 See the excerpt from Annika Ström's performance *Seven Women Standing in the Way*, 14 June 2014 at Moderna Museet Malmö during Feministisk fredag. https://www.youtube.com/watch?v=Gbx QyGEN5Qo (accessed 30 April 2020).

77 Email correspondence with the artist, 27 June 2020.

78 This is a line from Hito Steyerl's video *How Not to be Seen. A Fucking Didactic Educational. MOV File* (2013). Her mock instructional video tackles the serious issue of contemporary surveillance. One of her most acute and yet hilarious solutions to evade being seen is simply to be female and over fifty.

79 Casey Miller, 'Men Who Don't Move'. https://caseymm.github.io/men-who-dont-move/ (accessed 11 May 2020).

80 Angelica Mesiti website http://www.angelicamesiti.com/selec tedworks#/citizens-band/ (accessed 4 May 2020).

81 Short excerpts of all four performers can be viewed on vimeo https://vimeo.com/55522269 (accessed 10 November 2017).

82 Bree Richards, 'Citizens Band 2012', *Angelica Mesiti: A Communion of Stranger Gestures* (Melbourne Schwartz City and Sydney Artspace, 2017), 153.

83 Ibid.

84 Ibid.

85 Susan Rosenberg, *Trisha Brown: Choreography as Visual Art* (Middletown: Wesleyan University Press, 2017), 102–3.

86 Jean-Luc Nancy, *The Inoperative Community*, trans. Christopher Fynsk (Minneapolis: University of Minnesota Press, 1991); Maurice Blanchot, *The Unavowable Community*, trans. Pierre Joris (Barrytown: Station Hill, 1988); Alphonso Lingis, *The Community of Those Who Have Nothing in Common* (Indiana: Indiana University Press, 1994); Giorgio Agamben, *The Coming Community*, trans. Michael Hardt (Minneapolis: University of Minnesota Press, 1993).

87 Ian James, 'Naming the Nothing: Nancy and Blanchot on Community', *Culture, Theory and Critique* 51, no. 2 (2010): 173.

88 Byung-Chul Han, *In the Swarm: Digital Prospects*, trans. Erik Butler (Cambridge, MA: MIT Press, 2017), 11.

89 Ibid., 12, 11.

90 Ibid., 12–13.

91 Ibid., 10.

92 Richard Sennett, *The Fall of Public Man* (New York: Norton, 1974), 318, 419.

93 Angelica Mesiti cited in Bree Richards, 'Conversation with the Artist', in *Angelica Mesiti*, exh. cat. (Canberra: National Gallery of Australia, July 2017), n.p.

Conclusion

1 I am indebted to discussions with Ann Stephen and Tim Bass for triggering me to think about this work in this way.

2 Robert Leonard, 'Everything has Changed', *Blog for City Gallery Wellington*, 27 April 2020. https://citygallery.org.nz/blog/everything -has-changed/

3 There is some discrepancy about the number of deaths that the work commemorates. The online Biennale of Sydney entry for Tania Bruguera puts the number of deaths at 753; however, the printed biennale catalogue puts the number at 751. See 'Tania Bruguera' https://www.biennaleofsydney.art/artists/tania-bruguera/ (accessed 7 July 2020) and 'Tania Bruguera', *Nirin: 22nd Biennale of Sydney*, exh. cat. (Sydney: Biennale of Sydney, 2020), 276.

4 'Tania Bruguera', *Nirin: 22nd Biennale of Sydney*, 276.

5 See the report by Monica Ulmanu, Alan Evans and Georgia Brown published with the Guardian. 'The defenders: 207 environmental defenders have been killed in 2017 while protecting their community's land or natural resources' https://www.theguardian .com/environment/ng-interactive/2017/jul/13/the-defenders-tracker and the website of Global Witness https://www.globalwitness.org/ en/ (accessed 7 July 2020).

6 'Tania Bruguera', *Nirin: 22nd Biennale of Sydney*, 276.

7 Ibid.

8 Ibid.

9 Ibid.

10 Kathy O'Dell, *Contract with the Skin: Masochism, Performance Art and the 1970s* (Minneapolis: University of Minnesota Press, 1998), 60.

11 Leonard, 'Everything Has Changed'.

Bibliography

Agamben, Giorgio. *The Coming Community.* Translated by Michael Hardt. Minneapolis: University of Minnesota Press, 1993.

Andre, Carl. *Cuts: Texts 1959–2004*, edited by James Meyer. Cambridge, MA: MIT Press, 2005.

Andre, Carl. 'Preface to Stripe Painting' (1959). In *Theories and Documents of Contemporary Art: A Sourcebook of Artists' Writings*, edited by Kristine Stiles and Peter Selz, 124. Berkeley: University of California Press, 1996.

Antin, Eleanor. 'Notes on Transformation' (1974). In *Theories and Documents of Contemporary Art: A Sourcebook of Artists' Writings*, edited by Kristine Stiles and Peter Selz, 773–5. Berkeley: University of California Press, 1996.

Appiah, Kwame Anthony. *The Lies that Bind: Rethinking Identity: Creed, Country, Colour, Class, Culture.* London: Profile Books, 2018.

Archias, Elise. *The Concrete Body: Yvonne Rainer, Carolee Schneemann, Vito Acconci.* New Haven and London: Yale University Press, 2016.

Banes, Sally. *Democracy's Body: Judson Dance Theatre, 1962–1964.* Durham: Duke University Press.

Barthes, Roland. 'Rhetoric of the Image'. In *Image/Music/Text.* Translated by Stephen Heath, 32–51. New York: Hill and Wang, 1977.

Barthes, Roland. 'The Death of the Author'. In *Image–Music–Text.* Translated by Stephen Heath, 142–8. New York: Hill and Wang, 1977.

Benjamin, Jessica. *The Bonds of Love: Psychoanalysis, Feminism and the Problem of Domination.* New York: Pantheon, 1988.

Benjamin, Walter. 'The Author as Producer'. Translated by Edmund Jephcott. In *Art after Modernism: Rethinking Representation*, edited by Brian Wallis, 297–309. New York: New Museum of Contemporary Art, 1984.

Best, Susan. *Visualizing Feeling: Affect and the Feminine Avant-garde.* London: I B Tauris, 2011.

Best, Susan. *Reparative Aesthetics: Witnessing in Contemporary Art Photography.* London: Bloomsbury, 2016.

Biennale of Sydney. *Nirin: 22nd Biennale of Sydney.* Exh. cat. Sydney: Biennale of Sydney, 2020.

Bion, W. R. *Experiences in Groups and Other Papers*. New York: Tavistock Publications, 1961.

Bishop, Claire. 'Antagonism and Relational Aesthetics', *October* 110 (Fall 2004): 73–6.

Bishop, Claire. *Artificial Hells: Participatory Art and the Politics of Spectatorship*. London: Verso, 2012.

Bishop, Claire. 'Performance Art vs Dance: Professionalism, De-Skilling, and Linguistic Virtuosity'. In *Is the Living Body the Last Thing Left Alive? The New Performance Turn, Its Histories and Its Institutions*, edited by Cosmin Costinas and Ana Janevski, 40–5. Berlin: Sternberg Press, 2017.

Blanchot, Maurice. *The Unavowable Community*. Translated by Pierre Joris. Barrytown: Station Hill, 1988.

Blocker, Jane M. *What the Body Cost: Desire, History and Performance*. Minneapolis: Minnesota University Press, 2004.

Bochner, Mel. 'The Serial Attitude'. *Artforum* 6, no. 4 (December 1967): 28–33.

Bochner, Mel. 'Serial Art, Systems, Solipsism' (1967). In *Minimal Art: A Critical Anthology*, edited by Gregory Battcock, 92–102. Berkeley: University of California Press, 1968.

Bois, Yve-Alain. 'Strzemiński and Kobro: In Search of Motivation'. In *Painting as Model*, 121–55. Cambridge, MA: MIT Press, 1990.

Bois, Yve-Alain. 'Dumb'. In *Eva Hesse Sculpture*. Exh. cat., 17–27. New York: The Jewish Museum and London and New Haven: Yale University Press, 2006.

Bois, Yve-Alain. 'The Difficult Task of Erasing Oneself: Non-Composition in Twentieth-Century Art'. Institute for Advanced Study, 7 March 2007. https://video.ias.edu/The-Difficult-Task-of-Erasing-Oneself

Bois, Yve-Alain. 'Chance Encounters: Kelly, Morellet, Cage'. In *The Anarchy of Silence: John Cage and Experimental Art*. Exh. cat., 188–203. Barcelona: Museu d'art Contemporani de Barcelona, 2010.

Bois, Yve-Alain. 'Ellsworth Kelly's Dream of Impersonality'. 2013. Accessed 30 July 2019. https://www.ias.edu/ideas/2013/bois-ellsworth-kelly.

Bois, Yve-Alain. *Ellsworth Kelly: Catalogue Raisonné of Paintings, Reliefs, and Sculpture, Volume One, 1940–1953*. Paris: Cahiers d'Art, 2015.

Bollas, Christopher. *The Shadow of the Object: Psychoanalysis of the Unthought Known*. New York: Columbia University Press, 1987.

Borch-Jacobsen, Mikkel. *The Emotional Tie: Psychoanalysis, Mimesis and Affect*. Translated by Douglas Brick and others. Stanford: Stanford University Press, 1993.

Borja-Villel, Manuel, ed. *Lygia Clark*. Exh. cat. Barcelona: Fundacio Antoni Tapies, 1998.

Bourriaud, Nicolas. *Relational Aesthetics*. Translated by S. Pleasance and F. Woods. Paris: Les Presses du Réel, 2002.

Brecht, Bertold. *Brecht on Theatre: The Development of an Aesthetic*. Translated by John Willett. New York: Hill and Wang, 1978.

Brett, Guy. 'Lygia Clark: Six Cells'. In *Lygia Clark*, edited by Manuel Borja-Villel. Exh. cat., 17–35. Barcelona: Fundacio Antoni Tapies, 1998.

Brett, Guy. 'The Logic of the Web'. In *Lygia Pape: Gávea de Tocaia*, 305–15. São Paulo: Cosac and Naify, 2000.

Brik, Osip. 'The So-called "Formal Method"'. In *Art in Theory 1900–1990: An Anthology of Changing Ideas*, edited by Charles Harrison and Paul Wood, 323–4. Oxford: Blackwell, 1992.

Brown, Veronica. 'Being a Part of Living Art: Lygia Pape's *Divisor* (Divider)'. Accessed 1 March 2019. https://www.metmuseum.org/blogs/met-live-arts/2017/divisor-lygia-pape

Bruguera, Tania. 'The Artist as Activist: Tania Bruguera in Conversation with Clair Bishop'. 6 April 2016. https://www.youtube.com/watch?v=4raYhes7Owl

Buchloh, Benjamin. *Neo-Avantgarde and Culture Industry: Essays on European and American Art from 1955 to 1975*. Cambridge, MA: MIT Press, 2000.

Budick, Ariella. 'Lygia Clark, Museum of Modern Art, New York – Review'. 14 May 2014. https://www.ft.com/content/c1eea3c8-d6cc-11e3-b95e-00144feabdc0

Cahan, Susan E. 'Regarding Andrea Fraser's *Untitled*'. *Social Semiotics* 6, no. 1 (April 2006): 7–15.

Calle, Sophie. *Exquisite Pain*. London: Thames and Hudson, 2004.

Cameron, Sharon. *Impersonality: Seven Essays*. Chicago: University of Chicago Press, 2007.

Candela, Iria. 'The Risk of Invention'. In *Lygia Pape: A Multitude of Forms*. Exh. cat., 2–15. New York Metropolitan Museum of Art, 2017.

Carvajal, Rina. 'The Experimental Exercise of Freedom'. In *The Experimental Exercise of Freedom: Lygia Clark, Gego, Mathias Goeritz, Hélio Oiticica and Mira Schendel*, edited by Susan Martin and Alma Ruiz. Exh. cat., 35–54. Los Angeles: Museum of Contemporary Art, 1999.

Chave, Anna C. 'Minimalism and Biography'. *The Art Bulletin* 82, no. 1 (March 2000): 149–63.

Chrisafis, Angelique. 'He Loves Me Not'. *The Guardian*, 16 June 2007. https://www.theguardian.com/world/2007/jun/16/artnews.art

Colpitt, Frances. *Minimal Art: The Critical Perspective*. Seattle: University of Washington Press, 1993.

Connor, Michael. 'First Look: Amalia Ulman – Excellences & Perfections'. *Rhizome*, 20 October 2014. http://rhizome.org/editorial/2014/oct/20/first-look-amalia-ulmanexcellences-perfections/

Cooke, Rachel. 'Joan Jonas: "You don't know what you are doing sometimes. You just begin"'. *The Guardian*, 4 March 2018. https://ww w.theguardian.com/artanddesign/2018/mar/04/joan-jonas-video-art-p ioneer-tate-modern-exhibition-interview

Crimp, Douglas. 'The Photographic Activity of Postmodernism'. *October* 15 (Winter 1980): 91–101.

Dean, Tim, Hal Foster, Kaja Silverman and Leo Bersani. 'A Conversation with Leo Bersani'. *October* 82 (Autumn 1997): 3–16.

Dean, Tim. 'T S Eliot: Famous Clairvoyante'. In *Gender Desire and Sexuality in T. S. Eliot*, edited by Cassandra Laity and Nancy K Gish, 3–65. Cambridge: Cambridge University Press, 2004.

de Beauvoir, Simone. *The Second Sex*. Translated by H. M. Parshley. New York: Vintage, 1973.

Del Rio, Petra Barreras and John Perreault. *Ana Mendieta: A Retrospective*. Exh. cat. New York: New Museum of Contemporary Art, 1987.

Doane, Mary Ann. 'Film and the Masquerade: Theorising the Female Spectator'. *Screen* 23, Issue 3–4 (September/October 1982): 74–88.

Durkheim, Emile. *The Elementary Forms of the Religious Life*, Translated by Robert Nisbet, 2nd edn. London: Allen & Unwin, 1976.

Dwyer, Genevieve. 'Selfies in the Name of Art: Progressive or Narcissistic?'. SBS, 25 January 2016. https://www.sbs.com.au/topics/ life/article/2016/01/25/selfies-name-art-progressive-or-narcissistic

Eco, Umberto. 'The Poetics of the Open Work'. In *Participation: Documents of Contemporary Art*, edited by Claire Bishop, 20–40. London: Whitechapel and Cambridge, MA: MIT Press, 2006.

Eler, Alicia. *The Selfie Generation: How Our Self-Images are Changing Our Notions of Privacy, Sex, Consent, and Culture*. New York: Skyhorse Publishing, 2017.

Eler, Alicia. 'Amalia Ulman's Instagram Performance Exposed the Flaws in Selfie Culture'. CNN Style, 29 March 2018. https://edition.cnn.com /style/article/amalia-ulman-instagram-excellences-perfections/index .html

Eliot, T. S. 'Hamlet' (1917). In *Selected Essays*, 2nd edn, 141–6. London: Faber and Faber, 1934.

Eliot, T. S. 'Tradition and the Individual Talent' (1917). In *Selected Essays*, 2nd edn, 13–22. London: Faber and Faber, 1934.

Elise, Jacqueline. 'I Tried the "Abramović Method" (And I think I Passed Out)'. *VICE*, 30 April 2015. http://thecreatorsproject.vice.com/blog/i-tri ed-the-abramovic-method-and-i-think-i-passed-out

Fer, Briony. *On Abstract Art*. New Haven and London: Yale University Press, 1997.

Fernández, María Emilia. 'At the Boundaries of Language: The Body Reads, The Body Translates'. In *Franz Erhard Walther: Objects, to*

Use/Instruments for Processes. Exh. booklet, 45–51. Mexico City: Fundación Jumex Arte Contemporáneo, 2018.

Filipovic, Elena. 'Sculpture Not to Be Seen'. In *Franz Erhard Walther: The Body Decides*. Exh. cat., edited by Elena Filipovic, 13–35. Brussels: WIELS Contemporary Art Centre; CAPC musée d'art contemporain de Bordeaux in collaboration with The Franz Erhard Walter foundation and Konig Books London, 2014.

Flatley, Jonathan. 'Allegories of Boredom'. In *A Minimal Future? Art as Object 1958-1968*, edited by Ann Goldstein. Exh. cat., 51–75. Los Angeles: The Museum of Contemporary Art, 2004.

Forti, Simone. '*Huddle*: Artist's Statement' (2011). In *Simone Forti: Thinking with the Body*, edited by Sabine Breitwieser. Exh. cat., 96. Salzburg: Museum der Moderne, 2014.

Foster, Susan Leigh. 'Choreographing History'. In *The Routledge Dance Studies Reader*, edited by Jens Richard Giersdorf and Yutian Wong, 377–88. London: Routledge, 2018.

Fox, Howard N. 'Waiting in the Wings: Desire and Destiny in the Art of Eleanor Antin'. In *Eleanor Antin*, edited by Nola Butler. Exh. cat., 15–157. Los Angeles: Los Angeles County Museum, 1999.

Freeman, Nate. '"I'm Laughing at Myself a Little Bit": Amalia Ulman on Her Show in London, and Ending Her Instagram Performance'. *ARTnews*, 4 October 2016. http://www.artnews.com/2016/10/04/im -laughing-at-myself-a-little-bit-amalia-ulman-on-her-show-in-london-and -ending-her-instagram-performance/

Freud, Sigmund. *On Metapsychology: The Theory of Psychoanalysis*. Translated by J. Strachey. Harmondsworth: Penguin, 1984.

Freud, Sigmund. 'Group Psychology and the Analysis of the Ego' (1921). *Civilization, Society and Religion, Vol 12 Penguin Freud Library*. Translated by James Strachey, 95–178. Harmondsworth: Penguin, 1985.

Fried, Michael. *Absorption and Theatricality: Painter and Beholder in the Age of Diderot*. Chicago: University of Chicago, 1988.

Fusco, Coco and Paula Herdida. *The Couple in the Cage: A Guatinaui Odyssey*. Accessed 20 October 2019. https://www.youtube.com/w atch?v=qv26tDDsuA8&feature=emb_logo

Gardner, Lyn. 'Time has Fallen Asleep in the Afternoon Sunshine – review Birmingham Central Library'. *The Guardian*, Tuesday 3 April 2012. https://www.theguardian.com/stage/2012/apr/03/time-has-falle n-asleep-review

Gareis, Sigrid, Georg Schöllhammer and Peter Weibel, eds. *Moments: Eine Geschichte der Performance n 10 Akten*. Exh. cat. Karlsruhe, ZKM, 2012.

Gilligan, Carol. *In a Different Voice*. Cambridge, MA: Harvard University Press, 1982.

Glaser, Bruce. 'Questions to Stella and Judd' (1966). In *Minimal Art: A Critical Anthology*, edited by Gregory Battcock, 148–64. Berkeley: University of California Press, 1968.

Goodeve, Thyrza Nichols. '"The Cat Is My Medium": Notes on the Writing and Art of Carolee Schneemann'. *Art Journal Open*, 29 July 2015. http://artjournal.collegeart.org/?p=6381

Gough, Maria. *The Artist as Producer: Russian Constructivism in Revolution.* Berkeley: University of California Press, 2005.

Green, André. *Life Narcissism Death Narcissism.* Translated by Andrew Weller. London: Free Association Books, 2001.

Han, Byung-Chul. *In the Swarm: Digital Prospects.* Translated by Erik Butler. Cambridge, MA: MIT Press, 2017.

Hardt, Michael and Antonio Negri. *Multitude: War and Democracy in the Age of Empire.* New York: Penguin, 2004.

Henze, Kimberley. 'Interfacing Femininities: Performance, Critique and the Events of Photography in Amalia Ulman's Excellences & Perfections'. Masters diss, University of Northern Carolina, Chapel Hill, 2017. https://doi.org/10.17615/2q9v-db56

Honneth, Axel. *The I in We: Studies in the Theory of Recognition.* Translated by Joseph Ganahl. Cambridge: Polity, 2012.

Howard, Jane. 'Radical Capability: Endurance and mutation in *The Second Woman*'. *Kill Your Darlings*, 17 June 2016. https://www.kil lyourdarlings.com.au/2016/06/radical-capability-endurance-and-mut ation-in-the-second-woman/?doing_wp_cron=1529467530.01408696 17462158203125

Hsieh, Tehching. 'For Me It Is Freedom: Six Hours with Tehching Hsieh'. Marina Abramovic Institute, 23 June 2016. https://mai.art/content/2 016/6/10/tehching-hsieh-for-me-it-is-freedom

Jagose, Annamarie and Lee Wallace. 'The Second Woman: A 24-hour Lesson in the Gendered Performance of Intimacy'. *The Conversation*, 28 February 2018. http://theconversation.com/the-second-woman-a -24-hour-lesson-in-the-gendered-performance-of-intimacy-90455

James, Ian. 'Naming the Nothing: Nancy and Blanchot on Community'. *Culture, Theory and Critique* 51, no. 2 (2010): 171–87.

Jonas, Joan. 'Mirror Check, Interview with Joan Jonas for 14 Rooms'. Accessed 1 September 2019. https://www.dailymotion.com/video/x 20nmo1

Jones, Amelia. *Body Art: Performing the Subject.* Minneapolis: Minnesota University Press, 1998.

Joy, Jenn. *The Choreographic.* Cambridge, MA: MIT Press, 2014.

Judd, Donald. 'Yale Lecture, September 20, 1983'. *RES: Anthropology and Aesthetics* 7/8 (Spring–Autumn, 1984): 147–54.

Judd, Donald. 'Specific Objects' (1965). In *Art in Theory 1900–1990*, edited by Charles Harrison and Paul Wood, 809–13. Oxford: Blackwell, 1992.

Jurgenson, Nathan. *The Social Photo: On Photography and Social Media*. London: Verso, 2019.

Kee, Joan. 'Orders of the Law in the *One Year Performances* of Tehching Hsieh'. *American Art* (Spring 2016): 72–91.

Kelley Jr., Bill and Grant H. Kester, eds. *Collective Situations: Readings in Contemporary Latin American Art, 1995–2010*. Durham: Duke University Press, 2017.

Kester, Grant H. *Conversation Pieces: Community and Communication in Modern Art*. Durham: Duke University Press, 2004.

Kester, Grant H. *The One and the Many: Contemporary Collaborative Art in a Global Context*. Durham: Duke University Press, 2011.

Kinsey, Cadence. 'The Instagram Artist Who Fooled Thousands'. BBC Culture, 7 March 2016. http://www.bbc.com/culture/story/20160307 -the-instagram-artist-who-fooled-thousands

Kobro, Katarzyna and Wladyslaw Strzemiński. 'Composition of Space: Calculations of Space-Time Rhythm'. *Constructivism in Poland 1923 to 1936*. Exh. cat., 38–9. Cambridge: Kettle's Yard Gallery and Lodz: Muzeum Sztuki, n.d.

Kotz, Liz. *Words to Be Looked At: Language in 1960s Art*. Cambridge, MA: MIT Press, 2007.

Krauss, Rosalind E. *The Originality of the Avant-Garde and Other Modernist Myths*. Cambridge, MA: MIT Press, 1989.

Krznaric, Roman. *Empathy: Why It Matters, and How to Get It*. London: Random House, 2014.

Kuspit, Donald. 'Happiness, Health, and Related Anomalies of Avant-Garde Art'. In *Health and Happiness in 20th-Century Avant-garde Art*. Exh. cat., 7–50. State University of New York at Binghamton University Art Museum, 1996.

Lambert, Carrie. 'On Being Moved: Rainer and the Aesthetics of Empathy'. In *Yvonne Rainer: Radical Juxtapositions 1961–2002*. Exh. cat., 41–63. Philadelphia: University of the Arts, 2002.

Lambert-Beatty, Carrie. *Being Watched: Yvonne Rainer and the 1960s*. Cambridge, MA: MIT Press, 2008.

Laplanche, J. and J. B. Pontalis. *The Language of Psychoanalysis*. London: Karnac, 1988.

Lauer, Christopher. *Intimacy: A Dialectical Study*. London: Bloomsbury, 2016.

Le Bon, Gustave. *The Crowd: A Study of the Popular Mind*. New York: Macmillan, 1896.

Leonard, Robert. 'Everything has Changed'. Blog for City Gallery Wellington, 27 April 2020. https://citygallery.org.nz/blog/everything-h as-changed/

Lepecki, André. 'Zones of Resonance: Mutual Formations in Dance and the Visual Arts Since the 1960s'. In *Move. Choreographing You: Art and Dance Since the 1960s*. Exh. cat., 152–16. London: Hayward Publishing, 2011.

Le Roy, Xavier. 'Self Unfinished' (1998). In *"Retrospective" By Xavier Le Roy*, edited by Bojana Cvejić. Exh. cat., 157–72. Paris: Les presses du reel, 2014.

Le Roy, Xavier. 'SELF UNFINISHED – The Thing About … Art & Artists - Xavier Le Roy'. 26 August 2017. https://www.youtube.com/watch?v=QjUDY_54eLM

Le Roy, Xavier. 'The Self Unfinished'. Accessed 21 September 2019. http://www.xavierleroy.com/page.php?sp=d22f5301fc93b61aedfc31f0c3c53a88e553d8be&lg=en

Levi Strauss, David. 'Love Rides Aristotle Through the Audience: Body Image and Idea in the Work of Carolee Schneemann'. In *Imaging Her Erotics: Essays, Interviews, Projects*, 322–3. Cambridge, MA: MIT Press, 2002.

LeWitt, Sol. 'Serial Project No.1 (ABCD)' (1966). In *Minimalism*, edited by James Meyer, 226–7. London: Phaidon, 2000.

Leys, Ruth. 'The Turn to Affect: A Critique'. *Critical Inquiry* 37, no. 3 (Spring 2011): 434–72.

Lingis, Alphonso. *The Community of Those Who Have Nothing in Common*. Indiana: Indiana University Press, 1994.

Lippard, Lucy and John Chandler, 'The Dematerialisation of Art'. In *Changing: Essays in Art Criticism*, 255–76. New York: Dutton, 1971.

Lippard, Lucy R. 'Eccentric Abstraction'. In *Changing: Essays in Art Criticism*, 98–111. New York: Dutton, 1971.

Lippard, Lucy R. 'The Pains and Pleasures of Rebirth: European and American Women's Body Art'. (1976). In *The Pink Glass Swan: Selected Feminist Essays on Art*, 99–113. New York: The New Press, 1995.

MacRitchie, Lynn. 'Marina Abramovic: Exchanging Energies'. *Performance Research* 1, no. 2 (Summer 1996): 27–34.

Maddox, Garry. 'Nat Randall's The Second Woman is a Marathon Theatre Show for Bachelorette Fans'. Sydney Morning Herald, 19 October 2017. https://www.smh.com.au/entertainment/theatre/nat-randalls-the-second-woman-is-a-marathon-theatre-show-for-bachelorette-fans-20171019-gz3ysq.html

Magazine, T. 'Mostly True'. *The New York Times Style Magazine*, 13 February 2015. https://www.nytimes.com/2015/02/13/t-magazine/sarah-manguso-amalia-ulman-heidi-julavits-diary.html

Malevich, Kasimir. 'From Cubism and Futurism to Suprematism. The New Realism in Painting'. In *Malevich on Suprematism. Six Essays: 1915 to 1926*. Translated by Xenia Glowacki-Prus and Arnold McMillin, edited by Patricia Railing, 25–42. Iowa City: University of Iowa Museum of Art, 1999.

Mantock, Rachel. '"Being a girl is not a natural thing" – Why this Instagram Hoaxer Faked Her Cool-girl Selfies'. *Gadgette*, 10 February 2016. https://www.gadgette.com/2016/02/10/amalia-ulman-instagram -hoax/

Martin, Adrian. 'Film Review: Never Look Away – Unless It's Conceptual Art'. 20 April 2019. https://www.screenhub.com.au/news-article/rev iews/film/adrian-martin/film-review-never-look-away-unless-its-co nceptual-art-258232

MacRitchie, Lynn. 'Marina Abramovic: Exchanging Energies'. *Performance Research* 1, no. 2 (Summer 1996): 27–34.

McEvilley, Thomas. 'Tehching Hsieh, Linda Montano'. *Artforum* 23, no. 3 (November 1984): 98–9.

Meltzer, Eve. *Systems We Have Loved: Conceptual Art, Affect, and the Antihumanist Turn*. Chicago: Chicago University Press, 2012.

Merleau-Ponty, Maurice. *The Visible and the Invisible*. Translated by Alphonso Lingis. Evanston: Northwestern University Press, 1968.

Meyer, James. 'The Minimal Unconscious'. *October* 130 (Fall 2009): 141–76.

Miller, Casey. 'Men Who Don't Move'. Accessed 11 May 2020. https://ca seymm.github.io/men-who-dont-move/

Miller, Nancy K. 'The Text's Heroine: A Feminist Critic and Her Fictions'. *Diacritics* 12, no. 2 (1982): 48–53.

Miller, Nancy K. 'Changing the Subject: Authorship, Writing and the Reader'. In *Feminist Studies/Critical Studies*, edited by Teresa de Lauretis, 102–20. Bloomington: Indiana University Press, 1986.

Mitchell, Juliet. *Siblings: Sex and Violence*. Cambridge: Polity, 2003.

Montano, Linda and Tehching Hsieh. 'One Year Art/Life Performance: Interview with Alex and Allyson Grey' (1984). In *Theories and Documents of Contemporary Art: A Sourcebook of Artists' Writings*, edited by Kristine Stiles and Peter Selz, 778–83. Berkeley: University of California Press, 1996.

Morris, Robert. 'Note on Sculpture, Part 2'. In *Continuous Project Altered Daily: The Writings of Robert Morris*, 11–21. Cambridge, MA: MIT Press, 1995.

Morse, Meredith. *Soft Is Fast: Simone Forti in the 1960s and After*. Cambridge, MA: MIT Press, 2016.

Murdoch, Iris. *The Sovereignty of Good*. London: Routledge, 1970.

Nancy, Jean-Luc. *The Inoperative Community*. Translated by Christopher Fynsk. Minneapolis: University of Minnesota Press, 1991.

Nemser, Cindy. 'A Conversation with Eva Hesse' (1970). In *Eva Hesse*, edited by Mignon Nixon, 1–24. Cambridge, MA: MIT Press, 2002.

Neuner, Stefan and Wolfram Pilchler. 'Through the Looking Glass. Reflections on Bruce Nauman's *Live-Taped Video Corridor*'. In *Bruce Nauman: A Contemporary*, edited by Eva Ehninger and Martina

Venanzoni with Stephen E. Hauser, 55–84. Münchenstein: Laurenz Foundation Schaulager, 2018.

O'Dell, Kathy. *Contract with the Skin: Masochism, Performance Art and the 1970s*. Minneapolis: University of Minnesota Press, 1998.

Orta, Lucy. 'Questioning Identity'. In *GSK Contemporary: Aware Art Fashion Identity*. Exh. cat., 33–9. Bologna: Damiani editore via Zanardi, 2010.

Orta, Lucy. *Operational Aesthetics: The Work of Lucy + Jorge Orta*. London: University of the Arts, 2011.

Osborne, Peter. 'Conceptual Art and/as Philosophy'. In *Rewriting Conceptual Art*, edited by Michael Newman and Jon Bird, 47–65. London: Reaktion, 1999.

Osborne, Peter. *Anywhere or Not at All: Philosophy of Contemporary Art*. London: Verso, 2013.

Pape, Lygia interviewed by Lúcia Carneiro and Ileana Pradilla. 'Birds of Marvelous Colors'. In *Lygia Pape: A Multitude of Forms*. Exh. cat., 16–24. New York Metropolitan Museum of Art, 2017.

Phelan, Peggy. *Unmarked: The Politics of Performance*. New York and London: Routledge, 1993.

Praxis. 'Andrea Fraser in Conversation'. *Brooklyn Rail*, October 2004. https://brooklynrail.org/2004/10/art/andrea-fraser

Preston, Sammy. 'On this Weekend: A 24-hour Performance of a Single Scene'. *Broadsheet*, 18 October 2017. https://www.broadsheet.com.au/sydney/art-and-design/weekend-24-hour-performance-single-scene

Rainer, Yvonne. 'A Quasi Survey of Some Minimalist Tendencies in the Quantitatively Minimal Dance Activity Midst the Plethora, or an Analysis of Trio A'. In *Minimal Art: A Critical Anthology*, edited by Gregory Battcock, 263–73. Berkeley: University of California Press, 1968.

Rainer, Yvonne. 'A Manifesto Reconsidered' (2008). Serpentine Gallery, London. Accessed 15 August 2019. http://intermsofperformance.site/interviews/yvonne-rainer

Rancière, Jacques. 'Problems and Transformations in Critical Art'. Translated by C. Bishop and P. Lafuente. In *Participation*, edited by Claire Bishop, 83–93. London: Whitechapel, 2006.

Raskin, David. 'Judd's Moral Art'. *Donald Judd*. Exh. cat., 78–95. London: Tate Modern, 2004.

Raskin, David. *Donald Judd*. New Haven: Yale University Press, 2010.

Ravetto-Biagioli, Kriss. *Mythopoetic Cinema: On the Ruins of European Identity*. New York: Columbia University Press, 2017.

Reckitt, Helena. 'Forgotten Relations: Feminist Artists and Relational Aesthetics'. In *Politics in a Glass Case: Feminism, Exhibition Cultures and Curatorial Transgressions*, edited by Angela Dimitrakaki and Lara Perry, 131–56. Liverpool: Liverpool University, 2013.

Rice, Karen Gonzalez. 'Linda Montano and the Tensions of Monasticism'. In *Beyond Belief: Theoaesthetics or Just Old-Time Religion?*, edited by Ronald R. Bernier. Eugene: Pickwick Publications, 2010.

Richards, Bree. 'Citizens Band 2012'. In *Angelica Mesiti: A Communion of Stranger Gestures*, 152–3. Melbourne Schwartz City and Sydney Artspace, 2017.

Richards, Bree. 'Conversation with the Artist'. *Angelica Mesiti*, Exh. cat. Canberra: National Gallery of Australia, July 2017.

Richards, Mary. *Marina Abramović*. Second edn. Abingdon: Routledge, 2019.

Riley, Denise. *Impersonal Passion: Language as Affect*. Durham: Duke University Press, 2005.

Riviere, Joan. 'Womanliness as Masquerade'. *International Journal of Psychoanalysis* 10 (1929): 303–13.

Rodenbeck, Judith F., *Radical Prototypes; Allan Kaprow and the Invention of Happenings*. Cambridge, MA: MIT Press, 2011.

Rosenberg, Susan. *Trisha Brown: Choreography as Visual Art*. Middletown: Wesleyan University Press, 2017.

Pérez Royo, Victoria. 'Real Fictions: *Time has Fallen Asleep in the Afternoon Sun*'. Kunstenfestivaldesarts 2013, Brussels. Accessed 27 November 2019. https://www.kfda.be/en/program/time-has-fallen-asleep-in-the-afternoon-sunshine

Salecl, Renata. 'Cut in the Body: From Clitoridectomy to Body Art'. In *(Per)versions of Love and Hate*, 141–68. London: Verso, 1998.

Schneemann, Carolee. 'Interview with Kate Haug' (1977). In *Imaging Her Erotics: Essays, Interviews, Projects*, 21–4. Cambridge, MA: MIT Press, 2002.

Schneemann, Carolee. 'Notes on Fuses' (1971). *Imaging Her Erotics: Essays, Interviews, Projects*, 45. Cambridge, MA: MIT Press, 2002.

Sennett, Richard. *The Fall of Public Man*. New York: Norton, 1974.

Sennett, Richard. *Together: The Rituals, Pleasures and Politics of Cooperation*. London: Penguin, 2012.

Shalson, Lara. *Performing Endurance: Art and Politics since 1960*. Cambridge: Cambridge University Press, 2018.

Sharp, Willoughby. 'Body Works: A Precritical, Non-definitive Survey of Very Recent Works Using the Human Body or Parts Thereof'. *Avalanche* (Autumn 1970): 14–17.

Simmel, Georg. 'Metropolis and Mental Life'. In *The Blackwell City Reader*, edited by Gary Bridge and Sophie Watson, 11–19. Malden: Blackwell, 2002.

Singerman, Howard. *Art Subjects: Making Artists in the American University*. Berkeley: University of California Press, 1999.

Siqueiros, David A. et al., 'A Declaration of Social, Political and Aesthetic Principles'. In *Art in Theory 1900–1990: An Anthology of Changing Ideas*, edited by Charles Harrison and Paul Wood, 387–8. Oxford: Blackwell, 1992.

Slotkin, James S. *Readings in Early Anthropology*. London: Routledge, 2004.

Small, Rachel. 'Amalia Ulman'. *Interview Magazine*, 14 October 2015. https://www.interviewmagazine.com/art/amalia-ulman

Soldner, Anna. 'Artist, Feminist, Immigrant: An Interview with Amalia Ulman'. 30 April 2014. http://bullettmedia.com/article/amalia-ulman-interview/#article-carousel

Solomon-Godeau, Abigail. 'The Woman Who Never Was: Self-representation, Photography and First-Wave Feminist Art'. In *WACK! Art and the Feminist Revolution*, edited by Lisa Gabrielle Mark. Exh. cat., 337–45. Los Angeles: The Museum of Contemporary Art and Cambridge, MA: MIT Press, 2007.

Steinberg, Monica. '(Im)Personal Matters: Intimate Strangers and Affective Market Economies'. *Oxford Art Journal* 42, no. 1 (2019): 45–67.

Stephen, Ann. *1969: The Black Box of Conceptual Art*. Exh. cat. University Art Gallery, University of Sydney, 2013

Stigh, Daniela and Zoë Jackon. 'Marina Abramović: The Artist Speaks'. Inside/Out: A MOMA/MOMA PS1 Blog, 3 June 2010. http://www .moma.org/explore/inside_out/2010/06/03/marina-abramovic-the-arti st-speaks

Stimson, Blake and Gregory Sholette, eds. *Collectivism after Modernism: The Art of Social Imagination After 1945*. Minneapolis: University of Minnesota Press, 2007.

Strzemiński, Wladyslaw. 'B = 2' *Blok* (1924)'. In *Between Worlds: A Sourcebook of Central European Avant-gardes 1910–1930*, edited by Timothy O. Benson and Éva Forgács, 497–502. Cambridge, MA: MIT Press, 2002.

Strzemiński, Wladyslaw. 'Unism in Painting' (1928). In *Between Worlds: A Sourcebook of Central European Avant-gardes 1910–1930*, edited by Timothy O. Benson and Éva Forgács, 649–57. Cambridge, MA: MIT Press, 2002.

Tan, Teresa. 'The Second Woman: Performance Artist Stages 100 Intimate Moments with 100 Men in 24 Hours'. *ABC*, 20 October 2017. http://www.abc.net.au/news/2017-10-20/the-second-woman-nat -randall-stages-100-dates-with-100-men/9064390

Tatlin, Vladimir. 'The Initiative Individual in the Creativity of the Collective'. In *Art in Theory 1900–1990: An Anthology of Changing Ideas*, edited by Charles Harrison and Paul Wood, 309. Oxford: Blackwell, 1992.

Taylor, Charles. *A Secular Age*. Cambridge, MA: Harvard University Press, 2007.

The Frankfurt Institute for Social Research. *Aspects of Sociology*. Translated by John Viertel. London: Heinemann Educational Books, 1973.

Thompson, Nato, ed. *Living as Form: Socially Engaged Art from 1991–2011*. New York: Creative Time Books and Cambridge, MA: MIT Press, 2012.

Trebay, Guy. 'Encounter; Sex, Art and Videotape'. The Way We Live Now, 13 June 2004. https://www.nytimes.com/2004/06/13/magazine/the-way-we-live-now-6-13-04-encounter-sex-art-and-videotape.html

Tucker, Marcia. *Anti-Illusion: Procedures/ Materials*. Exh. cat. New York: Whitney Museum of American Art, 1969.

Twyford-Moore, Sam. 'Nat Randall's The Second Woman'. *The Saturday Paper* 189. 27 January–2 February 2018. https://www.thesaturdaypaper.com.au/2018/01/27/nat-randalls-the-second-woman/15169716005699

Ullrich, Jessica. 'Contact Zones – Where Dogs and Humans Meet: Dog-Human Metamorphoses in Contemporary Art'. In *Animals and Their People: Connecting East and West in Critical Animal Studies*, edited by Anna Barcz and Dorota Łagodzka, 53–6. Leiden and Boston: Brill, 2018.

Ulman, Amalia. *Excellences & Perfections*. Munich, London and New York: Prestel, 2018.

Vergine, Lea. 'Bodylanguage' (1974). In *The Artist's Body*, edited by Tracey Warr, 236–8. London: Phaidon, 2000.

Verhagen, Erik. 'The Work Can Never Be Finished. An Interview with Franz Erhard Walther'. In *Franz Erhard Walther: The Body Decides*, 49–72. Brussels: WIELS Contemporary Art Centre; CAPC musée d'art contemporain de Bordeaux in collaboration with The Franz Erhard Walter foundation and Konig Books London, 2014.

Wagley, Catherine. 'Funny and Unflinching – Eleanor Antin Bares all at LACMA'. 23 May 2019. https://www.apollo-magazine.com/eleanor-antin-times-arrow-lacma/

Ward, Frazer. *No Innocent Bystanders: Performance Art and Audience*. Hanover: Dartmouth College Press, 2012.

Weber, Eleanor Ivory. *Hyper Spectral Display (.hsd)*. Exh. cat., 55 Sydenham Rd, Marrickville, 28 June–14 July 2013. http://www.55sydenhamrd.com/wp-content/uploads/2014/01/55_hsd.pdf

Williams, Gilda. 'Amalia Ulman'. *Artforum* 55, no. 5 (January 2017): 227–8.

Wilson, William S. 'Eva Hesse: on the Threshold of Illusions'. In *Inside the Visible: An Elliptical Traverse of Twentieth Century Art, in, of and from the Feminine*. Edited by Catherine de Zegher, Exh. cat., 426–33. Boston: Institute of Contemporary Art; Kortrijk: Kanaal Art Foundation; Cambridge, MA: MIT Press, 1996.

Wood, Catherine. *Performance in Contemporary Art*. London: Tate Publishing, 2018.

Worringer, Wilhelm. *Abstraction and Empathy* (1908). Translated by Michael Bullock. New York: International University Press, 1953.

Index